Macro-control and Economic Development in China

T0298397

This book, together with *Economic Development and Reform Deepening in China* is a collection of papers written in recent years about maintaining economic growth, managing inflation, the relationship between growth and structural adjustment, controlling price growth, maintaining stable economic development, and other relevant aspects of macro control, economic development, and deepening reform. The Chinese government adopted many of the recommendations put forward by the book.

Chen Jiagui (1944–2013) was an Economist, Professor of the Academic Division of Economics of the Chinese Academy of Social Sciences, specializing in industrial economics and enterprise management.

China Perspectives Series

The *China Perspectives* series focuses on translating and publishing works by leading Chinese scholars, writing about both global topics and China-related themes. It covers Humanities and Social Sciences, Education, Media and Psychology, as well as many interdisciplinary themes.

This is the first time any of these books have been published in English for international readers. The series aims to put forward a Chinese perspective, give insights into cutting-edge academic thinking in China, and inspire researchers globally.

For more information, please visit https://www.routledge.com/series/CPH

Regulating China's Shadow Banks
Qingmin Yan, Jianhua Li

Macro-control and Economic Development in China
Jiagui Chen

Economic Development and Reform Deepening in China
Jiagui Chen

Forthcoming titles:

Internationalization of the RMB: Establishment and Development of RMB Offshore Markets
International Monetary Institute, Renmin University of China

The Road Leading to the Market
Weiying Zhang

Research Frontiers on the International Marketing Strategies of Chinese Brands
Zuohao Hu, Xi Chen, Zhilin Yang

History of China's Foreign Trade, 2e
Yuqin Sun

Macro-control and Economic Development in China

Jiagui Chen

Routledge
Taylor & Francis Group
LONDON AND NEW YORK

中国社会科学出版社
CHINA SOCIAL SCIENCES PRESS

This book is published with financial support from Innovation Project of CASS

Translated by Yang Limeng and Wu Yisheng

First published 2017
by Routledge

2 Park Square, Milton Park, Abingdon, Oxfordshire OX14 4RN

52 Vanderbilt Avenue, New York, NY 10017

Routledge is an imprint of the Taylor & Francis Group, an informa business

First issued in paperback 2020

British Library Cataloguing in Publication Data
A catalogue record for this book is available from the British Library

Library of Congress Cataloging-in-Publication Data
Names: Chen, Jiagui, author.
Title: Macro-control and economic development in China / Jiagui Chen.
Description: London ; New York : Routledge, [2016] | Series: China perspectives series
Identifiers: LCCN 2015048190| ISBN 9781138898691 (hbk) | ISBN 9781315708423 (ebk)
Subjects: LCSH: Economic development—China. | China—Economic policy.
Classification: LCC HC427.95 .C433336 2016 | DDC 338.951—dc23
LC record available at http://lccn.loc.gov/2015048190

ISBN: 978-1-138-89869-1 (hbk)
ISBN: 978-0-367-51662-8 (pbk)

Typeset in Bembo
by Apex CoVantage, LLC

Contents

Illustrations

Figures

Tables

Preface

My research life can roughly be divided into two stages: the research on micro-economic and macroeconomic issues respectively. When I was an undergraduate, my major was national economic planning which should fall into the scope of macro-economy, but I was mainly engaged in business management after I graduated. Later, I studied business management for a master's and doctor's degree. Afterwards, I began work in the Institute of Industrial Economics of CASS and was mainly involved in the study of business management and industrial economy. I finally transferred my research interest to macro-economy to meet my job needs. In 1998, I was appointed Vice President of the Chinese Academy of Social Sciences. In 2003, I was elected a member of the NPC Standing Committee and the Financial & Economic Committee. In 2006, when CASS set up different departments, I was appointed Dean of the Department of Economics and Chief Editor of the Blue Book of Economy. Due to these job opportunities, in recent years, the issues I touched upon and discussed are basically about macro-economy. And the topics I researched and the academic activities I participated in are mainly on macro-economy as well. Therefore, the research findings I published are mostly about macro-economy.

This Collection (consisting of this volume and the companion volume *Economic Development and Reform Deepening in China*) mainly includes my published articles on macro-economy, and it falls into three parts, i.e., macro control, economic development, and reform deepening. The articles are arranged based on published time, from the most recent to the least. Though I have published several collected works, this Collection includes my newest articles. Most of them were never used in other collected works, but a few of them have been republished here due to their high degree of relevance.

Between the two volumes there are 18 articles included on macro control. A majority of them were originally published in the Theory Section of *People's Daily* after the year 2008. These articles are concerned with the current economic situation and macro-control policy, call attention to some problems, and put forward policy suggestions. They specifically make an in-depth analysis on how to balance economic growth, restructuring, and price control. After a systemic reading, the readers would be able to grasp the evolution of China's economic situation and macro-control policies in recent years. In this sense, this is also an important reason why this Collection is published.

Regarding Economic Development, this Collection includes 19 articles on crucial issues that China faces during its economic development, namely, the international economic environment, energy and resources, the development of the manufacturing industry, industrial modernization, regional development, sustainable development, industrial structure, and the coordination of rural and urban development. As to development, my concern has always been on China's industrialization. We have made a detailed analysis of the industrialization process from 1995 to 2010, and come to a decision on which stage China's industrialization is in. The research finding has produced a tremendous influence and most issues I touch upon are on the major background of industrialization. In the meantime, as I frequently made field surveys to local cities, I also put forward suggestions on local economic development. This Collection contains my proposals on how to develop the Round Beibu Gulf Economic Zone, the Yangtze River Midstream Economic Zone, and the Economic Zone on the West Side of the Straits. The opinions I proposed about Round Beibu Gulf Economic Zone were ahead of the times and were adopted and put into effect.

This Collection contains 14 articles about Reform Deepening. I have long been concerned with the reform of state-owned enterprises, and published many articles about reform results. But the 14 articles are concerned with the reform of the macroeconomic structure. It is worth mentioning that in 2008, at the 30th anniversary of the reform and opening-up, I summed up the characteristics of China's reform and opening-up, and analyzed its nature, direction, target model, methods, driving force, deployment, and measures; moreover, I am one of the earliest scholars that advocated a socialist market economy in China. This Collection specifically selects two of my articles about socialist market economy published in 1993. So far, the viewpoints of the two articles still serve as a guideline for China to build a mature socialist market economy.

The research has no ending. There are many problems that need to be researched. With limited time put into no-limited research, mistakes and errors are unavoidable. Please don't hesitate to give your critical and constructive comments!

Chen Jiagui
December 1, 2012

Acknowledgements

We sincerely appreciate the input of China Social Sciences Press's President Zhao Jianying's support for this project and Xia Xia, Yang Yang, and Zhou Guanghuan in the department of international Cooperation & Publishing at CSSP who served as the editors and proofreaders. They have done much work in arranging the preparation of the English version.

We also sincerely appreciate the hard work of the translator, Mr. Wu Yisheng and Yang Limeng. Without their diligent work, this English version would not exist.

Finally we especially appreciate the financial support in the publication of this book from CASS Innovation Translation Fund.

December 3, 2015

Part 1

On macroeconomic regulation and control

1 To steady growth, regulate structure and promote reform

Since the beginning of 2012, we have witnessed weak market demand and economic downturn due to many domestic and international influencing factors. Regardless of some positive factors and signs that the economy is now stabilizing, the foundation to maintain stable economic growth remains fragile. At this time, we are caught in a dilemma: we must stay sober-minded to deal with the various problems in maintaining stable growth, and the underlying problems that may undermine long-term economic development, with the intention to promote the smooth, rapid, and sustainable development of Chinese economy.

1 To steady growth remains the vital task of current macroeconomic regulation and control

The Chinese economy has been on decline for seven quarters ever since last year; this year, the GDP grew 8.1% in the first quarter, but fell back to 7.6% in the second quarter, will probably sink further down to about 7.3% in the third quarter, and is likely to bottom out before bouncing back to above 7.5% in the last quarter; the expected growth target of 7.5% in the whole year will be hopefully surpassed. However, it seems less likely to regain a growth speed over 9% or maintain 10% long-term annual average of rapid growth in the following years. It will be possible and ideal to maintain an annual growth rate of about 8% as long as much progress is made constantly in adjustment of economic structure, transformation of economic development mode, and reform of economic system.

In the view of economic growth in the first three quarters of this year, the primary industry has developed quite well for the following reasons: 1) good harvests are achieved both in summer and autumn crops, 2) grain yield is expected to increase for nine years continuously, 3) crops including cotton and oil plants maintain a certain growth rate, and 4) the breeding industry develops with a steady pace. The tertiary industry has developed at a reasonably high rate and is expected to be about 8%. However, the growth rate of the secondary industry has slowed down considerably, especially the growth in secondary industry. The value added of industries above a designated scale remained a growth rate of 11.9% in March of this year, but, ever since April, it fell below 10% – a psychological threshold – for six months in a row, specifically 9.3% in April, 9.6% in May, 9.5% in June, 9.2% in July, 8.9% in August, and approximately 8.6% in September. In terms of quarter, the growth rate of industrial value added reached up to 11.6% in the first quarter, but it dropped to 9.5% in the second, and possibly to 9% in the third quarter; the accumulated growth rate between January and August was 10.1%, and maybe less than 10% in the first three quarters; whereas it was 14.2% in the same period last year, down 4.2 percent points year over year.

In the view of three major demands (consumption, investment, and export), the growth rate of consumption has slowed down modestly. In the first three quarters, the total retail sales of social consumables nominally grew 14.1% (data of the first eight months) year over year, down only 2.9 percent points from over the same period last year (year-over-year growth 11.4% with a deduction of price factor, which shows an increase of 0.1 percent points as compared with the same period last year). Among 16 categories of commodities by businesses above designated size, eight categories achieved a growth rate higher than that in the first half year, one category leveled off, and seven categories went down; commodity categories with a slowdown rate higher than 1% include communication equipment, automobiles, petroleum, and other petroleum products.

The slowdown in investment was remarkable. From January to August of this year, the nominal growth rate of the fixed assets investment was 20.2% only while it was 24.9% in 2011, down 4.7% year over year and lower than the growth rate in the last five years (it increased 18.2% in real terms, rising 1.3 percent points as compared with the same period last year). The reasons for the slowdown may vary, but they generally include: 1) dramatic decline in real estate investment. From January to August of this year, the investment in real estate development nationwide was RMB4.4 trillion Yuan, increasing only 15.6% year over year, with 17.6 percent points down compared to the same period last year. This slowdown rate is far higher than that of all fixed assets. Not only will it slow the total social investment, but it will also affect the urban infrastructure construction to be implemented by local government on account that a large portion of funds for infrastructure construction comes from land-transferring fees. In the current financial system, most of the local governments find it too hard for them to maintain daily operation, much less to carry out urban infrastructure construction without utilizing land-transferring fees. As land-transferring fees are cut down, the investment in urban infrastructure construction will decrease as well. In the meantime, a dramatic decline of investment in real estate will also affect the development of industries such as building materials, furniture, ceramic products, and household appliances that are correlated to house decoration; 2) slowdown in high-speed rail and expressway construction. In previous several years, high-speed rails and expressways developed at an excessive speed, especially the high-speed rails. Their construction funds largely came from bank loans: the railway authorities were indebted so heavily that many high-speed rail lines had a severe deficit after putting their railways into service. Now railway authorities have trouble financing and have to slow down construction, leading to less and less investment. From January to August of this year, the investment into railway construction failed to increase; instead, it fell 23.9%; and 3) elimination of local government funding vehicles has narrowed the financing channels and methods of local governments to such an extent that the investments of local governments into infrastructure construction are minimized.

Among three major demands, export has encountered the severest decline in growth rate. From January to August of this year, China's export only grew 7.1%, showing a downward trend of about 15% from the first three quarters of last year, which was 22.7%. Dramatic decline in export growth rate was caused mainly by changes of the international environment. Under influence of the American financial crisis and the European sovereign debt crisis, China's exports were inhibited due to international market collapse, increasingly serious trade protectionism, and problems concerning China's trade development mode; accordingly, the contribution rate of export to economic growth declined significantly. Judging from the expected trend of export-related industries, we will feel that it is more difficult to increase export volume in a big way because of American and European influences, as well as other recent influencing factors; consequently, we must get well prepared and figure out reasonable countermeasures.

In a word, there is certain inevitability in economic growth this year, but the slowdown in growth rate beats people's average expectation. The dramatic decline in the economic growth rate is caused by the combination of multiple factors, varying from domestic factors to international ones, from economic factors to non-economic ones, from institutional factors to economic structure and growth mode, and from long-term accumulated factors to newly-added ones in this year. Among these influencing factors, some are controllable while some others are not. Those that affect economic growth of this year not only exist at present but will do for a long time; the underlying factors such as the institutional factors, economic structure, and economic development mode, in particular, will restrict the sustainable development of China's economy for years. To steady economic growth is not only the priority of current economic work but also a long-term task for economic administrators. At present, we still need to follow the general policy of moving forward while maintaining stability, abide by proactive financial policy and prudent monetary policy, accelerate the adjustment of the economic structure while steadying the economy, deepen reform on economic systems, and focus on improving people's livelihood.

2 Properly handle the relationship between steadying economic growth and adjusting industrial structure

The dramatic decline in economic growth has resulted in the unreasonable industrial structure of China and uncovered extensive economic problems. For a long time, China's industrial structure and economic growth mode were characterized by being dominated by government and driven by investment. In the view of GDP components during the "11th Five-Year Plan", the proportion of investment to GDP has been rising year by year from 50.9% in 2006 to 69.3% in 2010; the rate of capital formation was 41.8% in 2006 and up to 48.6% in 2010; in the view of investment growth rate during the "11th Five-Year Plan", the average annual real growth of investment was 21.9%, which was far higher than the 11.2% average annual growth rate of GDP; in the view of contribution to economic growth, the contribution rate of investment went up from 43.9% in 2006 to 54.0% in 2010, with 91.3% in 2009. Though the decline in export growth rate is faster than that in investment, the latter has the greatest impact on economic growth rate because investment contributes much more to GDP than exports, with the most affected industries including iron and steel, cement, flat glass, large electromechanical equipment manufacturing, etc.

We should make the best use of the circumstances to promote an adjustment of the industrial structure. While correcting the incompatible development problems in the primary, secondary, and tertiary industries, we must modify the unreasonable inner structure of industry that was generated by investment-driven policy.

We should capitalize on the trend to adjust the proportion of light industry and heavy industry. At the initial stage of reform and opening up, the proportion of China's light industry as a whole was only 43%; after several years' adjustment, it went up to 47.4% in 1985; in the following dozen years, the proportion of light and heavy industry fluctuated around 50%, basically maintaining a coordinated development trend. Since the end of the 20th century, a noticeable trend featuring heavy and chemical industries emerged in China's industrial structure under the influences of change in stages of economic development and investment-driven policy. In 12 years, from 1999 to 2011, the proportion of light industry output value fell from 41.9% down to 30% while the heavy industry jumped from 58.1% up to 70%. The proportion of heavy industry was much higher before the reform and opening up. This created a lot of pressure on China's energy supply and environmental protection, and also suppressed consumer demands. We should seize the opportunity of sharp decline in investment growth rate to cut down the proportion of heavy industry so as to achieve coordination development between light industry and heavy industry.

We should restrain the expansion of energy-intensive industries with excess capacity and close down enterprises with outdated production facilities. In China, industries with huge overcapacity include iron and steel, electrolytic aluminum, cement, shipbuilding, automobile manufacturing, and textile and garment. The steelmaking capacity of China is close to one billion tons, but the capacity utilization rate in the first half year is no more than 74.7%; in addition, not a few enterprises have slipped into loss due to a meager profit as a result of excessive competition. According to the statistics of more than 70 key enterprises by the Iron and Steel Association, these enterprises achieved profits of RMB2.4 billion Yuan in the first half year, down 95.8% year over year; the profit margin of prime operating revenue was no more than 1.6%; the whole industry was hence put on the edge of loss. The cement capacity in China, which was already over three billion tons, has substantially surpassed 2.2 billion tons – the planning target to be achieved by the end of the "12th Five-Year Plan". In 2011, the capacity utilization rate of the cement industry was no more than 71.9%; in the first half of the year, dozens of new dry production lines were forced to halt production, resulting in a further decline in the capacity utilization rate, a 51.4% fall in achieved profit of the whole industry and more than a third percentage of loss-incurring enterprises. In China, there are too many energy intensive enterprises that are expanding excessively fast. The electricity utilization of energy intensive enterprises accounts for around 80% of the total industrial electricity. According to statistics by the Ministry of Industry and Information Technology (MIIT), the outdated capacity of 18 industries, such as iron and steel, steelmaking, electrolytic aluminum, coke, cement, and chemical fiber, make up 15–25% of the total industries. In ironmaking industry, there is still 100 million tons of capacity to be generated by blast furnaces, which makes up 20% of the total ironmaking capacity. In cement industry, there is still 500 million tons of capacity to be generated by small and backward cement plants, which makes up 20% of the total cement capacity. These are two typical examples to illustrate that outdated or backward production facilities in both ironmaking industry and cement industry should be closed down as soon as possible because they can waste resources and contaminate the environment.

We should carry out the technical transformation of traditional industries by means of advanced technology to accelerate the updating of traditional industries. The global industrial development history has indicated that there is no backward industry, but there is outdated technology. Traditional as these industries are, including textile, iron and steel, and automobile and mechanical manufacturing, they present an entirely new appearance with increased technical content and value added after they are modified with new and high technology in some industrially developed countries. In China, the traditional industries remain low in the level of modernization, which is estimated to be around 40% for most of them. Therefore, we should quicken the pace of technical transformation to improve the level of modernization, increase independent intellectual property rights, create famous brands, raise the added value of products, and enhance the core competitiveness of enterprises in these industries.

We should try to develop emerging industries and increase their proportion in the industrial economy. In recent years, we have witnessed the booming development of the new high-tech industries in China; from a global perspective, however, our emerging industries are engaged mostly in low-technology manufacturing links of high-tech products in an international division system and global value chain, with a low added value and labor return rate. While expanding the scale of emerging industries, we should push them into middle- and high-end links of the industrial chain. In addition, we should steadily boost progress of strategic emerging industries, carry out key technology R&D, address various problems in the process of industrialization, avoid haphazard development, reduce market risks, and ultimately occupy the commanding heights in global economy with strategic emerging industries.

We should carry forward adjustment of industrial organization structure, encourage and support mergers and acquisitions, centralize production factors into preponderant enterprises, and weed out those enterprises that are technically backward, are low in management level, are high in wasting resources and polluting the environment, and are on the verge of insolvency. We should foster large enterprise groups, raise scale economic efficiency, encourage large enterprises to expand, alter the industrial organization structure of some industries that are "small-sized, chaotic, dispersed and poor in management", raise industrial affinity, encourage and support small enterprises to move toward a "specialized, precise, unique and new" pattern, and constantly improve overall quality and efficiency of all industries.

3 Properly handle the relationship between steadying economic growth and deepening reform

To steady economic growth and maintain a long-term, stable, fast and sustainable development of China's economy, we must deepen the reform and build a mature market economic system. At present, we particularly need to accelerate reform of the administrative system.

According to the progress of the whole economic system reform, the administrative system reform is obviously lagging behind and becomes a large problem, though the reform of enterprises and the market needs deepening. Because of this regression and diversion, the reform in many key fields and important links has stalemated, and some even retrogressed. This requires us to solve the problem immediately and make breakthrough progress in administrative system reform to drive reform in fields such as financial taxation, allocation, investment, finance, state-owned enterprises, resource products pricing, etc.

What is more important for the administrative system reform is to streamline administration, delegate power to lower levels and transform the government functions in addition to exploring a new framework of administrative system, optimizing governmental organization structure, and developing a scientific administrative organization system by following a downsizing, unitary, and efficient principle. The ultimate purpose of all government administrative activities is to bring maximum well-being to citizens at minimum cost, i.e. the optimal portfolio of tax burden and public services. "Centering on economic construction" does not necessarily mean that governments at all levels should engage directly in production and operating activities. When defining the functions of government, we should always uphold the principle that some of the government functions must be delegated to the market, to an enterprise, or to a social organization whenever deemed appropriate. The government needs to transform gradually from an omnipotent system into a limited system which can provide public services effectively so that the market and social mechanism can play a greater role in resource allocation and social ordering.

In recent years, the government has intervened heavily in micro-economy and proudly boasted its administrative measures in economic management. Facts have repeatedly proved that any economic issues can only be solved using economic measures, and that it is not advisable to control economic behavior by easily taking administrative measures. For a short period, the administrative measures seem effective, but they will distort price signals; go against the law of value; escalate, intensify, and complicate conflicts; and ultimately incur huge economic loss.

The Law of Administrative Permit has been enacted in China. Before and after this law came into effect, the government canceled some approval systems; recently, the State Council decided to call off part of the items that require administrative approval. But this is far from enough. In the process of economic operation, some of the approval systems that should be canceled are not, and a large number of new items requiring administrative approval are unveiled. People from some department reported that if a private enterprise wants to get into some monopolized industry for expansion, it has to go through miscellaneous procedures and spend a lot of time because its application form needs to be stamped with more than 200 official seals. If the reform of the administrative system is not accelerated, if the administration is not streamlined and power is not delegated to lower levels, and if the government functions are not transformed, it will be hard for us to achieve the goal of building a mature market economic system and to maintain long-term, stable, fast, and sustainable economic development.

(Published in *People's Daily*, Nov 19, 2012)

2 To steady growth, not to protect growth

The forecast based on the contemporary economic situation

In 2012, the general policy of economic work in China was progressing while maintaining stability; "progressing" meant advancement in deepening reform, transforming the economic development pattern, adjusting economic structure, and improving people's livelihood. Whereas "stability" meant steadying the economic growth rate, the general price level, and the macroeconomic policy. We will carry out this general policy in a direct and unswerving manner.

1 Correctly understand the current economic situation

The expected growth target of GDP in 2012 was reasonably set at 7.5%. It was well grounded that the expected growth target of China's GDP was set at 7.5% in the *2012 Plan for National Economic and Social Development* that was adopted at the 5th Session of the 11th National People's Congress held in March.

First, we need to gradually link to reach the target of 7% average annual growth during the "12th Five-Year Plan". The 7% growth rate of the "12th Five-Year Plan" was determined on the basis of serious study and coordination among all sectors, so it was scientific and realistic. In 2011 (the beginning year of the "12th Five-Year Plan"), the economic growth rate of China reached up to 9.2%, laying a sound foundation for economic development in the following years. As long as the growth rate could remain around 7.5% in the next four years, the economic growth target set for the "12th Five-Year Plan" would be definitely accomplished and even surpassed.

Second, we need to take into consideration the actual situation of gradual decline in China's economic growth rate ever since the second half of last year. The economic growth rate of China was on a quarterly decline throughout last year. Objectively, it will be very difficult for China's economy to grow at a rate above 9% under the context of feeble economic recovery in developed countries, grim international economic environment, insuperable contradictions challenging domestic economy, and some uncertainties.

Third, we need to retain a certain leeway for actual work. The target of 7.5% is merely anticipated; such a low target can help reduce pressure for all local governments and all sectors. As an anticipated target, it may be deemed higher or lower in the process of implementation. In practice, the growth rate is higher than 7.5% in the development plans laid down by a majority of provinces, municipalities, and autonomous regions – except for a few regions.

Fourth, we need to guide the macroeconomy. This is especially important, and its purpose is to guide all local governments and sectors not to blindly pursue growth rate, but to focus on deepening the reform of the economic system, accelerating the transformation of economic development, adjusting the economic structure, improving the quality of economic development, and showing concern about people in order to maintain the long-term, steady, harmonious, and sustainable development of economy.

Finally, economists argue about the current economic situation. From the performance in previous years, the fundamentals of economic development are quite well. The GDP in the first quarter increased 8.1% (which is 1.1 percent points less than the 9.2% of last year, and is 0.8 percent points less than the 8.9% from the fourth quarter of last year). This is to be expected, and is acceptable to all sectors.

Since the beginning of April, however, some new problems have emerged: 1) the value added of industrial enterprises above designated size was reduced to below 10%, growing only 9.3% in April and only 9.6% in May; 2) the growth rate of financial revenue slowed down to 6.9% in April and 13.1% in May (the actual growth rate was 5% after deducting banking final settlement of income tax, according to interpretation by the Ministry of Finance); 3) prices declined remarkably (CPI grew 3.4% in April and 3.0% in May over the same period last year, and grew 3.5% from January to May, as was expected). But the producer price index for industrial products (PPI) dropped dramatically, falling 0.7% in April and 1.4% in May year over year, and falling 0.4% month over month, the lowest since November 2009; the purchasing price index for raw materials (PPIRM) declined 0.8% in April and 1.6% in May, falling 0.3% month over month. PPI dropped beyond expectation.

This sparked a debate on the current economic situation that led to the following two opposite views.

The first view argued that the gradual decline in China's economic growth rate, while slowly stabilizing, was something anticipated and acceptable. But there were different views about when it stabilized, some thinking it stabilized in the first quarter while some held that it would bottom out in the second quarter and it would go up steadily in the third and fourth quarters. People holding these views argued that we should currently follow the general policy of progressing while maintaining stability, that we should remain sober-minded in dealing with the current economic situation, and that the macroeconomic policy could be fine-tuned but the purpose was to "steady growth" rather than "protect growth".

The other view argued that China's current economic situation was similar to the situation in the fourth quarter of 2008 and the first quarter of 2009. Some people even believed that the current economic situation was worse than it was at that time, manifesting fears of a hard landing for Chinese economy, that the primary task of macro regulation and control should shift from "steadying growth" to "protecting growth", and especially that investment should be increased on a large scale to drive economic growth. Therefore, under dispute were several programs for investment amounting to RMB2 trillion, 3 trillion, and even 4 trillion; some government sectors hurried to finish project approvals, and the National Development and Reform Commission was crowded again with applicants.

An analysis is conducted on the current economic situation in comparison with the situation when the economic crisis happened. Is China's economy really going back to the situation at the outbreak of the economic crisis? I think that the situation currently facing China's economy is both similar to and different from the situation at that time. Three similarities are as follows.

First, the international economic environment is complex and volatile. As the American economy got out of the slump, the European sovereign debt crisis took place. This crisis is very likely to spread out, gloomy in prospect. The Japanese economic downturn has continued for years, and the economic recovery was suffocated by a nuclear power plant accident. Under the inflationary pressure, some major, large developing countries have lowered their economic growth rate by varying degrees. Inevitably, these challenges will have negative effects on the Chinese economy, and especially will bring mountains of difficulties to expand exportation.

Second, the economic growth rate slows down. In 2008, the economic growth rate slowed down on a quarterly basis, as high as 10.6% in the first quarter, 10.1% in the second quarter, down to 9.0% in the third quarter, and 6.8% in the fourth quarter, bottoming out in the first quarter of 2009, i.e. 6.1%. Since 2011, the Chinese economic growth rate has also slowed down quarterly, 9.7% in the first quarter, 9.5% in the second quarter, 9.1% in the third quarter, and 8.9% in the fourth quarter, and down to 8.1% in the first quarter of 2012 (see Fig. 1.2.1).

Finally, macroeconomic policy turns from tightening to easing. In the first half of 2008, China exercised a prudent financial policy and a moderately tight monetary policy in response to rapid economic growth. Not until the third quarter of 2009 did China begin to exercise a proactive financial policy and a moderately easy monetary policy in response to the financial crisis. This is a turn from tightening to easing. As of the fourth quarter of 2010, China readjusted the proactive financial policy and moderately easy monetary policy to the proactive financial policy and prudent monetary policy, and appropriately reduced the financial deficit. Last year, the Central Bank raised the deposit reserve ratio for the sixth time consecutively and raised the benchmark interest rate for the third time to tighten up monetary policy; as of the fourth quarter, however, China began to ease monetary policy moderately by lowering the deposit reserve ratio in May for the third time, and recently lowered deposit and loan interest rates. This is also a turn from tightening to easing.

But the current economic situation is quite different from the situation when the financial crisis broke out, which mainly includes the five points discussed below.

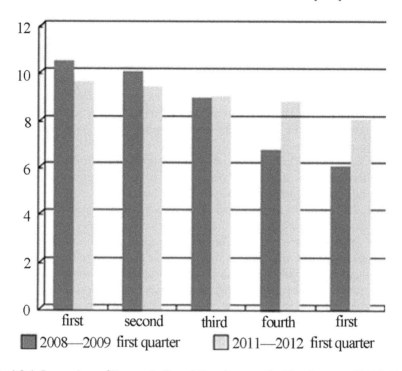

Fig. 1.2.1 Comparison of Economic Growth Rate between the First Quarter of 2008–2009 and the First Quarter of 2011–2012

First, even if the economic growth rate of China in the first quarter of this year has slowed down, the rate and reasons of slowdown are obviously different from the situation at outbreak of the financial crisis in 2008. In the view of the rate of slowdown, it is not as much as in that time. The growth rate of GDP was 8.1% in the first quarter, 0.6 percent points higher than the 7.5% expected, 1.3 percent points higher than 6.8% in the fourth quarter of 2008, and 2 percent points higher than 6.1% in the first quarter of 2009. This is even more so for industries that contributed the most to economic growth. The value that was added by industrial enterprises above a designated size only grew 6.4% in the fourth quarter of 2008 from a year earlier, only 5.1% in the first quarter and 9.1% in the second quarter of 2009; it grew 8.7% only in the first half of this year; and the rate of decline surpassed that of the first five months this year. In the view of reasons, although two slowdowns were caused by a decline in the industrial growth rate, the specific reasons varied a lot. In 2008 and 2009, the decline in the industrial growth rate resulted largely from a dramatic decline in exports of manufactured goods while this decline in industrial growth rate was mainly caused by a potential slowdown of China's GDP and a rapid increase of the appropriate control over industries in the last two years (e.g. high-speed rail). To some extent, the decline in the current industrial growth rate fits in with the expected target of government regulation and control.

Second, in recent years, China's economic growth has been driven largely by domestic demands, and the contribution rate of exports to economic growth has sharply dropped. The contribution rate of exports to China's economic growth usually remained above 2.0 percent points in years before 2008, but down to −3.6 percent points in 2009 and only 0.9 percent points in 2010. In other words, China's economy has been driven largely by domestic demands in recent years, and the decline in the export growth rate may have some impact on economy, but it is unlikely to surpass that of 2009 (see Table 1.2.1).

Third, the decline in the economic growth rate has little impact on employment that currently remains in sound condition. At the very time when the financial crisis happened in the United States, about 20 million rural migrant workers employed in southeastern coastal area of China were forced to return home as exports stumbled. But this phenomenon does not reoccur as the economic growth rate slows down, and the employment situation goes quite well. The reasons behind it may be that on the one hand, the labor-age population of China has scaled down dramatically in recent years, with an average annual decrease of about 5 million people; on the other hand, this decline in economic growth rate is a gradual process where pressure is released step by step; furthermore, a large number of rural workers get employed after they return to the Midwest of China where the economy is growing at a high rate.

Fourth, while all macroeconomic policies turn from tightening to easing, they differ in nature and intensity. Before the financial crisis, China adopted

Table 1.2.1 Contribution Rate of Three Demands to Economic Growth since 2005

Year	Final consumption		Investment		Net export	
	Contribution rate (%)	Percentage driven (percent points)	Contribution rate of capital formation (%)	Growth rate driven by capital formation (percent points)	Contribution rate (%)	Percentage driven (percent points)
2005	37.9	4.3	39.0	4.4	23.1	2.6
2006	40.0	5.1	43.9	5.6	16.1	2.0
2007	39.2	5.6	42.7	6.1	18.1	2.5
2008	43.5	4.2	47.5	4.6	9.0	0.8
2009	47.6	4.4	91.3	8.4	−38.9	−3.6
2010	36.8	3.8	54.0	5.6	9.2	0.9
2011	50.8	4.5	53.3	4.9	−4.0	−4.0

a prudent financial policy and a moderately tight monetary policy, and when faced with financial crisis, China began to implement a proactive financial policy and a moderately easing monetary policy, a transition from a tightening policy to an expansionary policy with changes in nature and direction, at least so far. However, the policy turns from tightening to easing but fine-tunes the economy under the premise of maintaining a proactive financial policy and a prudent monetary policy. This is a transition from tightening to easing at the operation level. It remains to be seen whether the government will change the nature and direction of macroeconomic policy.

Finally, the society is better prepared in mind than it was for negative effects caused by international economic changes. The enterprises and citizens are not put in a panic such as they were in the fourth quarter of 2009 and the first quarter of 2010; instead, voices with sober-minded solutions are heard here and there in the society, and an increasing number of people are quite critical about the proposition that the government should adopt a significant increment of investment to stimulate economic growth.

2 Currently there is no internal and external economic environment to "protect growth" in China

According to the above analysis, the current economic situation of China is quite different from the situation dealing with international financial crisis. For this reason, the macroeconomic policy should not shift from "steadying growth" to "protecting growth". From literal expressions, there is a difference of only a single word between "steadying growth" and "protecting growth"; as an economic policy, however, it refers to the government's judgments of the economic situation and a significant difference in nature and direction of macroeconomic policy.

"Steadying growth" is an expected target to be achieved by the government in order to avoid booms and busts in the economy in no case of emergent events, for which the neutral macroeconomic policy is usually adopted. Contingent upon varying economic situations and targets, the financial policy and monetary policy may work with each other in several ways: if the economy runs smoothly with a moderate growth rate, we can adopt a double prudent macroeconomic policy (double neutral), i.e. prudent financial policy and prudent monetary policy. If the economic growth rate fluctuates, we can adopt "one tightening and one prudent" macroeconomic policy, e.g. a proactive financial policy (expansionary) and a prudent monetary policy (somewhat neutral), or a moderately easing monetary policy (expansionary) and a prudent financial policy.

"Protecting growth" is an unconventional macroeconomic policy adopted by the government in response to a constant sharp decline in the economic growth rate caused by significant change in internal and external economic environment, for which strong stimulating measures are usually taken, e.g. expansionary financial policy and monetary policy, which we often call a proactive financial policy and moderate easing (or easing) monetary policy.

In China, the targets of "steadying growth" and "protecting growth" are achieved by means of industrial policy, land policy, real estate policy, and even administrative measures apart from financial policy and monetary policy.

To steady the economic growth rate at present, the government adopts a proactive financial policy and prudent monetary policy. The author deems it as appropriate. Of course, this policy can be fine-tuned timely and appropriately to make the economic growth rate stabilize during decline. For instance, with regard to the financial policy, we can reduce tax on enterprises, or introduce policy to stimulate consumption; with regard to monetary policy, we can properly reduce the deposit reserve ratio or adjust the interest rate. We should secure high-speed economic operation by appropriately fine-tuning macroeconomic policy and intensifying forces to steady economic growth, but we should in no case alter the nature and direction of the macroeconomic policy, or let the government dominate the policy that is intended to stimulate economic growth by increasing investment in a big way.

First, the international economic environment has many adverse effects on China's economic development, but it leads to few significant emergent events. While the American economy was hit heavily by financial crisis, it has bottomed out and begins to turn up. The European sovereign debt crisis is likely to deteriorate, but it is no longer a new event that may happen unexpectedly, and can be tackled in the long term since the complex reasons behind it involve the economic system and mechanism problems of Eurozone and EU, as well as some underlying problems of economic and social development patterns and the consumption pattern in these countries. Thus, it can be seen that the international economic environment will have long-term effects on China's economy, which cannot be solved by means of a short-term "protecting growth" macroeconomic policy.

Secondly, it is also recognized that the extensive economic growth pattern is unsustainable. The high growth rate of China's economy for more than 30 years has already created a wonder in the world. Now China lies at the second-half stage in the midterm of industrialization, so the intensive economic growth pattern dominated by the government and driven by investment is factually difficult to sustain itself. This therefore requires us to turn from scale expansion to improvement of overall qualities. In reality, China's economic growth leveled off during 1997–2002, varying between 7.6% and 9.3%; but it reached up to 10% in the five years between 2003 and 2007, owing to an increase of investment dealing with the Asian financial crisis and an accession to WTO. After the outbreak of financial crisis and European sovereign debt crisis, all countries have adjusted their strategy for economic development that enhanced the inclinations for trade protectionism. Both internal and external changes in the developmental environment compelled China to slow down economic growth and to change the economic development pattern and strategy. Do not make a fuss about the moderate decline in China's economic growth rate. It is a matter of course.

Third, even if the current economic growth rate of China declines sharply, it goes within a reasonable range and has stabilized while slowing down. Quite a few economists believe that the potential GDP of China remains around 8% at the present stage, but some argue that it remains around 7% only. In the real process of economic operation, the realized GDP fluctuates on the potential GDP without great deviation; otherwise, the economy may be too hot or too cold. The economy is expected to grow 7.5% this year, considering the actual decline in the potential GDP and other influencing factors. In other words, it will be deemed reasonable if the economic growth rate maintains around 8%. In the first quarter of this year, the economic growth rate is 8.1%; from April to May, the value added of industrial enterprises above designated size has dropped, but it is still close to 10% against less than the accumulative growth rate of 10.7% from January to May. The industrial value added in May has increased 0.3 percent points year over year and 0.89% month over month, showing positive signs of stabilization and recovery in industrial production; in June, it will be much better than April and May. Only by proper fine-tuning will it not be difficult for industrial value added to recover up to 10%. In addition, with a steady growth continuing in the primary and the secondary industries, it will be unlikely that the growth rate of GDP drops below 7% as it was in the fourth quarter of 2008 and the first quarter of 2009.

Finally, the decline in the economic growth rate leads to some positive changes in China's economy. The steady drop of CPI has created a good macroeconomic environment for us to control CPI below 4% this year; the industrial structure, especially the structure of light and heavy industries, is expected to improve, which helps to alleviate the contradiction between the supply and demand of energy resources (the coal in particular) and especially to fetch down the price of coal; some industries with excessive capacity will have to close down outdated production facilities under increasing pressure. All these signs suggest that a macroeconomic environment favorable for the transformation of economic development patterns and for the adjustment of economic structure is taking shape.

3 Be cautious about the macroeconomic policy of "protecting growth"

Since the 1990s, the macroeconomic policy of "protecting growth" has been implemented in China twice: the first time in 1998 to cope with the Asian financial crisis and the second in 2008 and 2009 responding to the global financial crisis caused by the United States. While dealing with two financial crises, the government resorted to a macroeconomic policy of "protecting growth" to secure a higher growth rate of the Chinese economy. In the whole process, we have gained considerable experience at considerable cost.

First, the government-leading and investment-driven pattern of economic growth is intensified. Since the beginning of the new century, as the investment-driven pattern of economic growth takes shape gradually in China, investment has become the impetus to stimulate economic development. It is all the more so during the "11th Five-Year Plan" (see Table 1.2.2).

Table 1.2.2 Proportion of Investment in GDP and Contribution to Economic Growth during
        2001–2010

Year	Proportion of fixed asset investment in GDP (100%)	Rate of capital formation	Growth rate of capital formation (100%)	Contribution rate of capital formation to economic growth (100%)	Percent points of economic growth driven by investment
2001	34.1	36.5	13.0	49.9	4.1
2002	36.1	37.8	16.9	48.5	4.4
2003	40.7	40.9	27.7	63.2	6.3
2004	25.0	43.0	26.6	54.5	5.5
2005	47.4	41.6	20.0	38.9	4.4
2006	49.5	41.8	23.9	43.9	5.6
2007	51.7	41.7	24.8	42.7	6.1
2008	54.9	43.9	25.9	47.5	4.6
2009	65.9	47.5	30.0	91.3	8.4
2010	69.3	48.6	23.8	54.0	5.6

In the view of GDP components during the "11th Five-Year Plan", the proportion of investment in GDP has been on the rise year by year, from 50.9% in 2006 up to 69.3% in 2010; the rate of capital formation was 41.8% in 2006 up to 48.6% in 2010. In the view of investment growth rate, it grew 21.9% in real terms during the "11th Five-Year Plan", far higher than the 11.2% average annual growth rate of the GDP. The contribution rate to economic growth was 43.6% in 2006 and up to 54.0% in 2010.

Investment is one of the impetuses to stimulate economic growth. We need to maintain a higher growth rate of investment in the following years, but a rate of capital formation close to 50% has already ranked highest in the world, which has never occurred in the history of economic development. This development pattern has squeezed residents' consumption, thus resulting in the disequilibrium of investment and consumption structure and of industrial structure such as to overload resources and environment and also reduce investment benefits. This unsustainable pattern is deemed to be one of the major problems to be tackled during the adjustment of the economic structure. Nevertheless, this structure is intensified by a "protecting growth" policy. According to data in Table 1.2.2, the contribution rate of investment to economic growth went up from 43.9% in 2006 to 91.3%, rising 47.4 percent points; the rate in 2010 went down dramatically as compared with that in 2009, but it remained up to 54%, rising 10.1 percent points as against 2006.

Second, the effect coefficient of investment is fetched down substantially. The effect coefficient of investment is an important index to measure economic effects, indicating newly added GDP of unit-fixed asset investment in a given period. In recent years, it shows a downslide, especially in years of protecting growth (see Table 1.2.3).

Table 1.2.3 Effect Coefficient of Fixed Asset Investment since 1996 (%)

Year	Coefficient	Year	Coefficient	Year	Coefficient
1996	45.2	2001	28.1	2006	24.0
1997	31.3	2002	24.6	2007	36.0
1998	19.1	2003	27.9	2008	25.0
1999	17.7	2004	34.1	2009	12.0
2000	29.0	2005	26.1	2010	21.7

According to data in the table above, the production efficiency of capital input drops as the investment scales up. This discloses a problem: the higher we input, the lower we will benefit. Due to insufficient and inefficient utilization, part of capital investment gives a low output that may compromise the benefit and quality of investment, all the more so in "protecting growth" years, e.g. 19.1% and 17.7% respectively in 1998 and 1999, and 12.0% and 21.7% respectively in 2009 and 2010. It was 12.0% in 2009, the highest level recorded, i.e. the GDP only increased RMB12 million Yuan per RMB100 million Yuan of fixed asset investment, reducing by RMB33.2 million Yuan as compared with 1996 and twice the decline of 2006. The GDP per RMB100 million Yuan of fixed asset investment increased RMB12 million Yuan as compared with 2006.

Third, it is more difficult to adjust industrial structure. The quite loose macroeconomic environment created by the "protecting growth" policy has enabled some industries with excess capacity to release their existing production capacity and also encouraged them to increase new production capacities, hence intensifying the degree of excess capacity of these industries; meanwhile, those enterprises that should be eliminated due to their high consumption of resources, low quality of products, severe contamination of environment, and low economic benefits have ways to survive. This is why we find it more difficult to adjust the economic structure.

Finally, the potential and actual financial risks are increased. When the macroeconomic policy of "protecting growth" is put into practice, there will be a massive increase in investment and loans. In previous years, governments at all levels increased several trillions of investment in response to the global financial crisis, but a large portion of this investment was raised by means of debt financing. According to statistics, more than 50% of RMB10.7 trillion debts of local governments, namely more than RMB5 trillion Yuan, were generated in three years around 2009. In addition, the "protecting growth" policy also led to an unprecedented increase in the bank's credit scale. According to relevant data, the total loan issued by all commercial banks nearly amounted to the sum of loans 30 years ago. The long-term loans made up a large proportion of these loans, increasing the potential financial risk and fiscal risk.

In brief, "protecting growth" is a double-edged sword, which we can never draw without hesitation. Currently in China, there is neither an internal nor external economic environment for the need of "protecting growth". Therefore, the macroeconomic policy cannot shift from "steadying growth" to "protecting growth".

(Published in *People's Tribune*, August 2012. All data referenced in this article are sourced from *China Statistical Yearbook [2011]*, China Statistics Press, 2011 edition)

3 Maintain smooth, rapid economic development, expand employment

Employment is always one of the socio-economic problems with which the Chinese government, experts and scholars, and the public are concerned. Since the reform and opening up over 30 years ago, a large number of jobs have been available for labor due to the rapid development of the economy, especially the high speed of the evolution of industrialization and urbanization in China, which, on the one hand, solved the employment problem of urban population successfully, and on the other, helped more than 200 million rural laborers get jobs after emigrating from the rural areas. This has facilitated the steady development of economic society beyond example. So far, the registered unemployment rate of the urban population in China remains below 4.3%, much lower than many foreign countries.

However, we should also see that the development of China's economic society has entered into a new period. The international environment of China's economy has changed dramatically. The American economy became too weak to recover after the financial crisis; many European countries suffered a severe economic recession after they were brought into the sovereign debt crisis; the long-term downturn of Japanese economy deteriorated after a seismic tsunami and a nuclear power disaster; and the developing countries went through severe inflation and decline in their economic growth rates. In response to these changes, many countries, especially the developed ones, chose to adjust their development strategies; as a result, the trade protectionism was reinforced, imposing a negative impact on China's exports such that the contribution rate of China's exports to economic growth turned to a negative. Considering the domestic situation, it is getting more difficult to create more job opportunities, owing to the decline in the growth rate and the intensification of the economic structure adjustment. It is important that we should properly analyze the favorable and unfavorable factors for enlarging employment under this grand background so as to come up with relevant policy measures.

1 Properly understand the economic development and employment situation in China

In the long term, there are still quite a few favorable factors to enlarge employment and maintain a higher rate of employment in China.

In the demand-side term (from the demand side and against the "supply side" in macroeconomics), China's economy will grow at a rate of more than 70% over a long period of time, and will offer quite a few jobs.

First, China now lies at a stage of rapid development of industrialization. Several years ago, we set up a research team to evaluate the process of industrialization throughout the country. Five types of indicators were chosen as the evaluation basis, including economic development level, industry structure, manufacturing structure, employment structure, and spatial structure: a system was thus built from these indicators. We put forward the hypothesis that a full mark of 100 points means the accomplishment of industrialization, and also divided the whole process of industrialization into three stages: initial stage (0–33 points), medium stage (34–66 points), and later stage (67–100 points), with each subdivided into two phases, i.e. early and later phases. For each stage, the flag value was set on the basis of predecessors' research findings. According to our evaluation, the process of industrialization in China by 2010 is still in the medium stage, uneven in development; seven provinces and municipalities, such as Beijing, Shanghai, Guangdong, Jiangsu, and Zhejiang, have moved into the later stage, but there are still twelve provinces and autonomous regions that stay in the initial stage and medium stage of industrialization respectively. We need at least 10–15 years to realize industrialization completely in China (see Table 1.3.1).[1]

Table 1.3.1 Evaluation Results of China's Industrialization Process (2007)

Regional stage		Mainland China	Four economic plates	Seven economic regions	31 provinces and municipalities
Post-industrialization stage (V)					Shanghai (100), Beijing (100)
Later phase of industrialization (IV)	Second half stage			Yangtze River Delta (76)	Tianjin (94), Guangdong (83)
	First half stage		East (68)	Pearl River Delta (68) Bohai Rim (67)	Zhejiang (80), Jiangsu (80), Shandong (73)
Medium phase of industrialization (III)	Second half stage	(52)			Liaoning (63), Fujian (59)
	First half stage		Northeast section (49)	Northeast (49)	Shanxi (45), Inner Mongolia (43), Jilin (42), Hubei (40), Hebei (40), Chongqing (37) Heilongjiang (36), Ningxia (36), Shaanxi (33), Qinghai (33)

Regional stage	Mainland China	Four economic plates	Seven economic regions	31 provinces and municipalities
Initial phase of industrialization (II)	Second half stage	Middle section (24) West section (18)	Six provinces in the middle section (24), great northwest (19), great southwest (17)	Henan (32), Hunan (30), Anhui (28), Sichuan (28), Jiangxi (27), Xinjiang (26), Gansu (23), Yunnan (22), Guangxi (21), Hainan (19)
	First half stage			Guizhou (16)
Pre-industrialization stage (I)				Tibet (0)

Second, China now lies at the stage of further development of urbanization. According to statistical data, the urbanization rate of China has been growing by more than 1 percent point since the "11th Five-Year Plan", which went up to 51.3% in 2011, the most remarkable feat ever achieved (see Table 1.3.2).

The current urbanization of China, however, is typically an incomplete urbanization. The urban population under the existing statistical caliber of China contains a large number of rural migrant workers who live permanently in towns and cities. Currently, the total number of rural migrant workers in China has exceeded 240 million people, and most of them live permanently in cities

Table 1.3.2 Changes of China's Urbanization Rate since the "11th Five-Year Plan"

Year	Number of urban population (10,000 persons)	Rate of urbanization (%)
2001	48,064	37.66
2002	50,212	39.04
2003	52,376	40.53
2004	54,823	41.76
2005	56,212	42.99
2006	58,288	44.34
2007	60,633	45.89
2008	62,403	46.99
2009	64,512	48.34
2010	66,978	49.95
2011	69,079	51.27

and towns. According to relevant data, there is a permanent resident population of 68.9283 million in four mega-cities such as Beijing, Shanghai, Guangzhou, and Shenzhen, but the registered population is 36.883 million only, which accounts for only 46.5% of the permanent resident population.[2] Though these rural migrant workers who dwell permanently in towns are reckoned in the urban population, they can hardly enjoy the same treatment as urban residents in labor and employment, wage and welfare, children's education, social security, and affordable housing purchase. If we exclude the population that is not completely urbanized, the urbanization rate of China will fall at least 10 percent points. For this reason, the current urbanization rate of China is merely a statistically incomplete rate of urbanization. In addition, the statistical figures have shown that the proportion of the urban population is increasing rapidly, but the urban residents' diathesis, living quality, consumer behavior, ideology, and management method can hardly keep pace with it. The low quality of urbanization is ill-adapted to the urbanization rate of population; besides, the growth rate of the urbanization of China will slow down as urbanization develops further. We need at least 10–15 years to push the urbanization rate above 60%.

Third, China's economy develops unevenly and a wide gap exists in regional development. In 2011, the per capita GNP of China went over USD5000 (IMF: USD5414); the GRP per capita in the eastern region surpassed USD7000 while that of many provinces in the middle and western regions were much less than the national average, equivalent to only 40–50% of the average in the eastern region. The gap in development level can be greater between the west and the east: the GRP per capita in the west is only 51.5% of that in the east, the financial revenue per capita in the west only 51.9% of that in the east, the financial expenditure in the west is only 8.3% of that in the east, the resident consumption level in the west is only 47.8% of that in the east, the disposable income of urban residents in the west is only 32.1% of that in the east, and the rural per capita net income is only 45.7% of that in the east. We also need at least 10–15 years to narrow this gap down to a reasonable level.

So, there is the possibility that the economic growth rate of China remains above 7% in the period of the next 10–15 years. What's more, this growth rate will be supported by such main production factors as high saving rate, enormous work force, rapid development in education, and steady improvement of the technological level. This is a reliable security to create more jobs and reduce the unemployment rate.

In the view of the labor supply side, the size of the population reaching labor age in China is on a yearly decline due to a sharp fall in the birth rate. The natural growth rate of China's population was up to 14.4% in 1990, but it fell to 4.8% in 2010. According to data from the National Bureau of Statistics, the amount of the population reaching labor age in the current year averaged out to 23.948 million during the "10th Five-Year Plan", 20.73 million people in the first four years of the "11th Five-Year Plan", decreasing 3.218 million per year on average. The labor force participation rate also fell from around 76% during the "10th Five-Year Plan" to around 74% during "11th Five-Year

Plan", decreasing nearly 2 percent points.[3] In the meantime, the growth rate of employed persons in China slowed down; during the "10th Five-Year Plan", a total of 25.62 million people were newly employed, increasing by 5.124 million people per year on average; during the "11th Five-Year Plan", a total of 14.58 million newly employed people were added, reducing by 2.916 million per year on average, with an average annual decrease of 2.208 million people.[4] This is one of the reasons for the "shortage of migrant workers" and the significant rise in the wage level of laborers. Some demographers and economists have predicted that there will be a negative growth in China's population reaching labor age by end of the "12th Five-Year Plan" at the latest.

As opposed to a downward trend in the employed population, China's urban population shows an upward trend. During the "10th Five-Year Plan", a total of 52.38 million people were newly employed in cities and towns, increasing by 10.47 million per year on average; during the "11th Five-Year Plan", the total number grew to 62.98 million, increasing by 12.59 million per year on average. The total number of newly employed persons in cities and towns during the "11th Five-Year Plan" increased per year by 2.12 million as against that during the "10th Five-Year Plan" (see Table 1.3.3).

Nevertheless, we should also see the unfavorable factors when enlarging employment.

First, the elastic coefficient of employment in China keeps falling under the influences of economic development, changes in industrial structure, and advances in technology. Since the late 1990s, China's economic growth has moved into a rapid development period of heavy industrialization and

Table 1.3.3 Changes in China's Employed Population since the "10th Five-Year Plan"

Year	Number of employed persons in current year (10,000 persons)	Number of employed persons added in current year (10,000 persons)	In current year, increased by (%)	Number of urban employed persons added in current year (10,000 persons)	In current year, increased by (%)
2001	72,797	712	0.98	982	1.1
2002	73,280	483	0.66	1,036	1.4
2003	73,736	456	0.62	1,071	1.5
2004	74,264	528	0.72	1,063	1.4
2005	74,647	383	0.52	1,096	1.5
2006	74,978	331	0.44	1,241	1.7
2007	75,321	343	0.46	1,323	1.8
2008	75,564	243	0.32	1,150	1.5
2009	75,826	262	0.35	1,219	1.6
2010	76,105	279	0.37	1,365	1.8

Source: Calculated based on figures available in *China Statistical Yearbook* (2011)

urbanization. In this period, one of the prominent features of economic development is that the capital-intensive industry has become the main engine to drive economic growth while the development of the labor-intensive industry has slowed. This change has undermined the driving effects of economic growth on employment growth. In the 1990s, the elastic coefficient of employment was basically trending up in China; but the specific value began trending down in the 21st century; it was 0.11 in 2000, i.e. GDP increased 1 percent point, the total population of employed persons increased 0.11 percent points, about 0.823 million persons; and it reduced to 0.04 in 2010, increased by about 0.3112 million persons.

Of course, we are also conscious of another phenomenon: there is a negative correlation between the employment elastic coefficient and GDP growth rate. The employment elastic coefficient tends to descend in years with a high growth rate; in other words, if the economic growth rate declines appropriately, the increased number of employed persons will possibly not grow per 1 percent point of GDP increased (see Table 1.3.4).

Table 1.3.4 Employment Elasticity Increased by GDP

Year	Annual growth rate of employed persons (%)	Annual growth rate of GDP (%)	Employment elasticity increased by GDP
1991	1.15	9.2	0.12
1992	1.01	14.2	0.07
1993	0.99	14.0	0.07
1994	0.97	13.1	0.07
1995	0.90	10.9	0.08
1996	1.30	10.0	0.13
1997	1.26	9.3	0.14
1998	1.17	7.8	0.15
1999	1.07	7.6	0.14
2000	0.97	8.4	0.11
2001	0.99	8.3	0.12
2002	0.66	9.1	0.07
2003	0.62	10.0	0.06
2004	0.72	10.1	0.07
2005	0.52	11.3	0.05
2006	0.44	12.7	0.03
2007	0.46	14.2	0.03
2008	0.32	9.6	0.03
2009	0.35	9.2	0.04
2010	0.37	10.4	0.03
2011	0.41	9.2	0.04

Source: National Bureau of Statistics website

Second, there is a serious phenomenon of structural unemployment such that some special groups are put under enormous pressure to get employed. While some groups find it hard to find jobs, some enterprises feel it is difficult to recruit eligible employees. The reasons may be as follows:

(1) Besides a huge population, the rural migrant workers are characterized by inadequate professional skills, high mobility, and unsteady employment. They are already an important part of China's workforce. According to data from the fifth census of China, the rural migrant workers account for 52% of total staff in the secondary industry, including 68% in manufacturing industry and 80% in building industry. In the next 10–15 years, quite a few of the surplus rural laborers will transfer from rural areas to cities and towns and get employed therein, but their employment is vulnerable to economic fluctuations. According to a survey by the Ministry of Human Resources and Social Security, there were at least 20 million rural workers returning home at the end of 2008 and in the first half of 2009 due to financial crisis.[5] To expand the employment of rural workers is frequently a big problem facing governments, enterprises, and various social organizations.

(2) The graduates from universities and colleges are faced with increasingly tough conditions and pressure to get employed. According to relevant data, the initial employment rate of college graduates has remained around 70% since 2003, but the absolute quantity kept rising constantly, totaling about 0.646 million persons in 2003, up to 1 million in 2006 for the first time, about 2 million in 2010, around 3 million including the unemployed by the end of last year; however, China is short of highly skilled talents, especially the skilled workers.[6] According to statistical data, the number of skilled laborers in China who are certified to national job qualification or its equivalence accounts for 33% of total urban laborers compared to 50% in developed countries; the number of highly-skilled talents of China, such as senior technicians, technicians, and senior workers, accounts for only 21% of all laborers compared to 30% in developed countries. According to a statistical analysis of labor market job supply and demand information in 93 cities conducted by the Monitoring Center for China Labor Market Information Network, the ratio between job vacancies and applicants at all technical levels remains greater than one even in the fourth quarter of 2008 when the financial crisis imposed a tremendous impact on the labor market, and the number of senior technicians, technicians, and senior engineers in demand is 1.94, 1.81, and 1.57 times the number of applicants respectively.[7]

(3) It is more difficult for laid-off and demobilized people to get re-employed, especially for those over the age of 40 (female) and 50 (male).

From the analysis above, while the contradiction of supply exceeding the demand of labor force will be alleviated to some extent in China, the employment problem can be solved only by means of creating millions upon millions of jobs every year in cities and towns. It remains an arduous task for us to expand employment.

2 Always regard job enlargement as an important job and a primary goal of the government's macroeconomic policy, industrial policy, and labor market policy, and endeavor to expand employment

First, maintain a steady and rapid growth of economy. There is an alterable relation of negative correlation between economic growth and unemployment rate. According to studies on the relation between economic growth and unemployment in the United States by some economists in foreign countries, the unemployment rate falls by 1 percent point per 2 percent points of GDP increased, based on 3% potential growth rate of GDP; in turn, the unemployment rate rises by 1 percent point per 1 percent point of GDP decreased.[8] In the next 10–15 years, there is the possibility that the growth rate will remain above 7% in China, but having this possibility realized will depend on our economic policy. Not only shall we keep the growth rate above 7% but also achieve an inclusive growth in order to avoid an economic growth without increasing jobs or a higher economic growth rate with lower growth in employment. For this purpose, we will continue to uphold the principle of centering on economic work and giving priority to development, and adhere to a scientific, coordinated, and sustainable outlook on development.

Second, the government should promote development of the tertiary industry and labor-intensive industry during structure adjustment and upgrading of industries. According to the historical data on employment in various industries of China, the annual growth rate of employed persons throughout the country averaged out to 0.54% in 10 years from 2000 to 2010, including 2.63% in the primary industry, 3.02% in the secondary industry, and 2.88% in the tertiary industry. In the long term, the labor force remains surplus in the primary industry; in 2010, the rural employed population was up to 38%, but the output value of the primary industry accounted for only 10% of the GDP. With the development of industrialization and urbanization, a large quantity of the surplus rural labor force will migrate from the rural areas, so the employment rate of the primary industry will be on a further decline, trending towards a negative growth. More jobs will be created as China lies in the medium stage of industrialization and there is a broad space of development in the secondary industry. Currently, the proportion of the tertiary industry of the GDP remains low, only 44% in 2010, and the number of persons engaged in the tertiary industry was only 34%, far lower than developed countries and much lower than many developing countries; but the tertiary industry has broad space for development and will become the main force to expand employment in China. Therefore, priorities will be given to the development of the tertiary industry as well as to the secondary industry (see Table 1.3.5).

In addition, we should also properly deal with the relationship between capital-intensive industry and labor-intensive industry during the structure adjustment and upgrading of industries, take into account both subjective and objective conditions, and avoid the blind pursuit of capital-intensive industry. Especially,

Table 1.3.5 Annual Growth Rate of Employed Population Nationwide and in Three Major Industries (%)

Year	National	Primary industry	Secondary industry	Tertiary industry
2000	0.97	0.77	−1.23	3.22
2001	0.99	0.99	0.09	1.72
2002	0.66	0.66	−3.40	3.93
2003	0.62	−1.19	1.56	3.09
2004	0.72	−3.80	4.91	5.18
2005	0.52	−3.98	6.32	3.14
2006	0.44	−4.49	6.35	3.00
2007	0.46	−3.79	6.84	1.08
2008	0.32	−2.63	1.82	2.80
2009	0.35	−3.45	2.56	3.07
2010	0.37	−3.32	3.61	1.84
Average annual growth rate	0.54	−2.52	3.02	2.88

Source: *China Statistical Yearbook* (all years)

some areas in the middle and western regions should focus substantially on the development of labor-intensive industry to address employment of labor force, apart from making full use of advantageous resources.

Third, promote the development of non-public economy and small or micro enterprises. From employment growth situation of different economic types, the state-owned and collective-owned sectors have witnessed a negative growth rate of employment while the non-state sectors have become the main force to create job opportunities since the year of 2000. The population of employed persons in private enterprises grew from 12.68 million in 2000 to 60.71 million in 2010, increasing 17.0% per year on average and ranking the first of all economic types; next comes the "limited liability company", the population of employed persons which grew from 6.87 million in 2000 to 26.13 million in 2010, with an average annual growth rate of 14.3% (see Table 1.3.6).

Moreover, the medium- and small-sized enterprises are the main force to expand employment in China. Now there are millions upon millions of medium- and small-sized enterprises, accounting for over 99% of the total number of enterprises in China. They have contributed over 60% of the total output value, over 50% of tax revenue, over 70% of import and export volume, and, in particular, over 80% of jobs in cities and towns, with 44 million new jobs created in the "11th Five-Year Plan" period alone. We must endeavor to continue to develop medium- and small-sized enterprises, especially small- and micro-sized ones by reducing the burdens on them, and creating a loose environment for them.

Table 1.3.6 Changes in Employed Population in Different Economic Types of China (2000–2010)

Year	Year of 2000 (10,000 persons)	Year of 2010 (10,000 persons)	Average annual growth rate (%)
State-owned enterprise	8,102	6,516	–2.15
Urban collective-owned enterprise	1,499	597	–8.80
Joint-equity cooperative enterprise	155	156	0.06
Joint ownership enterprise	42	36	–1.53
Limited liability company	687	2,613	14.29
Incorporated company	457	1,024	8.40
Private enterprise	1,268	6,071	16.95
Enterprise with investment from Hong Kong, Macao, or Taiwan	310	770	9.52
Foreign-invested enterprise	332	1053	12.24
Self-employed enterprise	2,136	4,467	7.66

Source: *China Statistical Yearbook 2001 & 2011*

Finally, the government should adjust educational structure to promote development of secondary vocational and technical education of various types. The existing education system of China is ill adapted to the human capital demand for upgrading the industrial structure and for the development of urbanization. While the enrollment scale of regular institutions of higher learning is expanded, the development of a secondary technical education has fallen far behind, giving a mass of middle school graduates few opportunities to receive professional and technical education or training. According to data from the National Bureau of Statistics, the proportion of education spending on regular institutions of higher learning increased from 16.26% of the total expenditure of national education funds in 1996 to 28.98% in 2010; in the same period, however, the proportion of education spending on trade schools decreased from 13.18% to 7.26%. This leads to two ubiquitous social problems: a shortage of technical workers and job hunting difficulty among non-skilled workers and college graduates. We should properly deal with the relationship between higher education and secondary vocational education, enlarge investment into vocational education, and encourage private investment into secondary technical and vocational schools in order to produce more skilled workers and technical experts to satisfy the needs of industrialization and economic modernization (see Table 1.3.7).

Finally, the government should improve and perfect policy measures of active employment. We should refine various preferential policies for re-employment and increase the capital investment into the implementation of a re-employment policy; promote the construction of a social re-employment service system and raise the capability and efficiency of service institutions; further strengthen the construction of a labor market network, in order to set up a trans-provincial and trans-regional labor market network, and make available the information about

Table 1.3.7 Proportions of Technical and Vocational Schools in National Education Funds (%)

Year	Regular institutions of higher learning	Regular middle schools	Secondary technical & vocational schools	Primary schools
1996	16.26	30.76	13.18	33.87
1997	17.23	30.40	13.26	33.02
1998	20.28	29.69	12.34	31.19
1999	22.83	29.41	11.77	29.70
2000	25.54	29.42	10.59	28.11
2001	26.90	29.96	8.98	27.49
2002	28.89	30.48	7.92	26.43
2003	30.18	30.84	7.64	25.38
2004	31.17	30.74	7.08	24.92
2005	31.57	30.80	6.76	24.14
2006	31.15	29.67	6.64	23.43
2007	30.97	28.42	7.01	24.27
2008	29.98	28.48	7.24	24.49
2009	28.98	28.89	7.26	25.56

Source: *China Statistical Yearbook* (all years)

labor supply and demand as well as recruitments and jobseekers; provide various vocational trainings, especially the training of the rural migrant workers for job skills; and encourage enterprises to offer on-job training and job-transfer training for their employees so as to facilitate the job-transfer of more laid-off employees inside their enterprises. The government is supposed to help special groups get employed by implementing preferential policies such as encouraging college students' innovative undertakings, providing social service jobs, and encouraging enterprises to enroll unemployed persons. While carrying out the active employment policy, we should also improve the social security system, and expand and refine the unemployment insurance system to provide relief for the unemployed.

(Published in *China Yan'an Executive Leadership Academy*, Issue 5, 2012)

Notes

1 Chiefly edited by Chen Jiagui: *China's Economic Development – Medium Evaluation in the "11th Five-Year Plan" and Outlook of the "12th Five-Year Plan"*, China Social Sciences Press, 2010.
2 Chiefly edited by Pan Jiahua and Wei Houkai: *Annual Report on Urban Development of China*, Social Sciences Academic Press (China), 2011.
3 Calculated based on figures available in *China Statistical Yearbook* (2010).
4 Ibid.
5 Source: The Ministry of Human Resources and Social Security website.
6 Website of the Ministry of Education of the People's Republic of China.
7 Website of the Ministry of Human Resources and Social Security of the People's Republic of China.
8 Okun's Law.

4 Grasp the direction, focus, and effort of the macroeconomic regulation and control

In the first half of this year, China's economy developed steadily and rapidly as there was a good harvest of summer grain crops, a good trend in the industrial growth, a rapid growth in the service industry, a substantial increase in financial revenue, a rise in urban and rural residents' income, an efficient regulation and control of prices, and a generally good trend of economic operation. However, there still exist some underlying conflicts in economic development and some remarkable new situations and new problems, including the acceleration of high energy-consuming enterprises; an increasingly intense power supply; a tight operating environment for small and micro enterprises; the residents' income growth rate lower than the growth rate of financial revenue, lower than the growth rate of corporate profit, and lower than the growth rate of GDP; and an insecure foundation for the slowdown of rising prices that are likely to rebound. To create a good economic situation in the second half of the year, we need to make a proper judgment of the economic situation; grasp the direction, focus, and effort of the macroeconomic regulation and control; and properly deal with the relationship among the growth rate, structure, and prices.

1 Make a proper judgment of the economic situation and grasp the direction of macroeconomic regulation and control

Currently, people are talking much about China's economic situation and trend in the second half of the year. Some of them believe that China's economy is moving towards a hard landing, and that this trend is irresistible. Some argue that there will be possibly a double dip in China's economy. Some others hold the view that there is a symptom of economic stagnation. Some even say that economic stagnation has emerged. We must never be credulous about these opinions, but pay close attention to them.

In the first half of this year, neither a second dip nor a hard landing will occur in China's economy, notwithstanding the slight decline in economic growth rate. Under the influence of the global financial crisis, the economic growth rates of China dropped to 6.8% in the fourth quarter of 2008 and to 6.1% in the first quarter of 2009. Obviously, a second dip means the GDP growth rate drops below 7%. The growth rate of China's GDP was 9.5% in the first half of this year. Some well-known research institutions both at home and abroad have forecast that the growth rate of China's GDP this year is expected to be around 9.3%, despite the slight decline in the previous year. In a quarterly perspective, the growth rates of the GDP were 9.7% and 9.5% respectively in the first quarter and the second quarter, and were expected to be around 9% in the following two quarters, which were unlikely to incur a second dip. The hard landing is visualized by the economists commenting on the sharp turn from a "too hot" economy down to a "too cold" one. This will not happen in China's economy. In a yearly perspective, the growth rate of China's GDP was 10.3% in the previous year, perhaps only 1 percent point lower this year if GDP grows around 9.3%. In a quarterly perspective, the year-over-year growth rate of China's GDP was 9.7% in the first quarter of this year, 9.5% in the second quarter – which remained 9.5–10% for four continuous quarters from the third of last year to the second of this year, perhaps only 1 percent point of decline even if it drops to around 9% in the fourth quarter. In a monthly perspective, among the three major industries, the secondary industry has contributed the most to the GDP despite a fall in the value added by industrial enterprises above a designated size (falling from 14.1% in January to 13.3% in May, only a 0.8 percent points decrease, but resurging in June to a growth rate of around 15.1%); what's more, the growth rate of the value added by industrial enterprises above a designated size has remained around 14% from last June to this June, and this trend is expected to continue in the second half of this year. It is thus clear that the hard landing will not occur hot on the heels of a slow and reasonable decline in growth rates of both the industrial value added and the GDP.

Then, has China's economic stagnation emerged? The answer is "no". Stagflation, originally called *stagnant inflation*, is a concept coined by some western economists to explain a peculiar phenomenon of American economy in the 1970s when there was a sharp fall in American economic growth rate due to a sharp rise in oil prices during the world oil crisis, resulting in growing unemployment and rocketing prices. The concept is usually used by economists under two premises: 1) the economic growth rate falls below the potential growth rate of GDP or stops while prices soar and stay at the highest level; and 2) this phenomenon usually lasts for years rather than fluctuates during a short term; for example, this lasted for about 10 years in the United States after the oil crisis in the 1970s. Many economists have forecasted a potential growth rate of about 8% for China's GDP. In the outline of the "12th Five-Year Plan", the expected target of economic growth is set at 7%, with the annual expected target at 8%. It is predicted that the growth rate of China's GDP will remain up to 9%, within the reasonable range of growth. The decline from above 10% down to around 9% is one that drops from a record high, but this is a normal fluctuation in economy rather than a sharp decline in the economic growth rate. That prices are currently on the high side is also a matter of normal fluctuation in an economy. In addition, there are no signs indicating a long-term continuity of declining economic growth rate or rising prices. So, there is no ground for the argument that China's economic stagnation has emerged.

In conclusion, it is normal and acceptable that the economic growth rate of China declines moderately under the influence of the international economic situation, under the restraint of resources and environment, and under the pressure of rising prices. Considering the potent impetus for economic growth, the current growth rate is not as slow as it can be. In the first half of the year, the fixed assets investment grew 25.6% year over year, the total retail sales of social consumer goods grew 16.3%, and the exports, 24%. It is also noted that the economic growth rate and rising prices are likely to rebound. The direction of current macroeconomic regulation and control, therefore, is not to loosen control in order to facilitate growth and prevent a second dip and the hard landing of economy, but to make the economic growth rate stabilize ideally at 8–9% during the moderate decline so as to create a good macro environment for fighting inflation, adjusting economic structure, and altering the economic development pattern. No longer shall we relive the vicious cycle where the economic growth is contracted whenever it is overheated, voices of complaint are heard wherever it is contracted, it loosens wherever there are voices of complaint, and it heats up again as soon as it is loosened. Without suppression of an excessively rapid economic growth rate, it will be unlikely to make substantial progress in the adjusting economic structure and altering economic development pattern; and the underlying conflicts will deteriorate in economic development. All these will prejudice the deepening of reform and the long-term, smooth, steady, and healthy development of China's economy.

2 Highlight the focus of macroeconomic regulation and control, and try every means to steady prices

The Central Government of China has designated steadying the general level of prices as the primary task of macroeconomic regulation and control. This correct decision has achieved preliminary results after several months' effort. The uptrend of prices is already brought down to some extent. However, the economic development situation shows that the focus of macroeconomic regulation and control cannot be changed, i.e. the primary task still is to steady prices.

Currently, the general level of prices remains high. In the first half of this year, the CPI grew 5.4%, remained at 4.9% in January and February, but climbed over 5% in the remaining four months, including 6.4% in June – the highest rate this year. In the second half of this year, the rise in prices slowed, but it may climb over 5% in the whole year. In the first half of the year, the general level of PPI grew 7.0% on average, and up to 7.1% in June.

Some new phenomena occurred before the pressure of rising prices was entirely alleviated. In the view of consumer goods, the CPI showed a widespread upward trend. According to data published by the National Bureau of Statistics, among 39 items of main product categories included in the consumer price index statistics, the number of items with month-over-month rising monthly prices from January to May was 32, 31, 29, 33, and 33 respectively.

On a month-over-month basis, the rise in prices of consumer goods was slowing down, but it rebounded in June, increasing 0.3 percent points over May; the pork price, in particular, went up rapidly, rising 11.4% in June over May. This shows an insecure foundation for prices to slow down such that the prices will rebound if the control loosens a bit. Besides, the non-food prices rising rapidly from March to May will have a great effect on the rise in the general level of prices.

As there is no great change in the main factors that lead to a rapid rise in prices, steadying prices is confronted with many tough problems: 1) there is no radical change in excess liquidity since it needs a long time to absorb the huge quantity of currencies issued – this is due to a long-term foreign trade surplus and a large number of loans released in 2008 and 2009, together with the impact of global excess liquidity originated from the quantitative easing monetary policy implemented by the American government; 2) the insecure foundation of agriculture, the low productivity of agricultural labor, and the low commodity rate of agricultural and animal products. With a large population, China has a strong demand in agricultural and animal products, so the conflict between supply and demand cannot be resolved in a short time and the prices rise inevitably. Where a severe, natural disaster occurs, the conflict will intensify and the rise in prices will speed up. In addition, the rising costs of agricultural means of production and labor will also push up prices of agricultural and animal products; 3) the rising prices are caused mainly by rising costs; staff wages will rise definitely with a declining growth rate of labor force population as well as further implementation of the nationally important policy designed to raise proportion of residents' income in national revenue and proportion of labor remuneration in primary distribution; the product cost of part of enterprise will increase with promotion of price reform and rationalization of unreasonable price relations; the rise in prices of some commodities and services was deferred in the first half of the year due to macroeconomic regulation and control, but it will continue as operating cost rises in the second half of the year; and 4) enormous pressure of exported inflation remains there; the prices of bulk commodities, such as crude oil, iron ore, grain, oils and cotton, fluctuating at high level, will push up prices of domestic goods.

3 Enhance coordination of macro-control policy and grasp its effort and rhythm

Currently, the development of China's economy lies at a critical moment, so we need to study carefully and decide prudently on how to keep the direction, highlight the focus, maintain the continuity, and grasp the focus and rhythm of macroeconomic regulation and control.

Since the beginning of this year, the Central Bank has raised the deposit reserve ratio for the sixth time consecutively and raised the benchmark interest rate of banks for the third time, so as to curb rapid economic growth and inflation. Some of the deflationary measures laid down by the Central Bank have achieved results, but though not until several months later. The proactive financial policy has played an important role in alleviating the impact of the global financial crisis on China's economy, facilitating adjustment of economic structure, and improving people's livelihood. Currently, there are quite a few uncertainties in the international economic trend. The American economy becomes too weak to recover; the Japanese economy feels faint to revive under the influences of earthquake, tsunami, and nuclear power plant disaster; some of the European countries are undergoing the sovereign debt crisis; and the major, developing countries are under the pressure of inflation. All these problems will inevitably generate adverse effects on China's economy. For this reason, the macro-control policy should focus on steadying the economic growth rate in the second half of the year. We may take a wait-and-see approach in the third quarter, and carry out an overall evaluation of the macro-control effects at the end of the third quarter, then decide whether it needs fine-tuning. The macro-economic policy should stay neutral as long as the economic growth rate drops to 8–9% and the inflation rate drops to around 4%.

In order to solve these economic problems, we need to enhance the coordinating roles of macro-control policies and measures. To achieve this purpose, we should combine macro control with deepening reform to improve the effectiveness of macro-control policies and measures; consolidate financial policy and monetary policy; alter the past practice that laid more emphasis on the control-of-demand side rather than on the supply side; gradually change monetary policy that laid more stress on utilizing the tool of a deposit reserve ratio than on the price of funds; actively promote reform on interest rate liberalization, especially in the current case of negative interest rate; alter the proactive financial policy that stressed the enlargement of government debts and increase of government investment, but overlooked reform of the tax system and reduction of enterprises' tax burden; and as for the application of macro-control measures, practices that preferred administrative measures should be altered. Some of the administrative measures should not be applied excessively for a long time, because they have covered up and built up contradictions and would cause negative effects though they seemingly achieved fast results.

(Published in *People's Daily*, Aug 5, 2011)

5 Properly deal with the relationship between steady growth, structural adjustment, and inflation

This is the beginning year of the "12th Five-Year Plan". This year, it will be of vital importance to accomplish the target tasks of the "12th Five-Year Plan". In the meantime, China's economic development is confronted with an extremely complex situation this year. Premier Wen Jiabao pointed out in his *Report on the Work of the Government* that we should maintain continuity and stability of macroeconomic policy, improve its pertinence and flexibility, deal with relationship between the steady and rapid development of the economy, and adjust the economic structure and control of inflation expectations. Properly balancing steady growth, structural adjustment, and inflation will be of great significance to accomplishing the goals of socio-economic development and to preventing possible drastic fluctuations in the economy.

1 Consider curbing inflation the primary task of current macroeconomic regulation and control

Since last May, the general price level of China has remained high; CPI (consumer price index) reached 4.9% in October, 5.1% in November, 4.6% in December, and 3.3% for the whole year; PPI (producer price index) remained high as well. CPI was up to 4.9% in January this year; though it leveled off in February, there were still as many factors as needed to increase inflationary pressure, some of which even have intensified their active force. It may be inferred that the inflationary pressure is likely to intensify in 2011. So we must take potent measures to hold down inflation. The reasons that inflationary pressure has increased are as follows:

(1) Excess liquidity. Prior to the outbreak of the international financial crisis, the problem of excess liquidity had begun to build up with accelerating issuance of paper money when an ample trade surplus appeared in China. Since the beginning of the fourth quarter of 2008, the moderately loose monetary policy was launched by the Chinese government in response to the international financial crisis, by which the total amount of loans in 2009 was scheduled to increase to RMB5 trillion Yuan, but it proved to be 9.69 trillion, increased additionally by 4.69 trillion. In 2010, the base amount of

5 trillion was allowed to increase by 16%, i.e. 5.8 trillion, but the actual sum of the loans amounted to more than 8 trillion. This has resulted in a serious problem of excess liquidity. From the beginning of the fourth quarter of 2010, China turned its moderately loose monetary policy to prudent monetary policy, with an attempt to tighten up, but this goal cannot be accomplished in one stroke. In January and February of this year, the scale of commercial bank loans grew 17.7% and 17.9% respectively, exceeding the expected growth rate despite a slight decline over the same period in 2009 and 2010. It needs several years to absorb the paper money issued in the preceding years and the massive credit loans. China's economy is also affected by the American quantitative easing monetary policy. In the following several years, the excess liquidity will continually be the main factor that leads to inflationary pressure.

(2) Excessively rapid rate of economic growth. It is generally acknowledged that the potential growth rate of China's economy stays around 9%. Thus, the 7% anticipated target of economic growth set in the outline of the "12th Five-Year Plan" is scientifically justified and realistic. Of the eight years from 2003 through 2010, there were six years that the growth rate of China's GDP remained over 10%; the average growth rate was up to 11.2% during the "11th Five-Year Plan". The long-term rapid growth will inevitably push up prices.

(3) Insecure agricultural foundation. For quite some time, especially since the "11th Five-Year Plan", China has taken a series of measures to stimulate agricultural growth and increase farmers' income; in particular, the removal of an agricultural tax and a variety of subsidies granted to grain farmers have aroused farmers' enthusiasm to grow grain. However, farmers are generally dependent on the mercy of the elements due to the weak farming infrastructure, particularly the inadequate input in water conservancy facilities, feeble capacities to fight and reduce the natural calamities, lagging agricultural technology and farmland management, low level of modernization, less arable land area per household, poor scale economy, a large number of young adults migrating to cities and towns to hunt jobs, low quality of agricultural labor force, and lower comparative profit as against other industries. In addition, as China has a large population and the economic and social development has increased the demand for agricultural products, there will be a tight balance between the supply and demand of major agricultural products including grain, such that any slight fluctuation may affect supply. The prices of major agricultural products will be on the rise.

(4) Rising costs. First, the wage cost is rising. As wages have hiked in the recent two years and the social insurance fund has expanded its coverage, the wage expenditure of enterprises has risen. Second, the prices of energy resources and raw materials are soaring. So are the prices of petroleum, iron ore, and cotton. As a result, the prices of downstream products are pushed up. The rising prices of industrial products cause the prices of agricultural products to climb. Third, the price of land is rising. This, on the one hand, pushes up

the prices of real estate, and on the other, increases the residents' expenses. In addition, the rise in product costs and service prices is also forced up by the reform of resource products pricing, a rise in environment cost, and a rise in prices of other elements.

(5) Imported inflation. In the past few years, the prices of some bulk commodities rise quickly on the international market. China is highly dependent on the international market for energy resources and some fundamental raw materials, e.g. 50% of petroleum and iron ore depend on import. As the world economy revives and the economic growth increases, the demand of bulk commodities such as energy resources, iron ore, and cotton, and the prices of these commodities, begin to rise in a big way. Last year, there was some increase in imports of bulk commodities in China, including crude oil, iron ore, plastics, copper, petroleum products, and soybean, but there was a sharp increase in corporate expenditures due to a dramatic rise in prices, and the prices of industrial products were raised accordingly. In recent years, China's CPI has climbed as a result of the uptrend in prices of agricultural products, including grain and oils, as well as the increasing import volumes of soybeans and oils.

The five factors are closely interrelated, but they work differently. Some people argue that the deflation policy will have no effect on the current cost-push rise in prices. This argument deserves discussion. Of the five factors mentioned above, the first three have played a bigger role; in particular, the "excessively rapid rate of economic growth" did the most. For this reason, the economic growth rate must be put under control, apart from increasing the supply of agricultural products and appropriately tightening liquidity.

2 Properly dealing with the relationship between steadying the economic growth rate and curbing inflation

An excessively rapid rate of economic growth and strong demand will inevitably push up prices and lead to inflationary pressure and even serious inflation. Instead, the cost will be controlled if the economic growth rate is harnessed within a reasonable range and the demand is stabilized. This is because the rise in prices will be slowed when there is less demand of labor force, energy resources and raw materials and the economic growth rate is under control. Evidences are provided in historical data. Of the 21 years from 1990 through 2010, the growth rate of GDP in 10 years remained below 10%; only three of the ten years witnessed CPI over 3%, and the remaining seven years saw CPI below 3%. Especially in the period from 1992 to 1995, the GDP grew excessively: it ranged between 11% and 15%, and it was followed by CPI, which ranged between 6% and 25%. A similar relation exists between the increased rate of PPI and the growth rate of the GDP.

The anticipated target of economic growth is set at 7% in the outline of the "12th Five-Year Plan". If we consider it the minimum growth target, the optimal range of growth rate will be 8–9%, and the suboptimal will be 9–10%; any economic growth rate over 10% can be interpreted as overheated. In reality, however, if the economic growth rate falls below 10%, someone will raise objection that it is too slow; if it falls below 9%, the dissenting voices will get louder. This leaves us an impression that the economic growth rate should be as rapid as possible. Considering the potential growth rate of the economy stays around 9% in the present period, it is not difficult to accomplish it as long as the economic growth rate remains at 8–10% and the inflation rate stays below 4%, though it is ideal to achieve economic growth by 8–9% and have only a 3% inflation rate.

Those who advocated a rapid rate of economic growth have provided a list of reasons, laying much stress on employment pressure. It makes sense in general, for China has a large population. In addition to total population, however, the employment pressure is also contingent on population composition, economic aggregate, and industrial structure. Due to the implementation of family planning policy in China, the natural growth rate of the population remains consistently low, and the aging problem is getting increasingly serious to such an extent that the amount of the population reaching labor age in recent years is reduced by around 5 million per year. This trend still continues. In the past several years, the phenomenon of "labor shortage" began to extend from eastern coastal areas to central and western areas. This has resulted from the reduced supply of labor force and the labor-intensive industrial structure. Therefore, an economic growth rate of around 9% will not lead to a large increase in the number of unemployed population.

Will the control of economic growth rate lead to stagflation? This is another question some feel concerned about. Stagflation will not occur in China's economy this year, and it is also impossible during the "12th Five-Year Plan". But great importance should be paid to the increasing number of aged persons, the diminishing supply of the labor force, the rapid rise in wages and benefits, and the vanishing amount of demographic dividends owing to long-term exercise of the one-child policy in China.

3 Properly deal with the relationship between steadying economic growth rate and adjusting economic structure

The economic structures subjected to adjustment vary from the structure of national income distribution to the structure of investment and consumption; from the structure of the primary, secondary, and tertiary industries to the internal structure of each industry and the structure of industrial organization; from the regional structure to the urban-rural dual structure; and from the ownership structure to the strategic adjustment of the state-owned economy.

There are some discrepancies between the economic growth rate and the adjustment of the economic structure, notwithstanding the consistency. Both of them are aimed to maintain a steady and rapid growth of the national economy and to facilitate transformation of an economic development pattern, but they differ in focus. Economic growth that focuses on short-term goals is a tactical measure; a structure adjustment that focuses on long-term goals is a strategic measure. But there is contradiction between them at times. Take the relationship between the rate of economic growth and adjustment of industrial structure as an example: a fast rate of economic growth contributes to employment and an increase of financial revenue; but if it gets too fast and demands become strong, then the backward enterprises and production facilities will have more space for expansion instead of being closed down. As a result, it will be more difficult to adjust the industrial structure. For instance, some of the enterprises in China had already met with serious problems before 2008, including excess production capacity, unreasonable industrial organization structure, etc. After the international financial crisis broke out, the proactive financial policy and the moderately loose monetary policy were enforced to avert a big slump in the economic growth rate; in particular, a huge quantity of currency and credit were put on market. As a result, though the rate of economic growth held on, the adjustment of the industrial structure was delayed in many trades and local industries. For another example: before 2008, we had proposed that the economic growth not be driven by investment; but there was a sharp increase in investment in many regions as response to the international financial crisis, thus resulting in a new height of the contribution rate of investment to economic growth. While this is an emergency move in an emergency period, it makes some sense.

So, we must properly deal with the relationship between steadying the economic growth rate and adjusting the economic structure, and combine them closely. When preparing the macroeconomic policy and making the arrangement of actual work, we must not aim at an annual high growth rate but lose sight of the adjustment of the economic structure with the result that the process of structural adjustment is delayed, nor shall we worsen the economic structure only to secure an annual high growth rate such that it gets more difficult to adjust the economic structure; rather, we should follow the instructions of the Central Government in all aspects, combine "protecting growth" with structure adjustment, and especially put the annual economic growth rate under appropriate control so as to create a good macro environment for adjusting the economic structure.

(Published in *People's Daily*, June 4, 2011)

6 Steady the economic development and control the inflation expectation

This is a year of transition from protecting growth to maintaining the steady and rapid development of the economy; it is also a year of transition from fulfilling all the anticipated goals of the "11th Five-Year Plan" to preparing for the implementation of the "12th Five-Year Plan". In the first three quarters, the national economy operates quite well on the whole, but there were some problems worthy of careful consideration. For macroeconomic regulation and control this year and next, priorities should be given to steadying the economic development and controlling the inflation expectation.

1 Steady the rate of economic growth

This year, China's GDP grew 11.9% in the first quarter, by 10.3% in the second, and by 9.6% in the third. If the economic growth rate comes to a halt, it is predicted that the economic growth rate in the whole year will be close to 10%. This is deemed as an optimal growth rate because, in the global context of economic development, the anticipated target or the minimum target of China's economic growth rate is 8%, with the optimal growth rate ranging between 8% and 9%, and the suboptimal between 9% and 10%. A growth rate over 10% can be considered overheated. Nevertheless, there is sufficient kinetic energy in government-dominated economic growth owing to high enthusiasm for economic development in all regions, strong investment impulsion, remarkable upgrading of consumption, and rapid development of industrialization and urbanization. In a month-over-month perspective, the current economy of China shows a trend of accelerating growth. According to some indicators used to measure economic sentiment, the manufacturing PMI was 53.8% in September, rising 2.1 percent points over the preceding month; the non-manufacturing PMI was 61.7%, rising 1.6 percent points over the preceding month. According to actual results of economic growth, the value added of industrial enterprises above a designated size in July, August, and September grew 1.14, 1.15, and 0.95 percent points respectively. There is the possibility that China's GDP growth rate will be greater than 10% if not well controlled. In this case, the economic development next year will face mounting pressure, such that it will be more difficult and complex to carry out macroeconomic regulation and control.

It is more noteworthy that the inflationary pressure in China is building up. This year, the CPI (consumer price index) rose on a quarterly basis, up to 2.2% in the first quarter, 2.9% in the second, and 3.5% in the third; the PPI (producer price index) was on the rise. Moreover, the inflationary pressure is likely to continue building up.

First, the problem of excess liquidity is not yet resolved. In 2009, calculated by the principle of moderately loose monetary policy, the additional amount of loans needed was 5 trillion only, but it turned out to be 9.7 trillion, increasing by 4.7 trillion; in 2010, the basic amount of 5 trillion could rise by 17% in normal cases, i.e. totaling 5.85 trillion, but it was expected to reach 7.5 trillion. According to data provided by the People's Bank of China, from August on, the monetary aggregate began to rebound, so did the growth rate of loans; the gross and net issuance of bonds hit a record high in a single month; the monetary supply volume was also raised when funds outstanding for foreign exchange were released. The amount of new bank loans is targeted for over 7.5 trillion Yuan this year; it may draw level to that for the previous year if off-balance-sheet lending is reckoned. Considering that it needs several years to absorb the large amount of credit loans released in 2009, the excess liquidity will always be the main cause for inflationary pressure in following years.

Second, the consumer price is likely to keep rising. From January to September of this year, the consumer price of China rose by 2.9%, which is very close to the anticipated target of 3%. The prices of food went up rapidly under the influences of natural calamities, rising costs, and a rise in international grain prices. In the next several months, it is likely that the prices of agricultural products remain high due to rising prices of grain in the international market and the rising cost of growing grain.

Third, the prices of bulk commodities are soaring with the advent of economic recovery worldwide as well as an increasing demand of energy resources, iron ore, and cotton for economic growth. Despite a slight additional import of bulk commodities including crude oil, iron ore, plastics, copper, oil products, and soybean in China, the prices of these commodities have risen significantly, hence pushing up the prices of industrial products.

Finally, the reform of domestic resource product prices, the rise in environment cost, and the rise in staff wages will raise enterprise costs, push up prices of industrial products, and heighten the inflation expectation. Besides, the inflationary pressure can be raised by other factors including the appreciation of the RMB.

In this case, if the economic growth rate is not controlled within a reasonable range, the overly rapid growth rate will further stimulate demand and push up the prices of commodities and assets, thus materializing the inflation expectation. For this reason, we must take steadying economic growth rate and governing inflation expectation as the primary task of macroeconomic regulation and control so as to 1) implement the "12th Five-Year Plan" successfully, and 2) to create a favorable macro-environment for accelerating the change of the economic development pattern and promoting the adjustment of economic structure.

2 Internal impetus for steady economic growth

As China has a large population and now lies in a rapid development stage of industrialization and urbanization, consumption is the most stable and sustainable impetus to stimulate economic growth. This year, the total retail sales of consumer goods of China grew 17.9% in the first quarter, by 18.5% in the second, and 18.4% in the third. With the price impact deducted, the growth rate remains as high as 15%, but it is far lower than the growth rates of investment and export. In the long run, both the proportion of consumption in national income and the contribution rate of consumption to the economic growth need to be raised. We should uphold the long-term policy of expanding consumption, particularly policies that can help narrow the urban-rural gap, enlarge employment and raise incomes of the low-income groups and the poor, improve residents' consuming abilities, and raise the contribution rate of consumption to the economic growth to around 50%.

Under the current systems of China, investment is a shock force to stimulate economic growth. It is appropriate to describe the effect of investment on China's economy with a proverb saying "Success or failure, Xiao He is the man behind it". When the economy appears sluggish, the investment, particularly the government investment, will be a powerful propeller to help it bottom out. For example, the contribution rate of investment to economic growth was up to 92% in 2009. However, investment is also a powerful propeller for the overheated economy. Whenever China's economy gets overheated, it is blamed on the over-size and over-speed of investment. The government increases investment significantly for a receding economy and cuts down on investment heavily for an overheated economy. This seems a sovereign remedy for economic upturns and downturns. But we paid a heavy price: excess production capacity in some industries, repeated and unchecked construction projects, waste of resources, deteriorating environment, sharp fall of investment benefits, buildup of potential financial risks and actual financial risks, etc. We must deepen the reform on the budget system and the investment system; endeavor to resolve a common malpractice of no one taking the responsibility for investment failure (in addition to the soft budget constraint on such public institutions as government sectors, state-owned enterprises, as well as colleges and universities), so as to maintain a reasonable size of government investment; and encourage private investment so that the volume of total investment and rate of investment are kept at a reasonable level to avoid rapid fluctuation. In the current stage of economic development, the actual investment rate of China should remain at around 20%, and the contribution rate of investment to economic growth rate should remain at around 40%.

The contribution rate of exports to economic growth depends not only on the quantity of exports, but also on the quantity of imports. It is directly under the influence of international economic changes, so it fluctuates in a wide range. For several years after China joined the WTO, the contribution rate of net exports to economic growth has remained around 3%, but that of 2009 was minus 3.9%, fluctuating by 6–7%. According to statistics from customs, from January to September, the gross value of imports and exports of China grew 37.9% over the same period last year, where exports grew 34% and import by 42.4%, with a trade surplus of US$120.6 billion and a year-over-year decrease of US$14.9 billion. If price factors are considered, the contribution rate of exports to economic growth remains very low due to the favorable balance of the whole year lower than that of last year, even if it turns from negative to positive. Since the outbreak of the international financial crisis, all countries have adjusted their strategies for economic development, and the trade protectionism in all forms has become increasingly intense so as to trigger a monetary war. Confronted with this serious situation of the international market, the export enterprises will meet with more obstacles and difficulties because their extensive export patterns are based on quantity expansion; sooner or later, they will be subjected to significant adjustment. The export enterprises must make up their mind as soon as possible to change the pattern of foreign trade, raise popularity of their brands, improve the quality and added value of their products, and endeavor to steady the contribution rate of exports to economic growth.

3 Steady macroeconomic policy

In the current economic situation, we should maintain the continuity and stability of macroeconomic policy, and see it as key to current macroeconomic regulation and control.

We will continue with the proactive financial policy. From the fourth quarter of 2008, China has exercised a more proactive financial policy in response to the international financial crisis, made greater efforts in governmental direct investment, and increased expenditure in "three agricultural services" (provided services for rural areas, agricultural activities, and farmers), and social security. As the financial policy is designed to address the problem of structural disequilibrium, it usually persists for a long time once established. As China now lies in a transitional period of economic society, it is urgent that the widening gap between regions, urban and rural areas, and different groups of people be narrowed, and the government is the main force to get it done. This year, China has witnessed a substantial increase in financial revenue and the financial deficit takes up less than 3% of GDP; so we have both the need and basic conditions to carry on a proactive financial policy. In the coming years, though, China needs to continue with a proactive financial policy, the structure of financial expenditure also needs to be adjusted so that more money will be spent on providing "three agricultural services"; on social construction of science and technology, education, and public health; on improving the social security systems; and on raising the availability of financial funds.

One of the major functions of monetary policy is to control economic aggregate. It is more flexible than financial policy, but it has less space for adjustment because the large amount of loans released in 2009 in response to the international financial crisis needs a long time to be absorbed; for this reason, the loose monetary policy was actually enforced this year, and only an economic fine-tuning can be done under such a loose premise in the fourth quarter of this year and even in the next year. Therefore, the moderately loose monetary policy should not be changed to deal with the uncertainties of international economic recovery and to avoid conveying a signal of change of monetary policy to the society; nevertheless, we must put it right, i.e. put into effect the moderately loose monetary policy. To steady economic growth rate and alleviate inflationary pressure, we should appropriately tighten up monetary policy this year and next.

(Published in *People's Daily*, Nov 11, 2010)

7 Promote the economic development to the new stage of steady and rapid development

At the meeting of the Political Bureau of the CPC Central Committee, convened not long ago, it was pointed out that the economic development of China now lies in a critical period of transition from economic turnaround to steady growth, and that it will be of great importance to, in the second half of the year, consolidate the results achieved in addressing impacts of international financial crisis, to maintain steady and rapid development of the economy, to accomplish all target tasks of the "11th Five-Year Plan", and to lay a solid foundation for development in the "12th Five-Year Plan" period. In the first half of 2010, China's economy operated generally well and moved towards the expected direction of macroeconomic regulation and control, but the economic development was still confronted with the complex internal and external environment in conjunction with quite a few conflicts and challenges that impose constraints on the smooth operation of the economy. We must conscientiously implement the decisions and arrangements of the Party Central Committee, deeply grasp the changes in economic development, strengthen the trend of economic turnaround, and promote China's economic development to a new stage of steady and rapid development.

1 Particularities of China's economy in 2010

The year of 2010 can be called "a year of transformation" or "a year of transition" because there are quite a few uncertainties and dilemmas as well as a variety of particularities in China's economic development.

(1) Transition from protecting growth to steady growth. Last year, the Central Government introduced a package of plans and a series of growth-protecting policy measures; as a result, China's GDP grew 9.1%, increasing 1.1 percent points over the anticipated target of 8% – what an amazing result! This year, there are three prospects for China's economic growth: a second dip if the growth rate falls short of 8%; an overheated economy if the growth rate climbs up to 10% in the whole year; and a steady rate of economic growth remaining at 9–10%. Judging from the economic operation in the first half of this year, we feel that the first prospect is less likely to arise, but we must take it seriously; we need to avoid the second prospect, or it may induce drastic fluctuations and complicate the economic development trend; the third prospect is most likely to arise, and it is also what

we have expected and will strive for, i.e. steady and rapid growth of the economy. Therefore, the acting point of China's macroeconomic regulation and control should be placed exactly on the transition from protecting growth to maintaining steady growth.

(2) Transition from accomplishing all expected targets of the "11th Five-Year Plan" to preparing for implementation of the "12th Five-Year Plan". According to the follow-up analysis by a research group of Economic Division of Chinese Academy of Social Sciences, an overwhelming majority of the targets prescribed in the "11th Five-Year Plan" will be realized, especially those quantitative targets; for example, the growth rate has been achieved ahead of schedule, but some targets including energy saving and emission reduction must be accomplished by making a final spurt. This is the last year and also a critical year for implementation of the "11th Five-Year Plan". This year, one of the primary tasks of economic work is to make substantial progress in aspects including energy saving and emission reduction, to strive for full-scale accomplishment of the intended targets of the "11th Five-Year Plan", and to lay a solid foundation for implementation of the "12th Five-Year Plan" so as to ensure a smooth transition of China's economy to the "12th Five-Year Plan" and ensure a good beginning of the "12th Five-Year Plan".

(3) Transition from laying particular stress on an economic growth rate in the past to focusing on the adjustment of economic structure and the transformation of economic development patterns. In order to remedy the tendency of laying more stress on the economic development speed than on the adjustment of economic structure as well as the quality and benefits of economic growth, which was formed in economic work over years, the Central Government has made arrangements for economic work at the beginning of the year, stressing that, henceforth, the top priority of economic work will be adjustment and optimization of economic structure and transformation of economic development patterns. This is a long-term but urgent task. A thousand-mile journey begins with the first step. We must act right now in a bid to have a good start this year; to make significant progress in curbing the too much and too-fast expansion of high energy-consuming enterprises, in reducing excess production capacity of some industries, in weeding out backward production facilities, in developing new energy and hi-tech industries, and in promoting the adjustment of the industrial organization; and to strive to achieve substantial progress in the next 5–10 years.

If these three transitions can be realized, China's economy will move up to a new stage of steady and rapid development.

2 Properly understand the downturn of economic growth in the second quarter of this year

In the second quarter of this year, the growth rate of China's GDP fell from 11.9% in the first quarter back to 10.3%, decreasing by 1.6 percent points; the growth rate of industrial value added fell from 19.6% in the first quarter back to 15.9%, down 3.7 percent points; and the growth rate of total social fixed asset investment fell from 25.6% back to 24.8%, down 0.8 percent points. In the meantime, the entrepreneur confidence index and the manufacturing PMI also declined. These declining indexes have aroused wide concerns in the society: Will there be a second dip? Will there be significant changes in macroeconomic policy? For this purpose, we need to carry out scientific and comprehensive analysis and research to avoid ideological discrepancies and misjudgment.

What are the reasons for the declining growth rate? We have concluded three reasons: 1) last year, the growth rate of China's GDP was lower in the first half than that in the second half, i.e. only 6.2% in the first quarter, up to 7.1% in the second, further up to 7.8% in the third, and 10.7% in the fourth, showing a quarterly uptrend. This year, in normal cases, the growth rate of GDP should naturally tend to be higher in the first half and lower in the second half. According to data provided by the National Bureau of Statistics, the year-over-year growth rate of GDP in the second quarter of this year should basically draw level with that in the first quarter if measured using the base period growth unchanged method; 2) the effect of policy measures issued at the end of 2008 in response to the international crisis manifested fully in the second half of 2009 and the first quarter of this year, and began to wear off in the second quarter of this year. Take investment, for example: in the first half of this year, investment in the Central Government's projects grew 13.0%, decreasing by 15.6 percent points over the same period last year, while investment in local government's projects grew 26.7%, down 7.4 percent points. Accordingly, the state-owned investment and state-owned state holding investment declined by 19.9 percent points year over year. In contrast, the investment of limited liability companies and foreign-funded enterprises grew respectively by 1.5 percent points and 1.2 percent points over the same period last year, while investment of private enterprises and companies from Hong Kong, Macao, and Taiwan dropped only by 0.8 percent points and 0.4 percent points respectively; 3) the economic stimulus was objectively brought down by the Central Government's fine-tuning of the macro-control policy, including enhancing control over real estates and closing down the outdated production facilities, especially the transition of monetary policy from an overly loose policy actually implemented last year to a moderately loose policy implemented this year. For example, the month-over-month housing sales price began to descend after ascending for a consecutive 15 months. In the first half, the growth rate of real estate development investment fell 1.7 percent points over that in the first quarter, with land acquisition cost deducted; and the selling area of commodity houses declined by 20.4 percent points over that in the first quarter. One more example: the growth rate of six major energy-consuming industries in the second quarter dropped 4.5 percent points over that in the first quarter, ascending for a consecutive two months. According to prediction by the National Bureau of Statistics, the decline in the growth rate of six major energy-consuming industries in June resulted in a decline of about 0.4 percent points in the growth rate of industrial enterprises above a designated size, accounting for about 14% of the whole declining rate.

Is the declining growth rate normal or abnormal? The growth rate usually declines from three levels: a record high level, a medium level, and a low level. In a quarterly perspective, China's GDP grew 10.3% year over year in the second quarter, consistent with the average growth rate in the first quarters from 2000 to 2009; the value added of industrial enterprises above a designated size grew 15.9% year over year, faster than the average growth rate of 14% in the first quarters from 2000 to 2009. In a yearly perspective, the expected target of China's GDP was 7% in both periods of the "11th Five-Year Plan" and the "12th Five-Year Plan", but it was much higher in practice, e.g. up to 10% from a consecutive five years since 2003. In order to narrow this gap and to increase employment, we raised the annual expected growth rate of China's GDP to 8%. If 8% is considered as a minimum expected target or a guaranteed safety target, we will have reasons to set a medium-level target at 9% and set a high-level target at 10%. The growth rate of China's GDP reached up to 11.1% in the first half of this year, even 10.3% in the second quarter. According to predictions by most of the research institutions both at home and abroad, the growth rate of China's GDP in the whole year may grow close to 10%. So the present decline in growth rate did not start from the level of 9%, much less from the level of 8%, but from the high level of 10%. This is a normal decline with a controllable rate. In an overall perspective, China's economic growth rate stays in a reasonable range of growth. Will the declining growth rate lead to a "second dip"? Or is it likely to continue? To answer this question, we need to know what the "second dip" implies. The bottom line of the "dip" does not for sure refer to the figure of GDP in the financial year from 2008 to 2009, for the figure climbed over 9%; rather, it should refer to the figure occurring in the fourth quarter of 2008 and the first quarter of 2009. The growth rate of China's GDP was 6.8% in the fourth quarter of 2008, and 6.2% in the first quarter of 2009. In the second half of this year, the growth rate of China's economy is likely to slow down moderately compared to that of the first half, but this will not lead to a "second dip". In an international perspective, the American economy has not completely climbed out of the shadows of the international financial crisis, but it has come at the end of the most difficult period and now moves in a good direction; though some of the European countries have gone through the sovereign debt crisis, they have worked out solutions to respond to it; Japanese economy is seeing some factors of positive changes; and major developing countries remain full of vitality. In other words, while there are some uncertainties in international economic development, the international environment for China's economic development is much better than last year. Because of this, the growth rate of China's export in the first half of the year grew 35.2% over the same period last year. In the second half year, despite the complex and volatile environment of China's exports and great difficulty in export expansion, it is predicable that China's exports will maintain a high rate of growth, and that the contribution rate of exports to economic growth is very likely to turn from negative to positive. In terms of domestic demand, China's consumption has been growing steadily all these years; with the price factor deducted, the total retail sales of social consumer goods has remained at a growth rate above 15%. In the first half year, the total retail sales of social consumer goods calculated by current prices grew 18.1% year over year; it grew 18.5% in the second quarter, rising 0.6 percent points over the 17.9% of the first quarter. With price factors deducted, the total retail sales of social consumer goods the first half year also grew at a rate above 15%. As the state policies aimed to raise the incomes of the medium- and low-income population and to stimulate consumption are constantly enacted and implemented, China's consumption will continue to maintain a rapid rate of growth. While the pattern overly dependent on investment for economic growth should be altered, it is still necessary to maintain a moderately steady growth of investment; however, the direction, focus, and structure of investment need to be improved. Investment is still a strong driving force to stimulate China's economic development.

3 Several noticeable problems in strengthening and improving macro regulation and control

We will consider maintaining the continuity and stability of macroeconomic policy as the foundation for strengthening and improve macro regulation and control, carry on the proactive financial policy and moderately loose monetary policy, and improve the pertinence, flexibility, and effectiveness of the policy. When we feel it necessary to fine-tune the macroeconomic policy, we will grasp the opportunity and ensure an appropriate strength, rhythm, and adaptability of adjustment. Government sectors that perform functions of macro regulation and control should not blindly follow the general trend, i.e. vie one another to introduce a stimulus package as soon as when the Central Government advocates it, or strive to introduce an exit policy no sooner than it is called upon. In this case, the superimposed effect of policy will come out to aggravate economic fluctuations.

We will consider properly dealing with the relationship between maintaining steady and rapid development of economy, adjusting economic structure, and controlling inflation expectation as the core of strengthening and improving macroeconomic regulation and control. First, we need to properly deal with the relationship between maintaining a steady and rapid development of the economy, adjusting economic structure, and controlling inflation expectation. Adjusting economic structure and transforming the economic development pattern cannot be done at one stroke, for it is closely related to the economic growth rate. China now has an extensive economy. Only a high growth rate can enable enterprises to obtain more profits, enable the country to higher financial revenue, and enable the government to alleviate the difficulty of employment. However, an excessive economic growth rate and a too-strong demand will impose less pressure on enterprises; as a result, the adjustment of the economic structure will at no time be put on the agenda, much less the transformation of an economic development pattern. What's more, the extensive high growth pattern is unsustainable; when conflicts accumulate to a certain point, they will burst out; at that moment, we will suffer far more losses. Therefore, we must properly deal with the relationship between short-term interests and long-term interests, between short-term high growth and long-term sustainable development, and determine to control the economic growth rate within a reasonable range so as to maintain a steady and rapid growth rate of economy, to create a suitable macro environment for adjustment of the economic structure and transformation of the economic development pattern, and to promote long-term steady rapid development of economy through optimization of the economic structure and transformation of the economic development pattern. Second, we need to properly deal with the relationship between maintaining a steady, rapidly developing economy and controlling inflation expectation. With the reviving world economy and the increasing demand of products, including energy resources and iron ore, the prices are skyrocketing. This year, there is some increase in China's import volume of bulk commodities such as crude oil, iron ore, plastics, copper, petroleum products, and soybean, but their prices have risen above 60%. These are the main factors to push up the prices of industrial products. The price reform of domestic resource products together with the rising environment cost and staff wages will also raise corporate costs, push up prices of industrial products, and magnify inflation expectation. The prices of consumer products also face great pressure to rise. In this case, if the economic growth rate cannot be controlled within a reasonable range, the excessive growth will further push up the demand and prices of products, thus likely to realize inflation expectations.

We will consider deepening the reform and improving the socialist market economy system as an assurance for strengthening and improving macro control. The macro control can only solve short-term economic problems, but the long-term underlying problems must be addressed by deepening the reform. In order to maintain a long-term, steady, and rapid development of China's economy, we must deepen the reform as well as strengthen and improve macro control. By reform, the system and mechanism in favor of macro control and long-term, steady, and rapid development of economy will be established. We should also deepen the reform of the financial system, adjust the interest relationship between the Central Government and the local government, and rationalize the financial system below a provincial level; deepen the reform of budget system, bring all of the special funds, incomes of state-owned enterprises, and social insurance funds into the national budget, and strengthen the binding force and authoritativeness of budget; improve public finance system, normalize transfer payment, and realize equalization of basic public services; actively boost the reform of the social security system, safeguard and improve democracy; deepen the reform of taxation system, fully implement value added tax transition, and accelerate the reform of resource tax and other taxes; deepen the reform of investment system, especially the situation where no one is responsible for state-owned investment; deepen the reform of state-owned enterprises and accelerate the reform of monopolized industries; advance the reform of the administration system, streamline administration and delegate power to lower levels, enhance service functions, and substantially reduce the government's direct intervention with micro economy. Although these reforms are long-term tasks and are very difficult to accomplish, we must actively push them forward. As arranged by the State Council, this year, we will accelerate the reforms of crucial areas and key links of reform, such as further eliminating institutional obstacles that have constraints on private investment, deepening the reforms of state-owned enterprises and monopolized industries, deepening the reforms of resource products pricing and environment protection charging, deepening the reform of the household register system, and deepening the reform of the income distribution system. In a word, we should closely combine macro regulation and control with deepening reforms, and give full play to the basic role of the market force in allocating resources. Only in this way will China's economy maintain long-term, steady, and rapid development under the guidance and leadership of macroeconomic policy.

(Published in *People's Daily*, Aug 4, 2010)

8 Maintain the stability of the policy and promote the economic development smoothly and rapidly

At the Economic Working Conference of the Central Government that was closed lately, it was pointed out that the general principle of making progress while maintaining stability should be followed in order to promote the development of the economic society next year. "Stability" means maintaining 1) steady macroeconomic policy, 2) steady and rapid economic growth, 3) a steady general price level, and 4) a stable society. "Progress" means continuing to seize and make good use of the period of important strategic opportunities for China's economic development, making new progress in the transformation of economic development pattern, making new breakthroughs in deepening the reform and opening up to the outside world, and achieving new results in improving people's livelihood. As the foundation of "progress", "stability" aims to create the basic conditions of a good environment. We should scientifically analyze and grasp the current economic situation; maintain the continuity and stability of the macroeconomic policy; consolidate the pertinence, flexibility, and foresight of macro control; and maintain steady and rapid development of the economy and stable general price level.

1 Properly understand the current economic situations

In 2011, China's economy witnessed a steady and rapid growth, a bumper harvest of grain crops, a rising trend of industrial growth, a rapid growth of service industry, a sharp rise in financial revenue, an increasing amount of employed population over expectation, a fast rise in incomes of urban and rural residents, a slowing down rise in prices, and a good economic trend on the whole. In 2012, China's economy is confronted with a more grim and complex economic situation both at home and abroad. We should conduct a serious analysis and proper judgment of the current economic situation, and try to raise the consciousness and initiative in implementing the decisions and arrangements of the Central Government.

There is an opinion stating that the current economic situation of China is very similar to that of 2008, so we must make significant adjustment in macroeconomic policy to avoid the economic hard landing and double dip. However, if we conduct a careful observation and analysis of the economic situation, we will find that the current economic situation of China differs greatly from that of 2008, notwithstanding some similarities.

There are three similarities: 1) a complex and volatile international economic environment. The American economy is too weak to recover; the Japanese economy is arrested to recover; some of the European countries are tortured with an intensifying sovereign debt crisis; and the major developing countries are confronted with inflationary pressure. These problems will inevitably exert adverse effects on China's economy, especially on China's export expansion; 2) decline in economic growth. In 2010, China's economic growth rate was 10.4%; this year, however, it descended on a quarterly basis, e.g. 9.7% in the first quarter, 9.5% in the second, and 9.1% in the third; 3) the macroeconomic policy turning from loosening to tightening up. In the first half of 2008, China's economic growth rate turned faster under the prudent financial policy and moderately tightening monetary policy. In the fourth quarter of last year, China adjusted the proactive financial policy and moderately loose monetary policy to the proactive financial policy and prudent monetary policy, resulting in an appropriate reduction of financial deficit; this year, the Central Government raised the deposit reserve rate consecutively six times, raised the bank's benchmark interest rate consecutively three times, and tightened up monetary policy.

We should also see that the current internal and external economic situation differs greatly from that of 2008. First, the feeble recovery of the American economy is rather a new problem than the continuation of the financial crisis in 2008. Studies of financial crisis and economic crisis have concluded that historically the economic crisis usually lasts several years and can hardly be corrected. While the European sovereign debt crisis is a new problem after the American financial crisis, it is related to the spreading of the American financial crisis to the rest of the world; in addition, its forming reasons are quite complex, involving such problems as development patterns, economic structure, and living styles, so it needs a long time to get resolved and will inevitably influence China's exports. This is what we should follow closely. Second, since the international financial crisis, the contribution rate of China's export to economic growth has dropped dramatically. Several years before 2008, China's exports used to contribute 2–3 percent points to economic growth, but the contribution rate dropped to minus 3.9 percent points in 2009, merely 0.8 percent points in 2010, and minus 0.1 percent point in the first half of this year. In other words, China's economic growth has been driven by internal demand in recent years. Though the descending growth rate of exports has some impact on China's economy, it is unlikely to be worse than what happened in 2009. Third, the decline in China's economic growth rate this year is not as drastic as it was, but remains within a reasonable range. In a yearly perspective, China's economic growth rate was 10.4% last year; if it rises to around 9.2% this year, it drops only by 1.2 percent points than it did last year. In a quarterly perspective, for five consecutive quarters from the third quarter of last year to the third quarter of this year, China's economic growth rate has varied between 9.1% and 9.8%, still a reasonable range. According to predictions by quite a few of domestic and overseas institutions, China's economic growth rate will remain at around 9% the next year. This is a rapid rate, considering the economic recession in major developing countries. Finally, the public are better mentally prepared for the negative effects produced by international economic changes than they were in the past years. Enterprises are not as passive as they were in the period from 2008 to 2009. China now is more experienced in response to international economic changes than it was, and the measures taken prove to be more pragmatic.

In 2012, the economic situation facing China differs greatly not only from that before and after 2009 but also from 2011. When there was a high rate of economic growth in 2011, China was confronted largely with the pressure of overly rising prices; so the primary task of macro control was to curb inflation. In 2012, due to the slowdown of the economic growth rate, the pressure of descending economic growth coexists with the pressure of rising prices; so, on the one hand, we need to steady economic growth rate, and on the other, we need to curb inflation. In addition, we will endeavor to strengthen the adjustment of the economic structure, deepen reform of the economic system, further improve people's livelihood, and safeguard social stability.

2 Promote the economic development smoothly and rapidly

At present, China's economy moves forward along the anticipated direction of macro control, and the economic growth rate has dropped to a reasonable range. We should endeavor to steady and stabilize the economic growth rate while it descends moderately in order to create a good macro environment for deepening the reform, fighting the inflation, adjusting the economic structure, and transforming the economic development pattern. An overly rapid rate of economic growth will make it more difficult to achieve substantial progress in adjusting the economic structure and transforming the economic development pattern and will also intensify some underlying conflicts; this is unfavorable to deepening the reform and will impede the long-term, steady, and rapid development of economy.

Stimulate and expand residents' consumption. As China has a population over 1.3 billion, consumption is the steadiest and most enduring impetus to drive economic growth. In recent years, with the inflation factors deducted, the growth rate of China's total retail sales of consumer goods has remained at around 13%, contributing a lot to the economic growth. In the first 10 months of 2011, China's retail sales of consumer goods increased 17.0%, only rising 11.2% with price factors deducted and lower than the growth rate in regular years. There are two reasons: 1) the rate of residents' income growth is lower than that of economic growth. In the first 10 months of 2011, the income of China's urban residents only grew 7.8% with price factor deducted, lower than the growth rate of GDP and much lower than that of the financial revenue and enterprises' realized profits; the farmers' cash net incomes grew 13.6%, but the growth is too feeble to drive consumption as they account for a rather low proportion in gross national income; and 2) the growth rate of the sales of bulk merchandise including automobiles is slowing down in the period of adjustment; the sales of commercial commodities are on a sharp decline, bringing down the sales of furniture and decoration materials involved. Therefore, in order to stimulate and expand residents' consumption, the trump card is to reasonably raise the income of urban and rural residents, especially the low-income groups, increase the proportion of middle-income groups, and synchronize economic growth with the increase of residents' income. In addition, we should further alleviate burdens on urban and rural residents, and put into practice the policy measures favorable for stimulating residents' consumption to ensure a steady growth of consumption.

Steady the growth rate of investment. In the first ten months of 2011, China's investment in cities and towns grew 24.9%, playing a positive role in driving the economic growth. Remarkable results of expanding consumption will be achieved over years' efforts; this year, the export has exerted a feeble driving force for economic growth; next year, it will not be optimistic as the world economy remains sluggish. Some construction projects approved in 2009 are not yet completed and need further investment; so, we need to develop some new projects in order to solve the "bottleneck" problems and strengthen future potentials of economic development. In this case, we must steady the growth rate of investment, particularly implement the policy measures that encourage and direct private investment, and strengthen the endogenous power of economic growth.

Strive to expand export. In the first 10 months of 2011, China's total import and export volume grew 24.3%; this is a very high growth rate, but the trade surplus declined over the same period last year and the contribution rate of imports and exports fell compared to that of the previous year: exports grew no more than 22.0%, lower than 26.9% of the imports growth rate. In 2012, we should promote the transformation of foreign trade development pattern, strive to expand export, increase the proportion of general trade and the proportion of new hi-tech products and high value added products in exports, actively respond to various trade protectionisms, and boost the contribution rate of exports to economic growth.

3 Maintain basically stable general price level

In 2011, the Central Government decided to consider fighting inflation as the primary task of macro control. This is a very correct decision. We have achieved preliminary results over one year's efforts; for example, the uptrend of prices is basically controlled. However, we should also see that the general price level remains high, despite some progress in fighting inflation. In 2011, the CPI (consumer price index) will be higher than 5.0%. Prices are brought down since July 2011 as a result of the "tail-rising" effect as well as macro control. Now, some essential factors that cause inflation are still present; so one of the important tasks of macro control is to fight inflation and stabilize prices.

(1) Insecure agriculture foundation, low agricultural labor productivity, and low commodity rate of agricultural and animal products. With a large

population and a strong demand of agricultural and animal products, China will face the perennial contradiction between the supply and demand of agricultural and animal products, so their prices will inevitably show an uptrend. In case of severe natural calamities, this contradiction will intensify and the rise in prices will speed up; the important factors that push up prices of agricultural and animal products will be ascribed to the rising cost of agricultural means of production and labor force.

(2) Prices are raised primarily by rising cost. One of the established state policies is to increase the proportion of residents' income in national income distribution and the proportion of labor compensation in primary distribution. With the policy being implemented and the growth rate of the labor force slowing down, the staff wages will inevitably show an uptrend; promoting price reform and rationalizing an unreasonable price relationship will also increase product cost of enterprises. The rising prices of part of the commodities and services were slowed by macro control in 2011, but, with rising operating costs, they will be possibly re-adjusted in 2012; and the new price-influencing factors will result accordingly.

(3) The pressure of imported inflation remains enormous. The prices of bulk import commodities including crude oil, iron ore, grain, oil products, and cotton are still fluctuating at a high level, likely to push up prices of domestic commodities.

The current general price level of China is influenced by both the supply-demand relationship and the rising cost. Comparatively, the PPI (producer price index) is more influenced by the supply-demand relationship and the CPI more by rising cost. With the descending rate of economic growth, the decreasing demand of enterprises for energy resources and raw materials, as well as the relative surplus of manufacturing production capacity, and the fierce competition among enterprises, the general level of PPI will be prone to fall preceding CPI. As CPI is more influenced by rising costs and the demand for products including grain is rigid, it will get tougher to curb the rising CPI. The rising CPI will directly affect the living level of urban and rural residents, especially of the low-income groups; so, at no time should we take it lightly.

4 Maintain the basic stability of macroeconomic policy, pre-tune and fine-tune it appropriately and timely

In 2011, China exercised the proactive financial policy and prudent monetary policy. Since it came into effect, the policy was moderately tightening up, the monetary policy in particular, as compared with the years of 2009 and 2010. Whether the macroeconomic policy will be adjusted has aroused public concern, leading to controversy. By comprehensive judgment, we should continue with the proactive financial policy and prudent monetary policy.

In the view of financial policy, as China now lies in the period of structural adjustment, many livelihood issues need to be solved urgently: along with keeping the proportion of financial deficit in GDP within 3%, and keeping the proportion of debts in GDP controllable, there is the need and condition for a proactive financial policy. However, we should take strict control over the deficit scale and debt balance scale; in particular, we should strengthen the supervision of local debts and fight against image projects and extravagance and waste to avoid crash expenditure at the end of the year. In addition, we should optimize the structure of financial expenditure and give full play to financial policy in improving people's livelihood and economic structure adjustment. We should also improve the structural tax reduction policy to alleviate burdens on enterprises, and strengthen financial and tax measures to support and promote the development of small- and micro-sized enterprises.

In the view of monetary policy, the idea of prudent monetary policy is neutral in itself, and the key lies in the direction of practical operation. As the uptrend of prices is preliminarily suppressed and the economic growth rate falls into a reasonable range, the monetary policy can be moderately loosened, but pre-tuning and fine-tuning should be enhanced. In addition, we should promote the reform of interest rate marketization and make economic adjustment effectively by leveraging the interest rate and exchange rate. When introducing monetary policy and exercising supervision, the financial authority should take into consideration the changes in the macroeconomic situation and properly deal with the interest relationship among depositors, industrial/commercial enterprises, and commercial banks so as to avoid prejudicing the interests of depositors and industrial/commercial enterprises and influencing development of entity economy.

As China is faced with a very complex economic situation both at home and abroad, the macroeconomic policy in 2012 should be prudent. Meanwhile, we should always keep an eye on the changes in the internal and external economic situation, and perform pre-tuning and fine-tuning appropriately and timely to address any problems during economic operation. Where the economic growth rate falls into the range of 8–9% and the inflation rate to around 4%, the macroeconomic policy should remain neutral.

(Published in *People's Daily*, Dec 21, 2011)

9 Deal with the relationship between steady growth and the adjustment of the industrial organization structure

In 2009, as China's economy began to rally as a whole by joint efforts under the influence of the international financial crisis, the anticipated targets of steady growth could be achieved, and the growth rate of the GDP in the whole year may reach around 8.3%. Nevertheless, with the rapid economic growth, we still have a tough job adjusting the economic structure and transforming the economic development pattern. To do a good job in economic activities in 2010 and beyond, we must properly deal with the relationship between steady growth and structure adjustment besides maintaining steady and rapid development of the national economy, and should concentrate on promoting adjustment of the economic structure and change of the economic development pattern.

1 Synchronize promoting structure adjustment and maintaining a smooth and rapid development of national economy

Adjustment of economic structure involves the following: adjustment of the national economy income distribution structure and adjustment of investment and consumption structure; adjustment of the primary, secondary, and tertiary industries and adjustment of internal structure and industrial organization structure; adjustment of regional structure and adjustment of urban–rural dual structure; and adjustment of ownership structure and strategic adjustment of the state-owned economy.

Steady growth and structural adjustment are closely correlated; both have a common goal that is to maintain a smooth and rapid development of the national economy and to promote the transformation of an economic development pattern, but they differ in emphasis. *Steady growth* is a tactical measure that emphasizes particularly on short-term goals, while *structural adjustment* is a strategic action that lays emphasis on long-term goals. For this reason, we must properly deal with the relationship between steady growth and structural adjustment by combining them tightly to realize the anticipated targets of steady growth and to promote structural adjustment. In no case should the macroeconomic policy and practical work deployment either lose sight of the economic structure adjustment or delay the structure adjustment process only to realize short-term targets, nor should they deteriorate the economic structure or complicate future adjustment only to maintain short-term steady growth. We should get them closely combined, coordinated, and collaborated. Significant research has gone into learning how to promote structure adjustment while steadying growth. In turn, how to maintain a smooth and rapid development of national economy while promoting structure adjustment is also a long-term task of macro control and economic work. In order to put them forward in concert, the current priority should be given to the relationship between steadying economic growth and adjusting industrial organization structure.

2 Noticeable problems in the current economic structure: excess production capacity and unreasonable industrial organization structure

Adjusting industrial organization structure is an important part of adjusting industrial structure, an essential guarantee to raise the industrial organization degree, and an important means to vitalize and improve the overall efficiency of the national economy. A reasonable industrial organization structure adaptable to the overall level of a country's industrial development will be helpful to prevent a market monopoly, facilitate an orderly competition and professional cooperative relationship among enterprises, and promote the coordinated development of large-, medium-, small-, and micro-sized enterprises.

Excess production capacity and unreasonable industrial organization structure have constituted the prominent problems in the current economic structure of China. At the end of 2008, according to relevant data, the production capacity of the iron and steel industry was 660 million tons, plus 58 million tons under construction, the total excess capacity was up to 200 million tons; the cement industry had a production capacity of 1.87 billion tons exceeding practical demand, but an additional capacity of 600 million tons is generated by over 400 production lines now under construction; the electrolytic aluminum has already had 18 million tons in contrast to the demand of around 12 million tons, but there are an additional 2 million tons under construction; and the problem of excess production capacity also exists in industries such as shipbuilding, chemical, and plate glass. In addition, some emerging industries with promising prospects, including solar energy and wind energy, have rushed headlong, leading to blind development and repeated construction. According to statistics, in the first quarter of 2009, the problem of excess production capacity hit 19 out of 24 industries in varying manner. The problem may be more serious as investment grows rapidly.

For businesses in the manufacturing industry of China, except for some with excess production capacity, most of them are characterized by the lower degree of organization and a lower level of specialized cooperation, as well as the drawbacks of being "large and all-inclusive" and "small and all-inclusive". Some of the so-called large-sized business are neither big in size nor in strength, the small- and micro-sized businesses are not unique, the superior businesses grow slowly, and it is difficult to weed out the inferior businesses.

3 The resultant force of industrial organization adjustment: the government working together with the market

In order to respond to the international financial crisis, to curb the short-term economic recession of China, and to promote the adjustment of the industrial structure and the transformation of economic development pattern, the State Council laid down the industrial adjustment and revitalization program at the end of 2008. This is a program for the mutual combination and promotion of steady growth and structure adjustment. We must accurately and comprehensively understand and grasp the spirit of this program and implement it in practical work. At no time does revitalization mean increasing production capacity: it means improving the quality of all industries. Therefore, we should combine adjustment and revitalization without any prejudice against either side. We should grasp the advantageous opportunities of insufficient external demand, low rate of economic growth, and great pressure on the part of enterprises to revitalize industries, improve industrial quality and benefits, and transform the economic growth pattern in adjustment of the industrial structure by means of relying on market force, making the best use of the circumstances, and taking the opportunity of the industrial organization structure adjustment.

In adjusting the industrial organization structure, we should take advantage of both the guiding role of the government and the fundamental role of the market mechanism. The government should not introduce some policy ministering to those enterprises that tend to produce outdated products, excessively consume energy resources, generate poor economic effects, and seriously contaminate the environment and destroy ecology. Rather, let them go bankrupt where appropriate. We should also encourage the superior to merge with the inferior and accelerate the process of merging, restructuring, and closing down the outdated production facilities.

4 Reshape large enterprises: guard against collaboration between administrative power and capital power

We should properly treat the idea to help enterprises expand with the attempt to raise the degree of industrial organization, strengthen international competitiveness of industries, and encourage a small number of enterprises to get bigger and stronger so as to constitute a large enterprise group.

Now there is a problem worthy of close attention: the government and state-owned asset sectors in some provinces and cities are piecing together all state-owned enterprises of the same industry in their region to create "big groups" one after another under the guise of helping enterprise to expand; however, some members of the "big group" used to be large-scale and equally powerful group companies that have produced similar lines of products and are always competing with each other instead of complementing each other's advantages.

For this sort of group, its headquarters was rather an administrative machine than a group company, i.e. the "children" preceding "parent" company pattern, which was criticized widely in the past. They retook power from grass-root enterprises and lusted for power from the superior authority, and adopted administrative means in managing grass-root enterprises. This practice created a lengthy and inefficient management chain composed of government's administration (the ministries and bureaus of industry), the State-owned Assets Supervision and Administration Commission, administrative group, listed companies and other companies (groups) parallel to them, grandchildren companies, and affiliated companies. History has proven that this management pattern is inefficient, making success impossible.

This pattern is a reproduction of the industrial companies that was denied in the 1980s. Incorporation of this group is a product of leading officials' will and also a genetic freak of the marriage between administrative power and capital power. There is no doubt that we should raise a loud voice against it. Practice has proven that large enterprise groups must be incorporated under the premise of complementing each other's advantages by economic means by getting them centered in one big business (Group Company) and linked with property relations, and by restructuring production capacity. Only in this way can we get twofold results with half the effort.

In the process of adjusting the industrial organization structure, we should encourage large enterprises to merge or acquire small ones across regions, for this trans-regional merger or acquisition is realized by economic means and can easily generate good effects. Currently, mergers and the restructuring of enterprises, especially those across provinces, autonomous regions, and municipalities, are constrained by administrative power and measures, so they are in urgent need of macro coordination. We should support competitive state-holding companies and national enterprises in trans-regional mergers and acquisition for the interest at a national level rather than a local level in order to accelerate the adjustment of product structure, give play to scale economy effects, and "rehearse" the "going-out" strategy to absorb and integrate global resources and participate in global competition.

5 Strictly define small enterprise: change its statistical caliber involving medium-sized enterprises

We should help small enterprises practically address difficulties during their development. They account for above 95% of the total number of enterprises; most of them are non-state-owned businesses and have contributed a lot to economic prosperity, employment enlargement, and export expansion. During the implementation of industrial adjustment and revitalization program, we should lay much more stress on the development of small and micro-sized enterprises by creating a loose environment and helping them address difficulties during development.

According to numerous surveys, there are problems in criteria determining enterprise scale. In China, the medium-sized enterprises are large in scale enough to compete with large-sized ones in business pattern, internal organization structure, and even the economic and social environment they are confronted with, but they are quite different from small and micro-sized enterprises.

In the terms of policy support, therefore, we should distinguish them from small and micro-sized enterprises; instead, treat them as large-sized ones. Take the matter of financing for an example, it is often reported that the small-sized enterprises find it hard to raise funds; but data from financial institutions have proven that this is not the case. How could this be? The answer lies in the fact that the data provided by financial institutions are all about medium-sized enterprises instead of small and micro-sized ones. During investigation, we found that it not as difficult for medium-sized enterprises to raise funds. In addition, the National Bureau of Statistics has over-designated the size of small enterprises and thus categorized into small-sized enterprises part of those that should be sorted into medium-sized ones.

In order to ensure policy more adaptable to small and micro-sized enterprises, we should redefine the criteria used to determine the enterprise scales as required by changing situation, with preference to upscaling micro enterprises.

In addition, the small and micro-sized enterprises are also confronted with the following challenges: 1) imperfect social support systems for the development of small and micro-sized enterprises in China, including an administration system, a financing and guarantee system, an information provision system, and a technical service system; 2) a lack of a pertinent, government policy. All measures issued to encourage the development of medium and small-sized enterprises are targeted at medium ones rather than small and micro-sized ones; and 3) the low quality of small and micro-sized enterprises. Apart from strengthening internal management, they should develop according to their real circumstances, focusing on being specialized, precise, unique, and powerful. Only in this way will an industrial organization structure with a reasonable division of labor and coordination be formed.

6 Reform of monopolized industries: the top priority in adjusting the industrial organization structure

We must accelerate the reform of monopolized industries. First, phase out regulation and control, lower entry threshold, and encourage non-state economic sectors into some of the existing monopolized industries so as to turn them into competitive ones. Second, phase out some of the privileges granted by the government to these monopolies. The government should no longer give them special support and care so that they can obtain monopolist profits, which allow them to not be responsible for any losses but to pay wages or bonuses at will if they make any profits and request state subsidies if they suffer any losses. We should push them onto the market, so they will become market-competitive subjects that can take care of their own management, development, and self-discipline as well as profits and losses. Finally, we should strengthen supervision over these industries, bring state-owned capital of these industries into the management of the state budget, and implement the paid use of state-owned capital. The pricing of products and services of these industries should be more transparent.

7 Reform of industry association: help administrative reform out of a vicious cycle

We should keep carrying forward the reform of industry associations. Since the reform and opening up, especially after some industry departments and bureaus were cut down, industry associations have developed rapidly and some of them are playing increasingly important roles; however, the existing industry associations have strong administrative features such that most of them fail to play their due roles: reform in this regard should continue. An industry association should be a voluntary NGO operating under internal democratic management. As a bridge for communication between enterprises and government, it is supposed to realize self-development in providing services for enterprises without financial appropriation; if otherwise, it will either become an administrative organization or be disguised as one. Meanwhile, the government should continue delegating powers to lower levels instead of ruling the roost; if not, the reform of administrative authority will yield little, and much less practical, results. This is why the reform is confined within a vicious cycle of institutions getting overstaffed as soon as they are reformed.

(Published in *Chinese Academy of Social Sciences Review*, Nov 19, 2009)

10 Strengthen the trend of economic consolidation and rise

At the meeting of the Political Bureau of the CPC Central Committee convened not long ago, it was pointed out that as China's economic development now lies in a critical period of stability and recovery, the macroeconomic orientation should remain unchanged, the macro control should be strengthened, and the focus of macro control should be explicit. The accurate judgment of the macroeconomic situation and the serious implementation of the decisions and arrangements of the Central Government will be of great importance in consolidating the economic uptrend and accomplishing this year's anticipated development targets of economic society.

1 China's economy is stabilizing and recovering, but has an insecure foundation

Since the fourth quarter of 2008 and in response to the impacts of the international financial crisis, the Central Government introduced a series of macroeconomic plans and a package of policy measures to stimulate economic growth. By several months' efforts, China's economy has shown positive signs turning from a downtrend to an uptrend, which is much better than expected. The main result is that the economic growth rate is on the rise. China's GDP grew no more than 6.8% year over year in the fourth quarter last year; it slightly dropped in the first quarter this year, only growing 6.1% year over year; in the second quarter this year, the growth rate of GDP rebounded to 7.9%, accumulating 7.1% in the first half of this year. The agricultural production trended up, for the summer grain yield increased for a consecutive six years. The growth rate of industry has also turned around and picked up steadily. The industrial growth rate rose only 3.8% in January and February, but up to 10.7% in June. The consumer goods market also went quite well. In the first half of this year, the total sales of national social consumer goods grew 15.0% year over year; with price factors deducted, it grew 16.6% in real terms, increasing by 3.7 percent points year over year. The investment of fixed assets continued with a rapid growth rate. In the first half of this year, the investment of social fixed assets grew 33.5% year over year, increasing by 7.2 percent points over the same period last year. The prices kept operating at a low level and the inflationary pressure was eased gradually. The employment of rural migrant workers was better than expected. More than 90% of rural workers that returned home during the Spring Festival went out to work again. Those who did not go out were also employed by local enterprises. The signs of economic recovery appeared on stock and real estate marketplaces.

We should also see that the severe recession of the international economy has not yet improved, that the China's economic recovery still has an insecure foundation, and that some new problems of economic development have emerged when some old problems remain unresolved.

The situation of foreign trade remained serious as exports fell constantly. According to data published by the General Administration of Customs, the foreign trade import and export of China fell 23.5% year over year in the first half year, with exports falling 21.8% and imports 25.4% year over year.

The first half year witnessed an oversized loan scale. At the end of June 2009, M2 grew 28.5% year over year, higher than the previous year and Q1 this year by 10.6 and 3.0 percent points respectively; M1 grew 24.8% year over year, higher than the previous year and Q1 this year by 15.7 and 7.8 percent points respectively, the highest level since May 1995; and M0 grew 11.5% year over year. At the end of June, the balance of RMB total loans from the financial institutions grew 34.4% year over year, 15.7 percent points higher than that at the end of the previous year. In the first year, the new bank loans of China amounted to RMB7.37 trillion Yuan, far higher than the expected macro-control target of 5 trillion increased in the whole year.

The economic recovery depended largely on investment of government and state-owned enterprises, but the private investment was not yet awakened. In the first half year, the investment of state holding companies grew 41.4%, increasing 22.1 percent points over the same period last year; and the private investment grew 34.3% only, decreasing by 1 percent point over the same period last year.

The declining enterprise benefits led to the increasing pressure on the balance of state revenue and expenditure. From January to May, the industrial enterprises over a designated size in China realized profits of RMB850.2 billion Yuan, decreasing 251.7 billion at the rate of 22.9%; the total of loss-incurring industrial enterprises over designated size was 23%, amounting to RMB234.7 billion Yuan, increasing 14.3% year over year. In the first half year, the total government revenue was RMB3.397614 trillion Yuan, down 83.205 billion over the same period last year at a year-over-year rate of 2.4%; but it began to recover since May, growing 4.8% and 19.6% respectively in May and June. The total government expenditure was RMB2.890256 trillion Yuan, increasing 602.054 billion at the rate 26.3% over the same period last year.

2 Several noticeable problems during macroeconomic regulation and control

At present, we should maintain the continuity and stability of macroeconomic policy, continue implementing the proactive financial policy and moderately loose monetary policy, and grasp the effort, direction, and focus of the policy.

We should fully consider and make a medium- and long-term preparation for any difficulties, and focus on coordinated and sustainable economic development during steady growth. The severity of this international financial crisis has led to a long duration of getting it adjusted. From an international perspective, all countries have concentrated on adjustment of domestic economy but lost sight of the rising trade protectionism. As their domestic consumption growth was greatly affected by the American financial crisis, it will not recover until asset prices have stabilized and the economic growth points have formed. At present, it may need a long time to create the conditions for these two aspects; therefore, it also needs a long time for the recovery of American economy. In a domestic perspective, there is no radical change in the extensive economic development pattern and structural contradiction that have formed over the years in China. Both the adjustment of problems accumulated during China's economic development and the periodical adjustment after China's economic growth for consecutive years have required slowing down the economic growth rate moderately. "Ensuring an economic growth rate of 8%" is the phased objective of China's economic growth, and it is also the requirement for employment growth. While steadying growth, expanding domestic demand, and reversing the downtrend, we should also accelerate the transformation of the economic development pattern, the strategic adjustment of economic structure, and the improvement of economic growth quality and benefits. Transformation of the economic development pattern, the strategic adjustment of economic structure, and the improvement of economic growth quality and benefits can help improve the coordination and sustainability of economic growth; whereas, steadying growth, expanding domestic demand, and reversing the downtrend can provide the necessary market demand as well as material and fund support for the transformation of the economic development pattern, the strategic adjustment of economic structure, and the improvement of economic growth quality and benefits. An organic combination of these two will not only help respond to the impacts of the current international financial crisis but also help address the long-standing problems during China's economic development so as to raise the quality of national economy and the competitiveness of the state.

We should take powerful measures to promote exports and stabilize foreign demand. The international financial crisis had much more impact on China's export than did the Asian financial crisis. So we should improve environment of foreign trade; take necessary measures to improve the import/export administration, the customs clearance facilitation, the import/export tax, the export insurance, and the foreign exchange control to support preponderant enterprise and product export; encourage financial institutions to increase loans for medium- and small-sized export enterprises; and expand direct financing channels for export-oriented medium- and small-sized enterprises. In addition, we should work out an appropriate policy for financial taxation to encourage enterprises to carry out self-dependent innovation; to produce piles of competitive products with proprietary intellectual property rights, proprietary brand,

and international competitiveness; and to facilitate the structure optimization of export products and improvement of quality and benefits.

We should take proper control of the scale and growth rate of investment and optimize the investment structure. At present, China's investment grows at a high rate and on a large scale. In the first half year, the total social investment amounted to RMB9.1321 trillion Yuan, growing 33.5% year over year and accounting for 65.3% of the GDP; the contribution rate of gross capital formation to economic growth was 87.6%, stimulating the economy to grow 6.2 percent points. It is impossible to maintain such a growth rate of fixed asset investment. What's important is to optimize the investment structure; at no time shall we return to the extensive and low-efficiency investment pattern only to stimulate short-term economic growth, nor shall we make blind investments only to carry out projects, which will lead to repeated construction and intensifying the excess production capacity of some industries. The ultra-high growth of investment is directly related to the loose environment of loans. What we need is moderately loose monetary policy rather than loose monetary policy. We should make "moderately" a concrete quantitative index such that it can be observed in practice; otherwise, this will result in hidden financial risks and the flow of surplus funds into stack market and real estate market, overly pushing up asset prices and rapidly generating inflationary pressure.

We should also take powerful measures to exploit the potentiality of consumption growth. The consumption level finally depends on people's income level and future expectations; therefore, we should raise the proportion of people's income in national revenue distribution and closely combine the long-term targets of consumption expansion and the short-term policy measures; give priority to enlargement of employment by implementing proactive employment policy; create a good environment for entrepreneurship and actively encourage residents' entrepreneurship; encourage the development of individual and private economic sectors, particularly of the tertiary industry; build a secondary distribution mechanism of wealth by means of tax, transfer payment to adjust excessive incomes and safeguard minimum incomes, and narrow the gap between residents' incomes; strengthen the services of public education and health by widening the coverage and accelerate the construction of urban indemnificatory housing; improve the social security system, the social insurance systems including pension, medical and unemployment insurances, as well as social assistance systems including subsidence allowances; and accelerate the construction of rural workers and rural social security systems.

We should utilize the opportunity of declining prices in the economic contraction period to adjust the economic structure and transform the economic development pattern. While the international financial crisis jeopardizes the economy, it also provides us with a good opportunity for mandatory adjustment. It is a period that generates new opportunities. The historical experiences of reform and opening up have shown that each external impact is an important opportunity for us to mobilize resources, promote institutional reform, foster new sources of economic growth, and push China's economy into a new stage.

We should seize this opportunity to promote the rapid development of high and new technology industries, new energy industries, and environment-friendly industries; to weed out enterprises with outdated production facilities that may cause severe environmental pollution; to encourage the merging of enterprises and the adjustment of industrial organization structure; and to seize the opportunity of rising prices of domestic agricultural products that may help mitigate the declining prices of bulk commodities, including international petroleum, to reform the pricing mechanism of resource products.

(Published in *People's Daily*, Aug 24, 2009)

11 Have a correct view of China's current economic growth fall and adopt a flexible and prudent attitude to control economic growth

While actively responding to the complex and volatile international environment from 2003 to 2007, China successfully promoted smooth and rapid economic growth and avoided significant fluctuations by concentrating on some prominent conflicts and problems during macroeconomic operation, properly grasping the direction, rhythm, and effort of macro control; comprehensively utilizing multiple macro-control means and methods; maintaining the continuity and sustainability of the policy; and adjusting the policy appropriately and timely according to changes in situations.

The macro control over the last five years is rich in contents and has achieved remarkable results. The overall national strength of China has been reinforced, the social undertakings have developed in an all-round way, and the people have benefited greatly. The gross domestic product was RMB24 trillion Yuan in 2007, growing 67% over 2002 and 10.8% in the whole year, rising from the sixth place to the fourth in the world; the total government revenue amounted to RMB5.13 trillion Yuan, growing by 1.71 multiples; and the total import-export volume amounted to RMB2.17 trillion Yuan, rising from the sixth place to the third in the world.

1 Reasons for the slowdown in China's economic growth rate

Macro control cannot be once and for all. The Central Economic Working Conference convened at the end of 2007 proposed a "double prevention" objective, i.e. keeping economic growth from growing too fast and too hot and keeping prices from turning against a structural rise to obvious inflation. These objectives take into consideration problems during China's economic operation in the second half of 2007, especially when confronted with the great pressure of economic growth going from being too fast to being too hot, and with the pressure of remarkably rising prices.

In 2008, as the American sub-prime mortgage crisis intensified, the world economic growth rate slowed down and quite a number of countries were confronted with inflationary pressure. Historically rare hazards occurred successively in China, such as a cryogenic freezing rain and snow disaster, a devastating earthquake, and flooding damage, caused heavy loss of life and property for people in disaster-stricken areas. To adapt to the changing situation, the Central Government timely put forward the "maintaining and controlling" guideline in July, i.e. maintaining smooth and rapid economic development and controlling the excessive rise of prices, which were seen as the primary task of macro control.

Despite significant changes in the international economic situation and the adverse impacts on China's economic development, China's economy shows good momentum in that 1) the economy has been growing rapidly on the whole, 2) the rise of prices has slowed down, and 3) the economic structure has been improved, and because we have laid great stress on agriculture, grain production in particular has made a comprehensive use of multiple policy tools and has grasped the focus, rhythm, and effort of macro control.

However, due to the spreading and deepening impacts of the American financial crisis on China's economy, the external impact has accelerated the falling economic growth rate of China that is cooling the economic growth, which fell from 12.7% in Q2 of 2007 to 10.7% in Q2 of 2008, down 2.6 percentage points; it was only 9% in Q3, down nearly 3 percentage points, and probably down over 2 percentage points from an annual perspective. The economic growth rate slowed down in 2008 for four reasons: 1) China's economy needs a phase of adjustment due to accumulated problems after five years' growth at a rate of above 10%; 2) the macro-control measures introduced by the government work efficiently; 3) the economic growth is influenced by the Olympic Games, even more significantly in Beijing and its peripheral areas; and 4) the most important one, the impact from the changing external environment. From 2005 to 2007, the contribution rate of net exports of goods and services to China's GDP rose to around 20%, driving the GDP to grow 2.2–2.6 percentage points; but this year, the contribution rate of net exports will be estimated as a negative value. The decline in growth rate was the original result anticipated by macro-control measures. This year, the economic growth rate still lies within a reasonable range and the fundamentals of China's rapid economic development remain unchanged. Nevertheless, the slowdown of China's economic growth rate is accelerated due to the constantly intensifying and deepening impact of the American financial crisis together with domestic macro-control factors of China and adverse factors of the international economy. We should pay great attention to it, but should not overreact to it. This is both a challenge and an opportunity to adjust the economic structure and deepen the reform.

2 Economic situation in the year of 2009

It is predicted that China's GDP will grow nearly 10% in the whole year of 2008, falling about 2 percentage points over the whole last year. The final contribution rate of the consumer spending is estimated to be around 50%, driving GDP growth to increase about 5.0 percentage points; the contribution rate of the gross capital formation will be around 53%, driving the GDP to increase about

5.3 percentage points; and the contribution rate of the net export of goods and services to GDP growth will be probably negative.

Currently, as the American financial crisis is intensifying, there will be many uncertainties about the world economy in 2009. In the *World Economic Outlook* published on October 9, the International Monetary Fund (IMF) predicted that the global economic growth rate in 2008 would be only 3.9%. The expected growth rate published in July by this organization was 4.1%. IMF lowered the expected global economic growth rate from 3.9% down to 3%, the lowest level since 2002; raised the expected American economic growth rate of 2008 from 1.3% in July up to 1.6%, but lowered that of 2009 from 0.8% to 0.1%; and lowered the expected economic growth rate of 2008 in Eurozone from 1.7% in July to 1.3%, and lowered the expected economic growth rate of 2009 from 1.2% to 0.2%. According to IMF's prediction, the Japanese economy will grow 0.7% this year, lower than 1.5% as estimated in July, then it lowered the expected Japanese economic growth rate of 2009 from 1.5% to 0.5%; and China's GDP of 2008 is expected to remain at 9.7%, but it lowered the expected growth rate of 2009 from 9.8% in July to 9.3%.

Under the influence of the sub-prime mortgage crisis, the domestic demand of the developed economies in 2008 and 2009 will fall further, which will exert an impact on emerging market and developing countries. The United States is the main export market of China. According to a rough estimate based on recent data (2002–2007) since China's entry into the World Trade Organization (WTO), there is a strong positive correlation between China's export growth rate and American GDP growth rate, i.e. when the growth rate of American GDP drops 1 percentage point, the growth rate of China's export will drop 5.2 percentage points on average. The impact of the sub-prime mortgage crisis on China's exports will depend largely on the slowdown of world economy. In 2007, the American GDP growth rate was 2.2%. If it drops to 1.6% in 2008 under the influence of the sub-prime mortgage crisis as predicted by IMF, the growth rate of China's exports in 2008 will fall about 3.1 percentage points as against that of 2007; if it drops to 0.1% in 2009 as predicted by IMF, the growth rate of China's export in 2009 will fall about 7.8 percentage points as against that of 2008.

As there is an increasing amount of uncertainty and instability in the current international environment, some conflicts begin to stand out during China's economic operation, and the challenges and difficulties begin to increase in maintaining smooth and rapid economic development. According to preliminary judgment, significant uncertainty remains in 2009, but we are expected to keep GDP growth rate above 9% in 2009, despite the likeliness of a continuing decline, and control inflation below 5%, as long as we take timely and appropriate macro-control measures. We also need to actively expand internal demand under the condition of decreasing foreign market demand (especially expanding consumer demand), stabilizing investment, appropriately increasing non-production investment, and accelerating the construction of a new socialist countryside and the transformation of both an economic development pattern and the process of reform in key fields.

3 Take a flexible and cautious approach to the current macro control

In the new situation, we should take a flexible and cautious approach in the current macro control in order to promote the sound and fast development of the economy. The focus of macro control should turn from curbing inflation to maintaining moderately rapid economic growth. For this purpose, we should shift the financial policy from being prudent to being moderately expanding, shift the monetary policy from tightening up to being moderately loose, and achieve coordination between the two policies. While fighting inflation remains an important problem about macroeconomic policy, we should properly deal with the following relationships.

First, we need to properly deal with the relationship between economic growth rate and inflation control. Despite apparent diversity and dissimilarity between economic growth and inflation in different countries and different periods, there is a certain correlation between economic growth and inflation in China as a developing country and in this development phase. If the economic growth rate is constantly too high, the inflation rate will rise; in contrast, if the too-fast economic growth rate is brought down, the inflation rate will definitely fall. However, as the American sub-prime mortgage crisis is deepening and there are increasing uncertainties in the international economy, we cannot expedite the decline of the economic growth rate; for this reason, we should control the inflation rate within an affordable range, but not necessarily bring it down immediately.

From the practical situation of China's macroeconomic regulation and control ever since the reform and opening up, it is appropriate to control China's economic growth rate around 9%. A too-fast economic growth rate will intensify many structural problems and may lead to inflation; whereas, a too-slow economic growth rate will be unfavorable for enlarging employment and building an all-around well-off society and may lead to deflation. After learning lessons from all previous macro-control activities, we will better deal with the relationship between the economic growth rate and inflation control, we will maintain smooth and rapid economic growth, and we will prevent against drastic fluctuations.

Second, properly deal with the relationship between farmer's income growth and inflation. Making every effort to increase farmers' income is an important and difficult point in building a well-off society: a policy of expanding domestic demand requires it. In recent years, the Central Government has viewed increasing farmer's income as the primary task of agricultural and rural work, and has taken a series of significant actions to turn around the sluggish growth of farmer's income towards a rapid growth trend. Since the beginning of this year, however, the farmers' income growth has been affected by the dramatically rising prices of agricultural production materials and the continuous decline of agricultural comparative benefits.

Under the influences of the rising oil price, the increasing demand of grain in emerging countries, and the depreciating US dollar, the grain prices are rising remarkably on the international market since the year of 2007. In China, the price of grain has risen to some extent in recent years, but it is currently much lower than international market price due to the policy of curbing grain export. The rising price of grain can be reasonable, for it helps increase farmers' income. The price of agricultural products in China, which is much lower than that of the international market, has provided an external condition for us to adjust the prices of the main agricultural products, including grain. Taking into consideration the consumers' bearing capacity and producers' interests, we will gradually adjust the prices of agricultural products to keep them within at a reasonable level; one of the adjusting actions is to raise the grain price gradually. Therefore, we should properly deal with the relationship between grain price and inflation control by getting them combined. After grain price is raised, we will probably increase subsidies for urban low-income residents.

Third, we need to properly deal with the relationship between resource factor price and inflation control. Price control implemented at the beginning of this year is an emergency action for the control of the refined oil price and the electricity price, and is also used as a temporary price intervention measure for commodities including food, steel products, and cement, which is effective in inhibiting short-term hyperinflation. But a long-term price control is less helpful in eliminating inflationary pressure, and may lead to a shortage of supply and a misallocation of resources. In the global context, the distorted price of resource factors means China's subsidy for the whole world. In the long run, once the inflationary pressure has eased, we should seize this opportunity to rationalize the price mechanism of resource factors.

Rationalizing the price of resource factors and eliminating distorted prices are the intrinsic requirements for us to save energy and reduce emission. At present, we need to properly deal with the relationship between the rationalization of the price of resource factors and the control of inflation by combining them. When the inflationary pressure has eased, we should rationalize the price of resource factors including electricity, coal, liquefied gas, and natural gas by stages, constantly improve the pricing mechanism of production factors and resources that have reflected the relation between market supply and demand, the shortage of resources, and the cost of environment damage, and constantly strengthen the sustainability of China's economy.

Finally, we must lay stress on the economic development pattern transformation while preventing a too-fast decline in the economic growth rate and maintaining smooth and rapid growth. In the period when the economy grows at a high rate, the employment rate has ascended and the incomes of residents, enterprises, and the government have increased, but many structural and underlying problems are covered up. When the economic growth rate remains high, the structural supply-demand contradiction will lead to inflation, even if the total supply can meet the need of expanding demand. The tightening policy adopted to curb intensifying inflation will bring down the economic growth rate and further expose the structural problems covered up in a period of fast economic growth. So, the moderate decline in the economic growth rate is an opportunity to address problems accumulated in the period of fast economic growth. Active adjustment of economic structure in the period of slowing economic growth rate can pave the way and store energy for long-term sustainable development of economy. We should be active in utilizing the opportunity given by the slowdown of rising prices when the economic growth rate decelerates to adjust the economic structure and transform the economic development pattern so that the slowdown of economic growth rate, at a certain degree, will generate positive significance.

As the foreign market demand is currently slowing, it is of important and practical significance to properly deal with the relationship between transforming the economic development pattern and maintaining smooth and rapid economic growth. We should uphold the policy of expanding domestic demand and take effective measures to transform economic growth from being driven mainly by investment and export to being driven mainly by consumption, investment, and export; from being driven mainly by the secondary industry to being driven jointly by the primary, secondary, and tertiary industries; and from being driven mainly by the increasing consumption of materials and resources to being driven mainly by advancing science and technology, raising the quality of the labor force and innovating management.

We must be fully aware that deepening the reform is a system and mechanism assurance for maintaining long-term, smooth, and rapid economic growth. For the short-term fluctuations in macroeconomic operation, we can tackle them by means of combined macro-control policies; but for some long-term and recurring problems and economic phenomena, we cannot depend on macro-control policy alone. These underlying problems persist for some time and are hard to tackle; one of the important reasons this is the case is due to inadequate reform in economic fields. For example, the key reforms of the financial and tax system and the monopolized industries have slowed. The underlying problems cannot be tackled by macro control alone, but must be tackled by deepening the reform in critical fields and improving the socialist market economic system.

In conclusion, we should adopt the flexible and cautious approach and an effective macroeconomic policy to maintain smooth and rapid economic growth, and lose no time to rationalize the prices of agricultural products and resource factors, transform the economic development pattern, and deepen the reform in critical fields so as to create favorable conditions for the long-term and sustainable development of economy.

(Published in *China Economic & Trade Herald*, Issue 22, 2008)

12 Inhibit the prices rising too fast; maintain the steady and rapid economic development

1 China's economy maintains a good trend of steady and rapid development

Since the beginning of this year, many new changes have taken place in the international and domestic situation of China's economy. After the American sub-prime mortgage crisis occurred, the world economic growth slowed down, the US dollar depreciated, prices of petroleum and grain rocketed continuously, and the world was confronted with great inflationary pressure. Recently, the financial situation of Vietnam deteriorated, the inflation intensified, and the potential financial risks increased. In China, historically rare hazards occurred successively, such as a cryogenic freezing rain and snow disaster, a devastating earthquake, and flooding damage, all of which caused heavy losses of life and property for people in disaster-stricken areas. These significant changes in the international and domestic situation have some adverse effects on China's economic development, but on the whole, the fundamentals of China's steady and rapid economic growth remain unchanged and now move towards the anticipated direction of macro control and sustainability.

China's economy keeps developing rapidly. In 2007, China's GDP grew 11.9% and maintained a growth rate above 10% for five consecutive years. In the first quarter of this year, GDP grew 10.6% year over year; the growth rate slowed down, but was still higher than the average growth rate from 2003 to 2005 and also higher than the average growth rate in the past 30 years. The agricultural production rose above the impact of severe natural calamities, with the output of summer grain increasing for five consecutive years. The industrial production grew rapidly; the value added of industrial enterprises above a designated size throughout the country grew 16.3% year over year in real terms from January to May. The income of urban and rural residents kept rising; in the first quarter, the disposable income of urban residents and the per capita cash income of rural residents grew 11.5% and 18.5% respectively. All these targets are better than the expected ones at the beginning of this year.

The momentum to stimulate economic growth remains powerful. From 2003 to 2007, the nominal growth rate of the total social fixed asset investment grew above 23% on average, with the actual growth rate above 20%. In the first five months of this year, the urban fixed asset investment of China was RMB4.0264 trillion Yuan, with a year-over-year nominal growth rate of 25.6%; with price factors deducted, the actual growth rate was less than 20%, but it remained at a high level. The retail sales of total social consumer goods in the first five months amounted to RMB4.2401 trillion Yuan, growing 21.1% year over year and showing a trend of rapid growth. Though the exports lowered, it still grew 22.9% in the first five months due to the strong overall competitiveness of China's export commodities. The imports grew 30.4% as the prices of international primary commodities rocketed. The trade surplus amounted to US$78.0 billion, decreasing US$7.3 billion year over year.

China's economy is developing toward the anticipated direction of macro control. One of the anticipated targets of macro control aims to address such problems as too-fast economic growth rate, too-fast investment growth rate, large trade surplus, and unreasonable demand structure. In the first five months of this year, the nominal growths of three major demands have indicated that the growth rate of urban fixed asset investment fell 0.3 percent points year over year; the growth rate of the retail sales of total social consumer goods accelerated 5.9 percentage points; and the trade surplus reduced US$7.3 billion year over year. The actual growths have indicated that the economic growth rate slowed down, the investment growth rate declined, the consumption growth rate leveled off, and the trade surplus decreased. The demand for consumption strengthened its momentum to stimulate economic growth, and the structure of demands was moving towards more balanced development.

2 Most prominent problem in China's current economy – the great inflationary pressure

The major problems facing China's economy are these: great inflationary pressure; dwindling supply of coal, electricity, petroleum, and transportation; insecure foundation for agricultural growth; excess liquidity of financial institutions; drastic fluctuations in asset price and stock market prices; grim situation of energy saving and emission reduction; etc. The most prominent problem is the inflationary pressure. From February to April this year, China's CPI grew 8% for three consecutive months, increasing 7.7% year over year in May, down 0.4% month over month; the main reason for this is that the production and sales of vegetables and fruits have come into the peak season, thus generating a decline in food price. But in the second half year, the CPI is still confronted with rising pressures, mainly including the following:

The pressure of global imported inflation will persist. Since the year 2007, prices soared in many countries, especially the prices of fuel oil, food, and ore. In 2008, the American sub-prime mortgage crisis broke out, the US dollar depreciated constantly, and the prices of energy resources and bulk commodities continued rising. The ratio of China's import dependence reached up to 47%; besides, as China lay in the stage of heavy chemical industry and there was a high consumption of energy resources, the pressure of the high oil price would persist.

Under the influences of crop fuels driven by rising oil price, increasing demand of grain in emerging countries and grain export control in many countries, the prices of most crops would remain a record high, though the world grain yield was expected to grow in 2008. On the whole, the international prices have limited effects on China's grain and food prices, but some of them are influenced remarkably by international grain prices, such as soybean and edible oil.

The pressure transited to CPI by PPI is increasing. In the first half of this year, China's producer prices of industrial products and the purchasing prices of raw materials, fuels, and power were rising rapidly. In May, the PPI grew 8.2% year over year, and the purchasing prices of raw materials, fuels, and power grew 11.9%. The pressure transmission from PPI to CPI was slowed by the price control and subsidy measures for refined oil products and electric power along with the temporary price intervention measures for commodities including food, steel products, and cement. The price control played a positive role in fighting short-term inflation, but there are still prominent problems such as shortage of supply and business operation difficulties. In the context where the growth rate of CPI slowed down in May, the National Development and Reform Commission recently raised the prices of refined oil products and electric power. This is an inevitable choice to safeguard market supply, mitigate difficulty in the business operation of some enterprises, and accelerate the transformation of economic development pattern. However, as the refined oil products and electric power are basic products, the influence of adjusting their prices covers a wide area. For this reason, the pressure transmitted by PPI to CPI will increase to some degree for some time in the future. While we do not make adjustment in prices of liquefied gas, natural gas, and electric power for residents' living and agricultural fertilizer production, these resource products are still confronted with the pressure of rising prices.

There is increase but no decrease in the pressure of excess liquidity. In recent years, China's foreign trade surplus remains at a high level, foreign exchange reserve increases rapidly, and the excess liquidity is hard to be effectively addressed. In the first half of this year, a mass of foreign exchange funds and hot money are flowing in quickly, notwithstanding the slowdown of foreign trade surplus. The RMB appreciation expectations and the interest rate differential with the US are the direct reasons for the large-scale inflow of hot money. The oversupply of RMB base money released by the rapid growth of the foreign exchange reserve has intensified the situation of excess liquidity. At present, as China's deposit reserve ratio is raised to 17.5%, the continuous excess liquidity has added much to the pressure of inflation and the difficulty in monetary policy operation.

The price tail-rising factors remain influential. The tail-rising influence is the important factor for difficulty in bringing down the growth rate of CPI in 2008. From January to May of this year, the CPI grew 8.1% accumulatively. According to prediction, the price tail-rising factor contributed 4.9% and the new price-rising factor, 3.2%. If the CPI in December 2007 is used as the benchmark, the price tail-rising factor from June to December only averaged out at 2.2%. Considering the new price-rising factors in the first five months of this year, if the CPI in May 2008 is used as the benchmark, then the average price tail-rising factors from June to December will rise to 5.0%. In other words, if there are not any new price-rising or price-falling factors from June to December (i.e. month-over-month price index is zero), then the growth rate of CPI in the whole year of 2008 will be around 6.3%. Considering the influence of new price-rising factors due to the adjustment of prices of refined oil products and electric power in June, if there are no new price-rising or falling factors, the growth rate of CPI in the whole year of 2008 will rise to around 7.0%. In the second half of this year, the new price-rising factors will originate mainly from the transmission of PPI to CPI and the likely rate of further rationalizing resource factor prices while the new price-falling factors will originate mainly from the seasonal decline of food prices in the summer and autumn. If the new price-rising factors prevail (i.e. month-over-month price index above zero), then the price tail-rising factors will rise further and the growth rate of CPI throughout the year will be above 7.0%; if the new price-falling factors prevail (i.e. month-over-month price index below zero), then the price tail-rising factors will be flat to some extent and the growth rate of CPI throughout the year will be below 7.0%.

3 Focus of macro control in the second half year

In the second half of this year, we should comply with the requirements of controlling economic gross, stabilizing prices, adjusting economic structure, and promoting balance development; continue to guard against in general the economic growth turning from being too fast to being too hot and avoid the prices turning from structurally rising to obvious inflation; and implement the prudent financial policy and the tightening monetary policy. The focus of macro control is placed on price control by means of giving priority to inflation control and stabilizing inflation expectation in order to prevent against financial risks, maintain healthy and steady macroeconomic fundamentals, and promote sound and rapid development of national economy. We should make every effort to inhibit a too-fast rise in the general price level by economic means, supplemented with legal means and administrative means (if necessary), laying emphasis on addressing both the symptoms and root causes, and combine long-term expectations and short-term expectations.

We should boost agricultural production and guarantee effective supply, enhance production of basic necessities and other commodities in short supply, and improve the reserve system; try to ensure an effective supply of important products and materials including refined oil products, electric power, and coal when price control cannot be completely deregulated; implement various policies of supporting agriculture and benefiting farmers, increased input into agriculture, and a raised overall agricultural productivity; endeavor to achieve domestic self-sufficiency in grain supply; and take initiative in addressing the food problem.

With easing inflationary pressure, we should promote the reform of resource factor price by stages and steps and focus on energy saving and emission reduction activities. In the "11th Five-Year Plan", China set two obligatory targets for energy saving and emission reduction, but no ideal progress has ever resulted over the past two years. Currently, as China's economic development pattern remains extensive and excessively dependent on the consumption of energy resources, there are severe phenomena of ecological damage and environmental pollution, so we still have a hard job to save energy and reduce emission. Rationalizing the resource factor price is an intrinsic demand of achieving objectives of energy saving and emission reduction as well as transforming the economic development pattern. In the past year, it was difficult to propel the reform of resource factor price due to the great pressure of rising prices. In June, the National Development and Reform Commission made an adjustment in prices of refined oil products and electric power, taking into consideration the various bearing capacities. In the second half year when the inflationary pressure was lessening, we can continue promoting reform of resource factor prices of liquefied gas, natural gas, and electricity by stages and steps; adopt price means to promote resource saving, guarantee market supply, and promote energy saving and emission reduction; and better combine fighting inflation by promoting the reform of resource factor prices.

We should strengthen financial regulation and supervision to ensure national financial security. In the first half of this year, the international financial market disruption intensified obviously. At the beginning of the year, the sub-prime mortgage crisis occurred in the United States; recently, the Vietnamese financial situation continued to deteriorate; and the prices on stock market and real estate market slowed down dramatically in some countries. With the complex and volatile international financial situation at present, we should further strengthen financial regulation and supervision. First, we should reinforce regulation and supervision over trans-border inflow and outflow of capital, stay vigilant against the reversion of short-term capital flow, keep a watchful eye on the trend of the changing international foreign exchange rate, grasp the rhythm and range of opening the capital market, and promote the healthy development of a capital market. Then, we should pay close attention to the changes in the real estate market and the tendency of real estate prices, stay vigilant against credit risks caused by the decline in house prices, maintain a steady real estate market, and ensure national financial security.

(Published in *People's Daily*, July 2, 2008)

13 Improve the effectiveness of macroeconomic regulation and control

This year, China's national economy maintains a good trend of rapid growth with the economic structure optimized, the economic benefits rose, and people's livelihood improved. But some prominent conflicts and problems accumulated over the years during economic operation are not yet fundamentally tackled; meanwhile, there have emerged some noteworthy new situations and problems. In this situation, the Central Economic Working Conference has made new arrangements for improving and implementing macro-control policies and maintaining the good trend of steady and rapid economic development. Only by earnestly implementing the Central Spirits, further improving the effectiveness of macro control and sparing no effort to address prominent problems during economic operation, shall we maintain the steady operation and long-term sustainable development of China's economy.

The Central Government stressed that the primary task of the current macro control is to prevent the economic growth from being too fast or being too hot, and to prevent the prices from turning from structural rise to obvious inflation, which is based on a scientific analysis of China's economic operation.

The economy grows at a fast rate. In recent years, China's GDP grows rapidly and shows an accelerating trend. In 2003, when a new round of macroeconomic regulations and controls commenced, China's GDP grew 10.0%; the growth rates from 2004 to 2006 increased 0.1, 0.4, and 1.1 percentage points respectively over the rates in 2003. In the first three quarters of this year, the growth rate of the GDP rose to 11.5%, indicating a strong uptrend. By three major industries, the industrial growth rate that has contributed the most to gross domestic product is accelerating; from January to September, the value added of industrial enterprises over a designated size grew 18.5% year over year, 1.3 percentage points higher than that in the same period of the previous year, and 1.9 percentage points higher than that in the whole of the previous year. It is forecast that China's economic growth rate in the whole year will reach up to 11.6%. The rapid rate of economic growth has brought about many difficulties for the adjustment of economic structure, the rational utilization of energy resources, and the protection of the environment.

The growth of investments and exports, which have in turn stimulated economic growth, remains robust. First, as the primary factor that has stimulated

China's economic growth, investment shows a rebounding trend in growth rate this year. The growth rate of total social investment was 27.7% in 2003, but fell to 24% in 2006 after three years' contraction. From January to September, the total social fixed asset investment grew 25.7%, falling 0.2 percentage points as against the first half year but rising 1.7 percentage points over the previous year. Then, foreign trade grows fast and trade surplus continues increasing. In the first three quarters of this year, the total volume of imports and exports amounted to US$1.5708 trillion, growing 23.5%, including the export of US$878.2 billion, increasing 27.1% with a year-over-year increase of 0.6 percentage points in growth rate. The trade surplus amounted to US$185.7 billion, which was beyond the level of 2006. Excessive trade surplus has intensified the international trade friction and the resource environment, and also increased the excess liquidity and the pressure on RMB appreciation.

The prices of consumer goods are rising remarkably. Since this year, the consumer price has terminated the long-term slump and begun to show a monthly rising trend. The CPI was 6.5% in August, 6.2% in September, 6.5% in October, and up to 6.9% in November. From January to November, CPI grew 4.6% accumulatively. China is a developing country with a higher Engel coefficient; the spending of residents on purchasing foods accounts for over 36% of CPI composition; this proportion may be much higher for low-income groups. For this reason, the recent, rapid rise in prices has had great effect on low-income and hard-pressed groups. The remarkable rise in consumer prices that has emerged since this year is an important signal of the macro economy turning from being too fast to being too hot.

The asset prices keep rising at a high level. Apart from CPI, the prices of asset markets including stock market and real estate market are constantly rocketing at a high level; in particular, the real estate prices in some big cities are rising excessively fast and high, which has already impacted the housing of residents and the immediate interests of the masses. On the securities market, a prediction based on the annual report data of listed companies in the first half of 2007 has indicated that, without considering long suspended stocks, the weighted dynamic price-earning ratio of the current 1,243 A-shares is 40.71 multiples. Without considering stocks with a negative net profit at the mid-term of 2007, there were only 261 out of 1,127 shares with a price-earning ratio below the average, accounting for 23.1% only, nearly 80% of the rest had a price-earning ratio higher than 40.71 multiples. In the context of excess liquidity and actual negative interest rate, a mass of money flowing into the stock market is likely to cause an asset bubble.

The "bottleneck" constraint of the resource environment is increasingly prominent. The domestic shortage of some resources may be relieved by means of high-price imports, but the environmental pollution, especially air pollution and water pollution, cannot be evaded. According to relevant data, China has 16 out of the 20 most-polluted cities in the world. As monitored by the State Environment Protection Administration, 27% of 411 surface water monitoring sections of seven major water systems in China are rated as Class V water of inferior quality, and the groundwater in urban districts of about one in two cities is heavily polluted.

In the situation of the national economy currently operating at a high level and tending to be too hot, the difficulty in macroeconomic regulation and control has increased due to some new problems such as the rising prices of consumer goods and assets, notwithstanding some problems are left unsolved.

The implementation and effectiveness of macro-control policy may be impaired by inconsistent understandings. Since the year 2003, China's GDP has been continuously growing at a rate above 10%, though it rose to 11.5% in the first three quarters of this year, far beyond the anticipated targets; however, there are still some people in disagreement with the economic growth turning from being too fast to being too hot. In the meantime, some local governments are less responsive to the macro-control policy of the Central Government. Under the existing economic system, local governments at all levels have control over many resources and quite a few of the state-owned enterprises can play vital roles in the implementation of the macro-control policy issued by the Central Government, for they are both objects of macro control and executants of policy. Indeed, some local governments only take into consideration their partial and local interests, and thus are actively implementing the macro-control policy that accords with local interests but take a negative attitude towards, or even boycott, the macro control policies that have disaccord with local interests. The implementation effects of macro-control policies are crippled accordingly.

The adjustment of the economic structure gets more difficult due to the expanding economic scale. In the 1980s and 1990s, when the economy became overheated or partly overheated, the economic growth rate could be brought down quickly only by tightening the macro-control measures. It is quite different this time. Ever since the year 2003 when this round of macro-control measures came into effect, the economy has been operating at a high level all the time. This shows, on the one hand, that our awareness of economic operation laws is deepening and that the scientific nature of macro control is strengthening; on the other hand, this shows that, with the rising degree of economic marketization and expanding economic scale, the inertial force of economic growth will be too strong to come to a halt once China's economy runs along the fast lane. If this is so, the growth of investment will keep operating at a high level and the foreign trade surplus will keep increasing; it is already too difficult to restrain the inertia in a short time, and the macro control will be faced with a more complex situation.

A too-fast rise in asset prices has become a key research subject of macroeconomic regulation and control. Apart from the pressure of a drastic rise in consumer prices, the price-rising pressure at present comes mainly from the rising asset prices, including security market price and real estate market price. There is plenty of private capital, but there are few investment channels available for it, which, in conjunction with the actual negative interest rate of deposits in a bank, helps masses of private money flow into the real estate market and stock market, thus expanding the demand of investment in real estates, pushing up stock market prices, and intensifying the inflation of asset price.

Inadequate reform of the system is an underlying problem that impacts the effect of macro control. Currently, the reform on investment system and financial system falls far behind the economic development. With the existing investment and financial systems, the non-standard sources and behaviors of investment dominated by local governments make it hard to restrain the impulse and thirst for investment. The excessively low cost of enterprises' use of resources and environmental pollution has added to the difficulty in energy saving and emission reduction. As the national income allocation structure inclines overly to investment and capital, the remuneration of labor turns down and the social security gets unsound, thus impairing the adjustment of the proportional relation between consumer demand and investment consumption. The macro-control effects are weakened by overabundant after-tax profits and self-owned funds of state-owned enterprises.

We should consider preventing against economic growth turning from being too fast to being too hot and preventing against obvious inflation as the primary task of macro control; accomplish macro-control work by following the principle of controlling the gross volume, steadying prices, adjusting the economic structure, and promoting balanced development; strengthen the effort of macro control; and improve the effectiveness of macro control.

We should be determined to bring down the too-fast economic growth rate, especially the growth rate of investment. We should thoroughly implement the scientific outlook on development and practically put the quality and benefit of economic growth in the first place so as to bring down the rapid economic growth rate, preferably down to around 9% in the following two years. To control the economic growth rate, we must first control the growth rate of investment by taking control of the investment scale through financial means, credit loans, land policy, and industrial policy. In addition, we should strengthen the effort to adjust the resource tax rate, accelerate the implementation of an environmental tax policy, strengthen the cost constraint on the capital of enterprises, control the direct investment scale of local governments at all levels, reduce support of financial policy for capital construction, increase the effort to adjust the structure of financial expenditure, put more financial funds into weak aspects (including education, health, and social security), and make contributions to boosting consumption rather than to enhancing production capacity. The state-owned enterprises with high profits, especially the monopolized enterprises, must pay part of their profits to the state, which will be used to cover the shortage of social security funds.

We should fully implement the prudent financial policy and the tightening monetary policy. In recent several years, the amount of financial revenue and overcharged tax have been big enough for the financial budget to reduce the deficit significantly; in particular, no more construction bonds shall be issued, and the investment put into leftover projects funded by bonds can be included into the budget. In recent years, the growth rate of credit loans has been on the rise. This year, the amount of originally planned new loans was RMB2.9 trillion Yuan in the whole year, but in the first three quarters, the amount of loans issued was RMB3.36 trillion Yuan, increasing RMB607.3 billion over the same period in the previous year. One explanation is that the size of loans should be increased due to the rapid economic growth rate. This explanation has virtually denied the idea that the monetary policy is designed to adjust to a too-fast growth rate. In practical work, we must strictly execute the tightening monetary policy.

We should stabilize prices and particularly prevent a further rise in consumer goods. Inflation is ultimately a monetary phenomenon. To prevent against a full-scale "inflation expectation", first, we should have control over the supply of money and scale of loans, and strengthen the flexibility of Renminbi exchange rate. Second, we should further increase inputs of financial sectors at all levels into agriculture and practically carry out all policies of supporting agriculture and benefiting farmers so as to increase the supply of grain, meat, and other foods; set up a price adjustment fund and special subsidy fund; and improve subsidy policy for providers of agricultural products (4.78%, 0.05%, and 1.06%), low-income groups, hard-pressed groups, and college students; and maintain social stability. Third, we should endeavor to increase the supply of medium- and low-price houses. The governments at all levels should adjust the structure of land supply to ensure sufficient newly-built houses on the market, and utilize resources in the hands of government to provide ample economically affordable houses and low-rent houses for people in need so as to curb the too-fast rise in housing prices. Finally, we should deter inside trading and prevent bank funds from illegally entering the stock market, and take effective measures to prevent stock market price bubbles.

We should deepen the reform and get rid of systematic obstacles that slow scientific development. For short-term problems during macroeconomic operation, we can tackle them effectively by means of a macro-control policy mix; but for some long-term or reoccurring problems and phenomena, such as "investment hunger", national income allocation, resource environment tax, and the soft budget constraint of some microeconomic subjects, we can hardly tackle them by means of macro-control policy alone. These underlying problems will be fundamentally solved only by deepening the reform, transforming government functions, standardizing government behavior, adjusting structures of national income allocation and financial expenditure, transforming the business operating mechanism of state-owned enterprises and banks, and constantly improving the degree of economic marketization.

(Published in *People's Daily*, December 26, 2007)

14 The current economic situation and the macroeconomic regulation and control

1 Measures and effects of macroeconomic regulation and control

Since the year of 2002, China's economy has entered a new rapid growth period. After SARS in 2003, it quickly recovered its strong growth momentum, with the GDP increasing 9.3% in the current year. In 2004, China's economy maintained the rapid growth momentum, realized a GDP of RMB13.6515 trillion Yuan, and grew 9.5% in the whole year, a year with the highest growth rate since 1997. With the rapid economic growth, local overheating phenomena occurred, including these: a too-fast growth rate and oversized scale of fixed asset investment; a rapid increase in the output of steel products, cement, and electrolytic aluminum (though short of supply); the tense situation of "coal, electricity, petroleum and transportation"; the excessively fast rising prices and considerable inflationary pressure; the falling output of grain in successive years; and a slow increase of rural income. The Chinese government has made a series of new macroeconomic policies since the beginning of 2004 to solve prominent economic problems and inhibit unhealthy and unstable factors during economic operation. These policies include the following: 1) the Central Bank has raised commercial banks' deposit reserve ratio twice, carried out a differential deposit reserve ratio system, increased floating rate loans, and the People's Bank of China has performed "window guidance" for financial institutions; 2) the Chinese government should clear up unapproved development zones in all regions – the Ministry of Land and Resources has exercised vertical leadership for land administration sectors below provincial level to enhance the land protection system, strengthen enforcement of land and environment protection law, and stop approving farmland for half a year in some industries and cities; 3) the Chinese government should impose constraints on loans issued to overheating industries including iron and steel, electrolytic aluminum, and cement – the China Banking Regulatory Commission has strictly investigated loans in overheating industries and regions to comprehensively clear up the use of fixed assets issued or promised by financial institutions for planned projects or those under construction – the National Development and Reform Commission has issued opinions on the control of investment in iron and steel industry, electrolytic aluminum industry, and cement industry, and seriously handled

"Tieben" incident;[1] 4) they should also introduce policy measures to facilitate agricultural production, increase grain acreage, raise protective grain purchase price, and actively enhance the supply capacity of coal, electricity, petroleum, and transportation; and 5) the Chinese government put financial expenditure under control, reduce issue volume of national debt, and adjust the structure of using the national debt fund.

   This new round of macro control has avoided drastic economic fluctuations and excessive price hikes, and maintained the good economic trend of steady and rapid development.

(1) The economy grows rapidly, without drastic fluctuations. The gross domestic product in the whole year was RMB13.6515 trillion Yuan, growing 9.5% over the previous year. In a quarterly perspective, the gross domestic products in four quarters grew 9.8%, 9.6%, 9.1%, and 9.5% respectively.

(2) A favorable turn has arisen in grain production and the adjustment of agricultural structure has pressed ahead. The grain acreage turned around from the trend of declining for a consecutive five years and restored to 101.61 million hectare, growing around 2% over the previous year. The total grain output amounted to 469.5 billion kilograms, increasing 38.8 billion kilograms.

(3) Too-fast growth of investment has been kept within limits, and the growth rate of fixed asset investment has begun to fall quarterly. The total social fixed asset investment amounted to RMB7.0073 trillion Yuan, growing 25.8%, decreasing 1.9 percentage points as against the previous year; the urban fixed asset investment was RMB5.862 trillion Yuan, growing 27.6%, with a decline of 1.5 percentage points; the rural fixed asset investment was RMB1.1452 trillion Yuan, growing 17.4%, down 4.4 percentage points.

(4) The growth of monetary and credit loans has decelerated. At the end of December, the broad money (M2) amounted to RMB25.3208 trillion Yuan, growing 14.6% as compared with that at the end of the previous year, with a year-on-year decline of 5 percentage points; the narrow money (M1) amounted to RMB9.5971 trillion Yuan, growing 13.6% and falling 5.1 percentage points; the currency in circulation (M0) amounted to RMB2.1468 trillion Yuan, growing 8.7% and falling 5.6 percentage points. The amount of all Renminbi loans from financial institutions grew RMB2.2648 trillion over the beginning of the year, 482.4 billion less than the growth in the previous year; total deposits increased RMB3.3315 trillion Yuan, 387.1 billion less than the growth in the previous year. The accumulative net cash injection in the whole year amounted to RMB172.2 billion Yuan, 74.6 billion less than that in the previous year.

(5) The consumer market has been revitalized in a steady situation. The total retail sales of social consumer goods amounted to RMB5.395 trillion Yuan, growing 13.3% over the previous year; with price factors deducted, it grew 10.2% in real terms, increasing 1 percentage point over the previous year. The total retail sales of urban consumer goods amounted to RMB3.5573

trillion Yuan, growing 14.7%, and the total retail sales of consumer goods at the level of county or below amounted to RMB1.8377 trillion Yuan, growing 10.7%.

(6) Foreign trade has leaped onto a new stage. The total volume of imports and exports in foreign trade amounted to US$1.1548 trillion; exports contributed US$593.4 billion, growing 35.4%; imports contributed US$561.4 billion, growing 36%; and the import and export trade surplus amounted to 32 billion. China has become the third largest trading countries in the world. At the end of the year, China's foreign exchange reserve amounted to US$609.9 billion, growing 206.7 billion as compared with that at the beginning of the year. In the whole year, the FDI contract value amounted to US$153.5 billion, growing 33.4% over the previous year; and the actually utilized FDI value was US$60.6 billion.

(7) The margin of price rise on the market has improved. The consumer price in the whole year grew 3.9% over the previous year, increasing by 2.7 percentage points as compared with the previous year, and it grew 3.2% year over year in the fourth quarter, with apparently lower than 5.3% of growth rate in that quarter. Under the influences of strong domestic demand and considerable rise in international crude oil price, the purchase prices of raw materials, fuels, and power grew 11.4% over the previous year; the producer price of industrial products grew 6.1%; the price of fixed asset investment grew 5.6%, and the housing sales price grew 9.7%.

2 Main problems existing in current economy

Since the beginning of 2005, there has been an overall good situation for China's economic and social development that has maintained the steady growth trend of high growth and low inflation. However, there are some problems and conflicts in the current economic activities, including achievements of macro regulation and control not consolidated yet; difficulty added to further increase grain output and rural income, especially the drastic rise in prices of essential production means; a strong possibility of expanding demand for fixed asset investment; increasingly fierce contradiction of resource and environment constraints; the short supply of coal, electricity, petroleum, and transportation, e.g. electric power growing 12% in January and February and power supply rationed in 25 provinces, cities, or regions, showing a tense relationship between economic growth and daily living; considerable pressure on the rise in general price levels as shown by rising prices of production means; the grim employment situation; the widening gap of residents' income that needs to be narrowed; the reform on state-owned enterprises and financial system that needs to be strengthened; and the unreasonable economic structure and the extensive pattern of economic growth that need to be solved fundamentally.

Some of these conflicts and problems are caused by short-term economic fluctuation, so they can be corrected by strengthening and improving macro-control measures; but some of them are underlying institutional defects, so they can be tackled by deepening reform step by step.

The following problems need special attention at present:

(1) *Preventing fixed asset investment from picking up again*

One of the unstable and unhealthy problems in China's economic operation in 2004 was the fixed asset investment inflation. After the macro control was strengthened and improved in a year, the blind investments of some sectors have been suppressed and the growth rate of total social fixed asset investment has slowed down as compared with the previous year. In the first quarter of 2005, however, the total social fixed asset investment grew 22.8% based on the high growth rate of 43% in 2004 over the same period last year; it was much higher than the growth rates of GDP and consumption; in particular, there was strong investment impulsion in various regions due to the excessive number of projects under construction currently and those recently approved. According to statistics, now there are more than 70,000 projects under construction in China, including more than 20,000 projects commenced in December 2004. The size of projects under construction amounted to about RMB20 trillion Yuan, a higher level in the history, almost equivalent to the gross volume of fixed asset investment in three years. Of the gross volume of investment in 2004, the extension projects and reconstruction projects only grew around 16%, but new construction projects grew over 36%. In 2003, the investment in new projects accounted for 55% of gross volume; in 2004, however, the proportion went up to 59%. Such big projects under construction added much to the difficulty in controlling the fixed asset investment scale in 2005.

While the fixed asset investment scale increased rapidly, there existed a problem of unreasonable structure of investment in industries. The growth of industrial investment remains fast at present; on the one hand, the scale of investment appears large in hot industries such as iron and steel, cement, and electrolytic aluminum, and on the other, new blind investments made by some local governments and enterprises in the illegal construction of a power station. The expanding investment demand that intensified "coal, electricity, petroleum and transportation" has increased investment in relevant industry and led to a new investment structure imbalance. Currently, there is an institutional condition for investment to pick up again, since all regions are highly motivated to develop economy; in addition, there is a funding condition, since there is considerable amount of capital in various aspects. From a financial perspective, though the financial policy has turned from an expanding nature to a prudent nature, it still features expansion. The use of funds needs to be strictly supervised, for a considerable quantity of long-term treasury bonds will be released in 2005 and the financial budget allows for a deficit of RMB300 billion Yuan. In a financial perspective, banks are witnessing a faster growth rate of deposits than that of loans, and the difference between them is widening. What's more, a mass of constantly accumulated private capitals are seeking channels for investment. In preventing investment from picking up again, we should pay close attention to the institutional and funding conditions that may contribute to rebounding investment. In 2005, the primary task of macroeconomic regulation and control is to keep the economy developing steadily and rapidly and avoid drastic economic fluctuations. To achieve this goal, we must restrain in time the too-fast growth of investment, adjust the economic structure, control investment in overheating sectors, and strengthen the weakness.

(2) Reducing pressure of rising prices

Ever since the second half of 2003, Chinese macroeconomic growth has begun an ascent stage of economic cycle; meanwhile, the pressure of rising prices has increased due to the tense relationship between the supply and demand of grain, the expansion of fixed asset investment, and the occurrence of new problems involving "coal, electricity, petroleum and transportation". While factors that generated the pressure from rising prices in 2004 remain there, we need to pay close attention to some new factors that may lead to a rise in prices, which includes the following:

First, China's CPI only grew 3.9%, increasing by 2.7 percentage points over the previous year; however, with expanding demand for investment, the dramatic rise in prices of upstream products is inevitably transferred to downstream products, thus leading to rise in the consumer price level. Though this transition is currently restrained by a supply-demand relation on the consumer market, the rise in prices of some upstream products will be definitely passed down.

Second, the production price keeps rising. At the beginning of 2005, the production price was on the rise with a strong possibility of resurgence in investment. In the first quarter, CPI grew 2.8%, but the production price grew 61% and the price of raw materials, fuels, and power grew 10.1%. From the present demand of investment, the uptrend in prices of production means cannot be curbed utterly in a short time; so, we will at no time lose sight of the possibility of cost-push inflation.

Third, the tight supply of "coal, electricity, petroleum and transportation" as well as water was an important reason for the rising price level that began in the second half of 2003. The tight supply of "coal, electricity, petroleum and transportation" in 2005 can hardly be improved, and it will definitely lead to a rise in prices.

Finally, the price of crude oil keeps rising in the international market and will increase both the production cost and living cost in China. It is predicted that the high price of crude oil will persist for quite a long time and will generate long-term pressure and a rise in the overall price level in China.

The above-mentioned four problems that formed in the second half of 2003 are factors that led to a rise in prices, but at present, we are also confronted with new problems that may cause the same result, which includes:

First, prices ascend and the bubble of real estate expands in some regions. In 2004, the average selling price of commodity houses in China showed a rising trend. In 2005, the trend persisted; the price of commodity houses grew 12.5% year over year, and the housing price grew 13.5%. It is inevitable that the price of real estate will keep rising due to the continuous rise in production price, including the iron, steel, and cement, as well as the price of land. The rising price of real estate will have remarkable effects on the rise in general price level.

Second, the shortage of rural migrant workers in some regions recently shows an uptrend of labor cost. According to statistics, the average labor remuneration of urban employed persons grew 12.5%, 14.1%, and 14.5% respectively in the first three quarters of 2004. The rising labor cost, on the one hand, can help raise the residents' income level, and on the other, it may have an effect on the general price level (that is, the average or aggregate of the fluctuating prices of all commodities and services of a country or a region in a given period).

Finally, in order to build a harmonious society and achieve sustainable development, we should pay more attention to environmental protection and require manufacturing enterprises to invest more in environmental protection. To improve the safety production level, we also need to increase the input of safety production. These new investments are quite necessary, but they will definitely have an effect on the price level to some degree.

On the whole, the problem of rising prices we have been confronted with in 2005 may not be as severe as it was in 2004; but, full attention must be paid to the possible effect of the rising price level on steady and rapid macroeconomic growth. In 2005, we should maintain the consumer price below 4% and also try to reduce inflation so as to create a favorable condition for all-round economic and social development.

(3) Price and output of grain

The basic principle of China's solution to "three agricultural services" (serving rural areas, serving agriculture, and serving farmers) is designed to increase farmers' income, and the fundamental and primary factor that affects farmers' income is the price of agricultural products. Since the year of 2003, the farmers' income has been increased substantially due to shortage of grain supply that drives drastic rise in grain price and prices of an overwhelming majority of agricultural products.

At present, we should stabilize the policy and measures that promote increases of grain production and farmers' income. The focus of "three agricultural services" should be placed on the construction of the rural public finance system, giving priority to public welfare establishments, to ensure that all citizens in different regions and from different classes are entitled to enjoy equal public services. To build a standard, transparent, and just financial transfer system, we should first satisfy the need to construct a basic level of political power based on defining the functions (power or authority of office) at the township level and village level. This seems particularly important after a cut in the agricultural tax.

(4) Cooling the overheated real estate market

From an industrial perspective, the fixed asset investment in 2003 and 2004 was mainly driven by real estate investment. This situation remains unchanged, so the government's macro control will focus on real estate investment in 2005. It is necessary for the government to intervene in the real estate market with the purpose of bringing down the growth rate of real estate investment.

Increasing the interest rate is one of the major measures currently taken. According to experiences since the year of 2004, however, the rise of housing prices is faster than the rise of interest rates in many regions. Though the increasing interest rate has boosted the pressure of repayment cost, monetary policy alone is not powerful enough to curb the demand for housing property.

The macro-control measures should be adapted to different relations between supply and demand.

First, we should promote the development of leasing houses including low-rent houses to meet needs of the wage-earning class, especially the large number of ordinary workers; properly understand the meaning of housing commercialization; and see house leasing as a main form of commercial residential building. Considering China's present development level, it is impractical to pursue a 100% rate of home ownership. In addition, due to the fact that the production factor market is underdeveloped in the current situation, the government needs to intervene in the housing lease business, which has the nature of public goods. The government should take hold of a certain quantity of available houses and invest in the house leasing market to stabilize house rent and ultimately stabilize housing price; after all, housing price is the capitalized rent. If so, these measures will fundamentally inhibit the excessively fast growth of real estate investment and prevent real estate bubbles.

Then, we should introduce a progressive real estate tax, impose restrictions on building too many high-grade luxurious houses, and increase the supply of ordinary commercial housing.

(5) Restricting production capacity of energy-intensive and resource-oriented products

According to relevant statistical data, the present production capacity generated by investment in the steel industry of China has exceeded 500 million tons; however, there were less than 300 million tons of steel products consumed in 2004. Inevitably, the excess capacity will turn to the international market to find the way out. Among most of the industrial products in China, steel products are competitive in price on the international market; but they are so energy-intensive and resource-oriented that they have overlooked their social cost, especially the environmental cost. For this reason, we should impose a restriction on this line of products with a high consumption of energy resources to alleviate resource and environmental pressure. This is also an important measure to put under control the drastic growth of fixed asset investment.

3 Current tendency of macroeconomic policy

In the current critical period, as the achievements of macro control have not been consolidated, a little slack may lead to a regression. Furthermore, the year 2005 is the key to fully accomplishing tasks of the "10th Five-Year Plan" and laying a solid foundation for development of the "11th Five-Year Plan". So, the macro control will, on the one hand, maintain sustainable, steady, and rapid development of the national economy, and on the other, pave the way for medium- and long-term economic and social development.

For macro-control policy orientation in 2005, we will implement the prudent financial policy and prudent monetary policy, strengthen the coordination of various macroeconomic policies, uphold the principle of differential treatment that may stimulate or inhibit investment, emphasize the role of market mechanism, and make full use of economic and legal means to limit the scale of fixed asset investment and expand consumer demand. Based on a macro-control system, we will continue advancing the reform on economic systems to ensure economic operation at a high level, say between 7% and 9%, with the hope to extend the ascent stage of economic cycle.

(1) Paving the way for addressing the issue of medium- and long-term economic structure

At present, we need to pay attention to the internal structure of industry as well as to the gap between investment and consumption and residents' income and to the structure problem of the secondary and the tertiary industries. In 2004, the growth rate of China's heavy industry was 3.4 percentage points higher than that of light industry; and heavy industry accounted for 67% of industrial value added, but light industry did less than a third. Heavy industry now leads industrial growth, but it also leads to the tense relation between the supply and demand of "coal, electricity, petroleum and transportation" and the excessive rise in production prices. The growth of heavy industry features both self-cycling and strong inertia. A disproportion in the industrial internal structure will deepen the negative effect of economic fluctuations on steady and rapid economic growth. Once heavy industry begins to grow, it will boost economic growth over a period of time; however, once heavy industry growth is flat in a downward spiral, it will be more difficult to get it started. When the problem of industrial internal structure interweaves with the structural problem of investment and consumption, the supply capacity in shortage of sufficient and effective demand support will give rise to excess production capacity and further to deflation.

(2) Implementing the prudent financial policy

The prudent financial policy has a new and important task under the new situation to strengthen and improve macroeconomic regulation and control. It is aimed not merely to control the economic aggregate but adjust the economic structure. During implementation of this policy, special care should be paid to the executing effect in order to prevent various problems that may occur and to ensure the practical effectiveness of the policy.

First, faced with the current pressure of rising price levels, we should concentrate macro control on fighting inflation. Considering that the issuance of treasury bonds is an expansionary action, during the implementation of the prudent financial policy, we should, on the one hand, guarantee a smooth rather than sharp transition from expansive financial policy to prudent financial policy, and on the other, adapt financial policy to the general trend in an ascent stage of economic cycle in accordance with the changing situation by weakening its expansiveness.

Second, during macroeconomic operation in China, the investment rate is too high and the investment growth rate is too fast, so much so that the issue of imbalance between investment and consumption is getting increasingly serious. The prudent financial policy should play its role in guiding the macroeconomic policy to solve or improve the issue of a too-high investment rate and the structural imbalance between investment and consumption.

Finally, one of the main contents of prudent financial policy is to put an appropriate amount of the national debt fund into "three agricultural services" and social undertakings; in the long run, however, the input and support of public finance for "three agricultural services" and social undertakings are mainly derived from normalized financial transfer payments.

(3) Bringing into full play the monetary policy

The monetary policy can play effective roles in controlling the expansion of investment demand and easing the pressure of rising prices. After one year of strengthening and improving macroeconomic regulation and control, the monetary policy has indeed performed its due functions. In macro-control practice, the indirect regulatory mechanism of China's monetary policy is taking shape gradually, and the guiding role of monetary policy is increasingly evident.

To stop investment from picking up again and effectively inhibit the pressure of rising prices, now we can consider signaling the monetary policy intended to raise interest rates, giving play to interest rate leverage. Macroeconomic regulation and control will be exercised in the supply and demand of money, even of macro-economy. In the existing situation, the real interest rate, especially the real interest rate of deposits from residents, is basically negative. If such a case persists for a long time, it will go against the interests of resident depositors, the economic relationships, and the normal order of market economy.

(A speech delivered on the 5th Sino-Russian Economists Forum held in Moscow on June 18, 2005)

Note

1 In 2004, Jiangsu Iron and Steel Co., Ltd. started illegal construction of an iron and steel project.

15 Several problems on the investment in real estate in China

Since the first quarter of this year, the CPC Central Committee and the State Council have continued improving the macro-control policy and consolidated the results achieved since the last year, so China's economy shows an uptrend in development on the whole and maintains sustainable and rapid growth, with the GDP up 9.5% and other targets including financial revenue shaping up. Nevertheless, China's economy is also confronted with some problems that require a prompt solution, e.g. too-high growth rate of investment in fixed asset and excessive, large-scale investment.

1 Excessively rapid growth rate and large scale of China's investment in fixed assets in recent years

Ever since the year of 2003, China's investment in fixed assets has grown at a rate above 20%. It was 27.7% in 2003, 25.8% in 2004, and 22.8% in the first quarter this year; in the whole year, it may maintain above 20%. This is one of the most rapid growth periods in history; after deducting price factors, it is only lower than the investment growth rate during 1992–1994 when the economy was overheated.

As the investment grows at a high rate, the proportion of investment in the GDP ascends sharply and the scale of investment expands quickly. Calculated by the proportion of gross capital formation in GDP, the rate of investment was 42.8% in 2003 and 45.2% in 2004; it is estimated to be above 40% this year. Calculated by the proportion of total completed investment in fixed assets in GDP, the rate of investment was 41.4% in 2002, up to 47.3% in 2003, and further up to 51.4% in 2004; this is one of the highest periods in history. By the above-mentioned calculating method, from 1978 to 2002, the rate of investment exceeded 40% only in the period from 1993 to 1995, i.e. 43.4% in 1993, 41.2% in 1994, and 40.8% in 1995. This is a period of an overheating economy accompanied by high inflation.

As compared with other countries in the world, China's investment rate is much higher. In 2002, the world average rate was 19.9%; but the investment rate was 19.7% in low-income countries, 22.9% in middle-income countries (19.0% in upper-middle-income countries and 25.2% in lower-middle-income countries), and 19.0% in high-income countries. One more example: the investment rates of countries equivalent to China's development level (i.e. per capita GDP around US$1000), such as the Philippines, Indonesia, and Thailand, were 19.3%, 14.3%, and 23% respectively. It follows that China's present investment rate is far higher than the world average and much higher than that of major developed countries and all developing countries.

China's investment rate is too high, though it exists for a certain objective reason. According to statistical analysis, it is advisable for China's investment rate to be below 40%, and the rate of investment growth to be below 20%. The investment growth rate above 20% (as was from 1984 to 1988, from 1991 to 1994, and after 2002) and the investment rate above 40% (as was from 1993 to 1995 and after 2002) will overheat China's economy entirely or locally.

The state-owned and local projects have occupied a large proportion of the present composition of China's investment. Although the growth rate of state-owned investment is much lower than other economic sectors, its proportion is much larger. Therefore, the issue of how to control the proportion of state-owned investment and local investment remains a major problem that needs attention from the Central Government. The state-owned investment accounts for over 40% of urban investment (state-owned investment was 39.1% in 2004, and solely state-owned corporations were 2.8%); and the local investment accounts for around 90% of total social investment. The lack of an explicit scope, and a sound mechanism of governmental investment at present in China, has given rise to egregious loans for some local governments in excessive pursuit of vanity projects and image projects to merely change a city's appearance. There are various borrowing methods; for example, they borrow money from banks via a state-owned urban construction corporation, which is guaranteed by the government. Some experts have estimated that the total liabilities of governments at the levels of prefecture, county, and township amount to about RMB3 trillion Yuan, and the total debt is also increasing; the level of indebted government is ascending from county and township to prefecture. Bank lending is playing a more important role in the management of public facilities, including urban construction. For example, the development bank released a medium- and long-term loan of RMB 366.7 billion Yuan in 2004 for projects with a total investment of RMB3.7 trillion Yuan, including RMB1.67 trillion Yuan pledged by the development bank. The loan for the management of public facilities, including urban construction, accounts for 31% of the total loans released for these projects. The Central Government has taken a series of macro-control measures one after another to inhibit blind investment in industries and real estate, and effective results have occurred; however, it has issued no effective measures specific to urban construction carried out by some local governments borrowing money from banks, where the local governments make the best of their administrative means. This is also an area of investment that breeds huge potential financial risk.

In history, China's overheating economy, either entirely or locally, was caused by both the excessive large scale and rapid growth rate of investment. Since the reform and opening up, the three periods when China's economy has been overheated entirely or locally occurred in this way. In the first period from 1985 to 1988, the rate of investment averaged out to 37.5%, growing 3.3 percentage points on average over three years from 1978 to 1984 when the growth rate of GDP went up to 10%, which resulted in a high inflation rate. In the second period from 1992 to 1994, the rate of investment averaged out to 41%, and the average growth rate of GDP surpassed 10%, giving rise to a high inflation rate. In the third period that began in 2002, the rate of investment exceeded 40% on a sequential basis, hitting a historical new high.

It is also obvious that the entirely or locally overheated economy of China caused by the excessively rapid growth rate of investment bears an administrative feature of the economic cycle. Ever since the year 1982, exclusive of 1997 and 1998 when China's economy was affected by Asian financial crisis, every leadership transition of the CPC and the government in power has caused economic fluctuations. For example, the rate of investment was 5.2% in 1981 but grew to 9.1% and 10.9% respectively in 1982 and 1983 when the transition occurred; it was 8.8% in 1986 but grew to 11.6% and 11.3% respectively in 1987 and 1988 when the transition occurred; it was 9.2% in 1991 but grew to 14.2% and 13.5% respectively in 1992 and 1993 when the transition occurred; and it was 7.5% in 2001 but rose to 8.3% and 9.3% respectively in 2002 and 2003 when the transition occurred.

The excessively rapid growth rate and large scale of investment will also go against the transformation of economic development pattern. In recent years, there has been a decline in investment benefits due to an unimproved investment structure. In 1993, new projects occupied 30.5% of state-owned investment; extension projects, 33.4%; and extensional investment, up to 63.9%. As compared with the 1990s, the extensional investment has increased significantly in recent years. Quite a few projects are under blind or redundant construction. From a macro perspective, the investment benefit of China is on the decline. For example, the effect coefficient of investment was 0.71 in 1994, down to 0.26 in 1997, and further down to 0.15 in 2002; the elastic coefficient of investment was 1 in 1997, down to 0.47 in 2002; and the marginal output ratio of investment fell from 3.34 in 1997 to 1.20 in 2002.

2 The arduous task to control the present growth rate and scale of investment

In the over one year's strengthening and improving macroeconomic regulation and control, blind investment of some sectors has been inhibited, and the growth rate of total social investment in fixed assets has declined as compared with the previous year. In the first quarter of 2005, nevertheless, the total social investment in fixed assets amounted to RMB1.0998 trillion Yuan, growing 22.8% year over year; though the growth rate fell 20.2 percentage points and 3 percentage points over the same period last year and throughout the last year respectively, it was deemed as a high growth rate based on a 43% growth over the same period last year, increasing 1.5 percentage points over last December. This is a sign that the growth rate is picking up again. In the first quarter, investment in commodity houses and commercial housing respectively grew 27.6% and 27.4% year over year, and investment in municipal public utilities grew at a high rate of 27%. The growth rate of investment is obviously higher than that of GDP and consumption; in particular, there are too many new projects and those under construction at present, so investment impulsion remains strong. According to statistics, there are more than 70,000 new projects in China; construction of 22,776 projects commenced in the first quarter, increasing 1,176 projects year over year, with a total planned investment of over RMB9 trillion Yuan, growing 26.7%. At present, the amount of total social investment in projects under construction exceeds RMB20 trillion Yuan, a historical record high, nearly equivalent to three years' investment in fixed assets. Of total investment in 2004, investment in extension and reconstruction projects only grew around 16%, but investment in new projects went up to 36%. Of the total investment in 2003, the proportion of new projects was 55%, but it rose to 59% in 2004. Such a large-scale project under construction will add to the difficulty in controlling the investment in fixed assets in 2005.

While the investment in fixed assets grows rapidly, unreasonable problems still exist in the industrial investment structure. At present, the industrial investment grows rapidly; on the one hand, the scale of investment remains large in some overheated industries including iron and steel, cement, and electrolytic aluminum; on the other hand, new blind investment is carried out illegally in some regions and by some enterprises. The expanding demand of investment that results in a tense supply of "coal, electricity, petroleum and transportation" has led to increasing investment in some industries and further to a new imbalance of investment structure.

Currently, there is an institutional condition for investment to pick up again, since all regions are highly motivated to develop the economy. In addition, there is a funding condition, since there is a considerable amount of capital in various aspects. From a financial perspective, though the financial policy has turned from an expanding nature to a prudent nature, it still features expansion. The use of funds needs to be strictly supervised, for a considerable quantity of long-term treasury bonds will be released in 2005 and the financial budget allows for a deficit of RMB300 billion Yuan. From a financial perspective, banks are witnessing a faster growth rate of deposits than that of loans, and the difference between them is widening. What's more, a mass of constantly accumulated private capitals are seeking channels for investment. In preventing investment from picking up again, we should pay close attention to the institutional and funding conditions that may contribute to rebounding investment. In 2005, the primary task of macroeconomic regulation and control is to keep the economy developing steadily and rapidly and to avoid drastic economic fluctuations. To achieve this goal, we must deepen the reform of government functions and state-owned enterprises, gradually eliminate institutional factors that lead to administrative interference in the economic cycle, strengthen and improve macro control, restrain in time the too-high investment rate and too-fast growth rate of investment, actively adjust the economic structure, control investment in overheating sectors, strengthen the weaknesses, and strive to improve investment benefits.

(Published in Journal of *Chinese Academy of Social Sciences*,
June 9, 2005)

16 Perfect the regulation system and promote healthy economic growth

Since the second half of 2003, the Central Government has introduced a series of macro-control measures. Particularly after the Meeting of the Political Bureau of the CPC Central Committee and the 47th Executive Meeting of the State Council, preliminary results have been achieved by active implementation of these measures in all regions and sectors: the growth of total urban investment in fixed assets has slowed down; the increases of money and credit have fallen, consolidation of the land market has achieved certain results, the growth of production capacity and output of some overheating industries has decelerated, and the rising product prices have declined, with some of them even down to normal level. However, we should also see that some fundamental conflicts remain unsolved in the process of economic operation. There are also many problems worthy of attention and research in the present macroeconomic regulation and control. We must pay close attention to these conflicts and problems.

1 Further study the objectives and grasp the efforts of macroeconomic regulation and control

The objectives and efforts of macro regulation and control may vary in different periods of economic development. The objective of macro control was to promote economic growth and fight inflation a few years ago when China's economy grew at low rate due to the Asian financial crisis and the world economic downturn; at that time, the proactive financial policy and the prudent monetary policy together with other policy measures were put into effect. Now, as China's economy has entered a new period of high growth rate and the economic growth is locally overheated, the objective and efforts of macro control have changed, and the primary task of macro control is to curb the ultra-high growth rate of economy so as to prevent the locally overheated economy from growing into an entirely overheated economy. Two problems are raised accordingly:

First, the macroeconomic policy must be subject to adjustment and the proactive financial policy must fade out. I put forward my opinion when the government work report was discussed at the beginning of this year, proposing the words "maintain the continuity and stability of macroeconomic policy" not be included in the report. Although not a single word of "fade out of the existing proactive financial policy" is mentioned in the Central Government's document, this policy is being adjusted in practical work. So, it is not appropriate for us to implement the proactive financial policy at the moment; rather, we should implement moderate macroeconomic policy after an economic "soft landing".

The second problem involves the objectives of macro regulation and control. How high of a rate of China's economic growth will be appropriate? According to plans for the year of 2004, the GDP should grow at the rate of 7%, investment at 12%, and exports at 8%. These targets were already surpassed in the first half year, with the GDP growing 9.7%; investment, 28.6%; and exports up to 36%. If the macro regulation and control were performed according to the original targets, a heavy decline or an economic downturn would have occurred definitely. It is not scientifically grounded that the growth rate of the GDP was calculated based on a quadruple of China's national economic aggregates in a period of 20 years. According to the current economic strength of China and historical experiences, I think it is advisable to maintain China's economic growth rate within the range of 8–9% at the present stage.

There is also a problem of prices. In 2003, one of the important foundations for some people not to accept China's overheated economy is the low consumer price index (CPI) of China. However, this situation has changed greatly in the first half of 2004. CPI is estimated to be just 3.6%, but it will increase step by step; its growth rates in the first five months are 3.2%, 2.1%, 3.0%, 3.8%, and 4.4% respectively, fluctuating in a V shape. In the second half year, the CPI is estimated to grow year over year up to around 4%, breaking the target of price regulation in the whole year. Experience has shown that a no more than 5% rise in prices is moderate and acceptable to a developing country like China, along with being beneficial to economic development. In other words, if the economic growth rate exceeds 9% and CPI is above 5%, the economy will be deemed entirely overheated, which should be avoided.

2 Make proper use of regulatory and control means

Currently, there is a heated discussion among people at all levels about macro control means, focusing on how to use administrative means. Quite a few people at local levels have complained that the Central Government has a preference for administrative means in economic management, while people in Beijing have complained that some local governments directly intervened in the economy by administrative means. According to the information we have at this time, both complaints exist and may be more serious in a number of regions. To build the socialist market economy system, it is inevitable that we rely heavily on economic and legal means for economic regulation and control. However, we must also see that China's market economy remains immature, that the governmental behavior is still less standardized, and that the government's direct intervention in the economy still prevails in China. Particularly, these phenomena can get more severe at the time of government re-elections, which may lead to a new administrative cycle of the economy. Therefore, when necessary, appropriate administrative means should be taken. But the administrative means can only be auxiliary and temporary. It is only used in order to correct the improper administrative means of the lower governments. And it can only be effective in this way.

3 Focus macro regulation and control on the adjustment of industry and the economic structure and the transformation of the economic development pattern

There is an imbalanced relationship among the primary industry, the secondary industry, and the tertiary industry of China. As the agricultural development lags behind, the problem of "three agricultural services" (serving the agriculture, the farmers, and the rural areas) will be the main obstacle in rapid economic development of China; attention is paid to agricultural problems not because of the reduction in grain yield, but because of research on long-term mechanisms to address the problem of "three agricultural services". We have reached a consensus regarding this problem, but we should pay close attention to acquisition and expropriation of rural land at low prices by some local governments.

According to a survey, some local governments pay very low compensation fees for land acquisition, about RMB30,000 Yuan per *mu* (a unit of area, equivalent to 0.0667 hectare), even the highest no more than RMB60,000, and only a tiny portion of the money can go into farmers' pocket. After consolidation of the land acquired, the government will make big bucks by selling it at a higher price, e.g. hundreds of thousands of Renminbi Yuan per *mu*, so much so that the land transfer fees in some developed regions have surpassed the local financial revenue. As this money is not included in the budget, the government puts it into vanity projects or image projects. This is the principal source of money for expanding the scale of investment. In some regions, the landless farmers without unemployment insurance and endowment insurance have become a serious social problem. With the advancing industrialization and urbanization, it is inevitable for the government to acquire part of the rural land, but it must take into consideration the farmer's interests and properly cope with farmer's social security; in addition, it must strengthen the management of the land fund and improve the utilization benefit of the fund.

In China, the scale of the secondary industry is already large enough; so priorities should be given to the problems of blind construction and low-level redundant construction, to the development of pillar industry, particularly to the development of high-level equipment manufacturing industry, to the new hi-tech industry, to the high value-added industry, and to the tertiary industry.

The extensive operation pattern of China's economy has not changed, but prevailed, in the last two years, being particularly conspicuous in maintaining a high growth rate by means of investment and the high consumption of resources. The input-output ratio of the developed countries is 1:1, the world's average is

2.9:1, but China's was 5:1 in 2003. In spite of abundant resources, China's per capita possession of resources is lower than the world's average; in particular, the per capita possession of resources including fresh water, arable land, and forest (which have strategic significance for human survival and China's industrialization) accounts for only 1/4, 1/3, and 1/6 of the world's total quantity; the per capita possession of the reserve of energy resources and the potential value of mineral resources accounts for only 1/2 of the world's average; the bulk mineral reserve, exclusive of coal, can hardly meet the demand. In addition, China has an enormous consumption rate and grievously wastes resources. If calculated by an exchange rate, China's GDP accounted for 3.8% of the world's GDP in 2003, but the consumption of steel, coal, and cement amounted to 36%, 3%, and 55% respectively of the world's gross product in 2001. China's energy consumption per unit of output value is three to four times that of the developed countries; the average utilization rate of energy resources is 30% only, 10–20 percentage points lower than developed countries; the unit water consumption by main products is more than 500 times that of developed countries, and the repeating utilization rate of industrial water is 3.5 to 4 times lower than developed countries; the utilization rate of timber is only 40–50%, the multipurpose utilization rate is merely 1/8 of developed countries; and in the period of the "8th Five-Year Plan", the area of arable land fell 2.11 million *mu* per year on average. This development pattern has to come to an end. In recent years, China's economic development has increasingly been under the constraint of resource and environmental factors. The only way out for China's economic development in the future will move towards the sustainable, intensive, and saving economy.

4 How to avoid constant administrative cycles in China's economic development

For a long time, drastic fluctuations in China's economic growth are caused primarily by administrative impulsion. The key to this problem is to deepen the reform of the planning system, financial system, investment system, and land acquisition and expropriation system, and especially of the commercial banks. The expanding scale of investment has revealed serious problems concerning risk control by commercial banks in China. In addition, we should strengthen the legal system by strengthening the reform of the political system. The root cause of the administrative cycle in economic operation also lies in the fact that the government functions are not changed fundamentally due to the integration of government administration with enterprises. Another important reason is the defective legal system, the weak legal awareness, and the illegal administration by the government. Only when significant progress is achieved in the reform on these problems will it be likely to reduce and ultimately avoid the administrative cycle that may give rise to drastic fluctuations in China's economy.

(Published in *Chinese Academy of Social Sciences Review*, Aug 3, 2004)

17 Control the scale of investment in fixed assets and reduce the investment in redundant construction

In 2003, China's economy grew at an unprecedented rate; GDP increased 9.1% over the previous year; imports and exports and financial revenue also witnessed a high growth rate. All these achievements should be highly appreciated, but there were some noteworthy problems, such as an excessively fast growth rate of investment in fixed assets and an excessively large scale of investment, that we should take seriously.

1 The scale of China's current investment in fixed assets is already excessively large

In 2003, the total social investment in fixed assets of China amounted to RMB5.5118 trillion Yuan, increasing 26.7%, and 9.8 percentage points higher than the growth rate in the previous year; the growth rate of investment in capital construction was 28.7%, increasing 12.3 percentage points. The scale of the fixed asset of projects under construct was about RMB16 trillion Yuan, the rate of investment up to 40%, and the contribution rate of investment to the GDP was close to 70%. As the growth rate of investment is higher than that of consumption, the formation rate of fixed assets of China rose from 35% in 1998 to 39.2% in 2002, possibly up to 40% in 2003.

There are a number of channels for high growth rate of investment in fixed assets: (1) own funds of enterprises. Last year, the own funds of enterprises and public institutions grew around 47%, with a year-over-year growth of 20 percentage points; (2) bank loans. Last year, the loans in Renminbi and foreign currencies issued by financial institutions increased 2.9 trillion Yuan, with a year-over-year rise of 1.07 trillion loans, including 2.77 trillion loans in Renminbi, which increased by 0.92 trillion Yuan year over year. The balance of loans in Renminbi and foreign currencies issued by financial institutions amounted to 16.97 trillion Yuan, increasing 21.4% year over year, including a 15.90 trillion balance of loans in Renminbi, which increased 21.1% year over year. From the uses of these loans, investment in fixed assets has the fast growth rate of about 45%, including an increase of 637.3 billion in loans for capital construction, which grows 319.9 billion year over year; (3) foreign direct investment (FDI). Last year, foreign direct investment grew 34.4%, basically equaling that of the previous year; (4) treasury bonds. From 1998 to 2002, the State has issued 660 billion Yuan of long-term treasury bonds for construction, and arranged 3.28 trillion Yuan of investment in projects together with bank loans and social investment. In 2003, 140 billion Yuan of long-term treasury bonds were issued for construction, which mobilized a considerable amount of investment; (5) administrative means. According to incomplete statistics, currently there are 3,837 development zones in China (more than 5,000 zones, according to some other source), including 232 development zones approved by the State Council, accounting for 6%; 1,019 zones approved by the provincial government, accounting for 26.6%; and the remaining, accounting for 67.4% of the total number of development zones, were approved by governments below provincial level that failed to follow the prescribed procedures. In order to seek for high economic growth, some local governments ratified a number of new projects with a high consumption of water and energy resources and severe environmental contamination, regardless of the bearing capacity of local resources and environment. A majority of these projects were built using bank loans; due to a shortage of money, some of them maintained the status quo by means of forced expropriation of farmers' arable land and arrears of construction party's funds or rural workers' wages.

2 An excessively large scale of investment in fixed assets has serious negative effects on economic development

While many underlying problems in China's economic development, such as the unreasonable economic structure, the extensive management, and the old system constraint, are still under dispute, a number of new problems have emerged during economic operation, mostly caused by an excessively large scale of investment in fixed assets.

There is a short supply of energy, transportation, and main raw materials. Last year, despite a yield of 1.7 billion tons last year, China remained short of raw coal supply so much so that there was a drastic decline in coal stockpiles of some enterprises; the electric energy production increased at the highest rate and the utilization ratio of electric energy was close to 60%, but there was a shortage of electric supply, and power cuts occurred occasionally at the main power grid. China's consumption of crude oil has reached around 250 million tons, one third of which are replenished through imports. The rail capacity also is insufficient; last November, the average daily fill rate of railway vehicles was no more than 55%, the annual average was only 68.2%, which was significantly lower than the 73.5% of the previous year. Apart from a shortage of coal, electricity, petroleum, and transportation, there is a short supply of some important, basic raw materials, such as aluminum oxide, copper, and iron ore, which largely rely on imports. Blind expansion and redundant construction have intensified in some industries, including iron and steel, cement, and electrolytic aluminum, due to a high growth rate of investment demand, especially the demand of investment in capital construction. Last year, the investment in iron and steel industry amounted to RMB140 billion Yuan, increasing more than 100% over the previous year. The production capacity of steel products has reached 250 million tons, and together with more than 80 million tons of production capacity under construction, it is estimated to reach 330 million tons by the end of 2005. Moreover, there is a planned capacity of about 70 million tons in all regions, according to incomplete statistics; the total capacity will exceed 400 million tons if all these planned projects are completed. The production capacity of steel products is obviously excessive, for the existing capacity plus those under construction has substantially exceeded the anticipated demand of 270 million tons of steel on the market in the year of 2005. Last year, the production capacity of electrolytic aluminum surpassed 7 million tons, much greater than market demand; however, there are also more than 5 million tons of production capacity from projects under construction and the planned projects. If the present trend persists, the production capacity of electrolytic aluminum will be 10 million tons in 2005 while the market demand will be estimated around 6 million tons only.

Severe impact is exerted on the transformation of the economic development pattern. Intensive management is an essential requirement for economic development and is also an important policy for the economic construction of China. Blind investment and redundant construction may lead to low-levels of redundant construction and waste of funds and resources. According to rough estimates, last year, China's consumption of steel products accounted for 25% of the world's total consumption, cement about 50%, coal about 30%, and electric energy production about 13%, while China's GDP accounted for less than 1/30 of the world's GDP, when converted into US dollars. Blind expansion and redundant construction in some industries will deteriorate the industrial organization structure and product structure; in the long run, it will be detrimental to the improvement of economic efficiency.

Increase the pressure of inflation and financial risks. The prices of main production means are rising comprehensively due to a rise in investment demand. The price of "ferrous metal" smelting and pressing industry increased 10.1% over the previous year, including medium plate at 20.4%, wire rod at 16.5%, and ordinary medium rolled steel at 15.4%. The ex-factory price of crude oil increased 19.8%, and prices of petroleum and diesel grew 17.1% and 16.3% respectively. The ex-factory price of "non-ferrous metal" smelting and pressing products increased 5.1%, including nickel at 22.4% and aluminum oxide at 19.9%. The prices of living materials including grain, cotton, and edible oil also are on the rise due to a decline in output and a change in the international market. In the first three quarters of 2003, CPI increased only 0.7%; but it increased 1.8%, 3%, and 3.2% respectively in October, November, and December. In 2004, the general price level is unlikely to rise and the pressure of inflation increases gradually. The rapid expansion of investment size, in the short run, will help dilute the bad and doubtful debts of banks. In the long run, however, after the economic growth slows down, loans used to support blind construction and redundant construction will inevitably lead to idle and wasteful production capacity that may affect the normal operation of enterprises, and even lead to the bankruptcy of some enterprises; if so, new bad and doubtful debts will result, increasing the pressure of financial risk.

3 Take various actions to keep a reasonable scale of investment in fixed assets

To address the problems above, a permanent cure is to control the growth rate of investment in fixed assets and the size of construction. According to historical experiences and China's current economic development, it is appropriate to maintain China's growth rate of investment in fixed assets and GDP at 2.0:1–2.5:1. In other words, if the GDP is planned to grow 8%, the rate of investment in fixed assets should range between 16% and 20%. For this reason, the problem concerning the excessive growth of investment in fixed assets, especially in capital construction, should be tackled by economic means, e.g. strengthening macro regulation and following a market-oriented principle, supplemented with necessary administrative means.

The control of the size of loans should continue. Due to measures including open market operation of negotiable instruments, increase of reserve ratio and strengthening window guidance, the growth rate of bank loans fell in the fourth quarter last year; nevertheless, it is the growth rate of short-term loans that fell; in contrast, the medium- and long-term loans put into capital construction continued increasing. Last year, the medium- and long-term loans occupied 40% of total loans from financial institutions, 18 percent points higher than that at the end of 1997. So, the Central Bank should take multiple measures to effectively control the supply of money and credit. In the meanwhile, other relevant sectors should cooperate closely so as to guide investment and impose strict restrictions on new projects in some industries through industrial policy and market access qualification.

The use of treasury bonds should be redirected, and the scale should be adjusted. The current economic situation differs greatly from the situation when treasury bonds were issued. The scale of the treasury bonds for construction should be adjusted in order to control the scale of investment, especially to control the excessive growth of investment in fixed assets. In addition, the focus of treasury bonds investment should turn from expanding investment demand and stimulating economic growth to promoting the adjustment of the economic structure and the coordinated development of the economic society, and the private investment should be directed accordingly.

We should regularize the behavior of the government at all levels, strengthen the financial discipline and the power of examination and approval, further clear up and rectify the construction of development zones, normalize approval procedures for land use, prohibit unlawful appropriation of cultivated land or forced expropriation of land at a low price, put a resolute stop to the construction of projects without secured funds or market prospect or economic effects or social benefits, put a resolute stop to arrears of workers' or teachers' wages only for the construction of projects, and put a resolute stop to a variety of "image projects" or "vanity projects".

(Published in People's Daily, Feb 24, 2004)

18 Improve the positive employment policy

In recent years, the implementation of a proactive employment policy and re-employment projects has aroused widespread concern in the whole society: the State Council has introduced a series of policies to encourage re-employment, and local governments have built labor markets at various levels and on different scales. From 1998 to the end of December 2002, we achieved remarkable results: hundreds of thousands of people received re-employment training, and more than 18 million people were re-employed, which outnumbered the total population of laid-off workers by 50% over the same period. In September 2002, the CPC Central Committee convened the "National Work Conference on Re-employment", stressing that the work of employment and re-employment is a long-term strategic mission and a significant political task aimed to maintain the overall situation of reform and development and to realize the lasting peace and stability for the nation, and requiring leadership at all levels to pay close attention to the re-employment of the laid-off or unemployed workers from state-owned enterprises. In addition, the State Council perfected some re-employment policies issued in the past. The 16th National Congress of the Communist Party of China explicitly pointed out that "employment is vital to people's livelihood; expanding employment is, and will be, an important and arduous task for a long time". This has established the long-term and strategic position of the proactive employment policy. In order to earnestly implement the guiding principles of the 16th National Congress of the CPC and the National Work Conference on Re-employment, and to give full play to the proactive employment policy, I'd like to propose some of my opinions and suggestions about problems in the current work of employment and re-employment.

1 Coordinate a proactive employment policy with a macroeconomic policy

The issue of employment is not isolated but correlated with many factors such as economic growth, economic cycle, structure adjustment, and system transition. So, the effectiveness of employment and re-employment policy depends largely on how closely the macroeconomic policy works with it. In order to provide a good macro environment for the implementation of the proactive re-employment policy and to grasp employment and re-employment policy from a perspective of macroeconomic decision, we should properly deal with the following four relationships:

(1) The relationship between proactive employment policy and economic growth. China's population occupies 21% of the world's total population and the volume of labor resources accounts for 26% of the world's total volume, but the volume of natural resources and capital resources is less than 10% of the world's gross volume. From 1978 to 2001, the net increase of China's population was 314 million persons, increasing 13.64 million persons per year on average; the net increase of employed population was 330 million persons, increasing 14.35 million persons per year on average. Every year, there are 8 million new laborers in the labor market in cities and towns while there are more than 22 million people hunting jobs; in addition, there are 150 million people of surplus rural labor migrating from the countryside. As a result, to solve the problem of employment will be a long-term arduous task for us. Re-employment is addressed relative to unemployment. Undoubtedly, it is deemed as a proactive policy to promote re-employment of the unemployed persons through multiple channels; but it may be deemed negative when addressed relative to maintaining a certain rate of economic growth and providing more jobs; or rather, the latter is more active than the former. According to economists' empirical studies, on the basis of GDP's 3% growth rate, if GDP growth rate rises 2 percentage points, the unemployment rate will fall 1 percentage point; conversely, if the GDP falls 1 percentage point, the unemployment will rise 1 percentage point. The negative correlation between economic growth and the unemployment rate is verified by both the experiences learnt from developed countries and the practical situation of China's economic development. Since the reform and opening up, it is the long-term high growth of China's economy that has provided a huge number of jobs and eased the difficulty of employment to some extent. According to pertinent data, from 1980 to 2001, the number of employed persons in cities and towns grew from 105.25 million to 239.40 million, increasing 1.27 multiples; the number of employed persons in township enterprises grew from 30 million to 130.86 million, including more than a hundred million rural workers. The elastic coefficient of employment of China has lowered in recent years for various reasons, but it remains quite necessary to maintain an economic growth rate above 7% over the next two decades in order to ease the contradiction of employment.

(2) The relationship between proactive employment policy and economic structure adjustment. In the process of adjusting industrial structure, we should give priority to applications of appropriate technology and development of the tertiary industry while promoting hi-tech industry development, facilitating continuous technological innovation, and modifying traditional industries with new technology, new equipment, and new processes.

According to statistical data, from 1991 to 2001, a total of 25.85 million persons were cut down in the primary industry, 22.69 million in the secondary industry, and 78.50 million in the tertiary industry. At the present stage, 170,000 jobs will be created if the output value of the secondary industry grows 1 percentage point, and 850,000 jobs will be created if the output value of the tertiary industry grows 1 percentage point. In China, the number of employed persons in the tertiary industry is only 27% of total population of the employed, but it is 74.5% in the United States, 74% in France, 72.8% in the United Kingdom, 63.1% in Japan, 62.6% in Germany, and around 50% in Malaysia. There is a huge space for the development of the tertiary industry; besides, it provides more and more job opportunities. While adjusting the ownership structure, we should be active in promoting the development of individual private businesses. According to data from the National Bureau of Statistics, in the year of 2001, as compared with the year of 1991, there was a net decrease of 53.61 million urban employed persons in the state collectively-owned enterprises, and 118 million in private individually-owned enterprises. We should attach importance on the development of the labor-intensive industries, mostly SMEs, which have provided 80% of the new jobs over these years.

(3) The relationship between proactive employment policy and economic system reform. In China, we have not completed the socialist market economic system; it is a hard job to carry out reform in an administrative management system, state-owned enterprises and financial system. In particular, the deepening of reform of state-owned enterprises will lay off a large number of workers and make it more difficult for us to enlarge employment and re-employment. While deepening the reform of economic system and introducing reform measures, we must make overall plans and take into consideration the social stability and social justice so as to coordinate the effort of reform and the bearing capacity of the society. In this regard, we should deepen the reform of the income distribution system, deepen the reform of the monopolized industry, rationalize the pattern of income distribution, and make a reasonable adjustment of the excessively high income of the monopolized industry so as to create a fair and just social environment where the laid-off workers from state-owned enterprises have a peaceful mentality in a competitive field. At the present stage, due to the hysteretic reform of state-owned enterprises in the competitive field, there are two extreme cases: on the one hand, there are a large number of laid-off workers from state-owned enterprises in the competitive field who live a hard life, and on the other, there are quite heavy administrative and departmental monopolies where the employees earn excessively high incomes despite inefficient state-owned enterprises, which may be detrimental to the market environment for fair play and the improvement of corporate efficiency, unfair to laid-off workers from state-owned enterprises by affecting their profession-choosing concept and mentality, and unfavorable for the effective implementation of re-employment policy specific to laid-off

workers. Therefore, strongly objecting to administrative and departmental monopolies (except the networking services of natural monopolies such as power grid, water supply, gas pipeline, telephone line, and trunk railway) and deepening the reform of state-owned enterprises in a monopolized field will be quite necessary to improve the efficiency of enterprises in said monopolized field, and it will also help the effective implementation of the re-employment policy.

(4) The relationship between a proactive employment policy and industrialization and urbanization. China still lies at the medium-term stage of industrialization. With the advancement of industrialization, the urbanization process will speed up; as a result, there will be more rural labor forces migrating into cities. According to relevant data, 150–200 million rural labor forces can transfer from rural areas, considering the present development level of agricultural labor productivity. As the level of urbanization rises, there will be an increasing number of labor forces migrating from the rural areas. We must take into consideration the problem of employment and re-employment while we are thinking about the process and pattern of urbanization. First, we should continue with the employment policy that weighs both urban and rural development, integrate employment with "three agricultural services", stimulate labor mobility between cities and the countryside, and find solutions to employment problems by market mechanism. Second, we should combine the development of non-agricultural industries with urbanization processes, boost industrial development by expanding the size of cities, and promote the upgrading of middle and small cities by industrial development so as to solve the problem of surplus rural labor force. Finally, while advancing urbanization and industrialization, we should not overlook the role of agriculture as an "impounding reservoir" absorbing the rural labor force. In a certain period, therefore, we need to constantly expand the employment capacity in rural areas.

2 Improve and perfect the organization system for the implementation of a proactive employment policy

In recent years, an organization system has taken shape at both levels, from the Central Government to local governments, for the implementation of the proactive employment policy and re-employment project, and it has operated quite well; but it needs to be improved and perfected. The re-employment service center of enterprises will be rescinded when it has fulfilled its historical mission and after the laid-off workers have exited. The main body of the organization system will be the social re-employment service agency based in large- and medium-size cities. Up to now, however, the social employment service agency in China still needs to be established and improved. According to the findings of a survey conducted in 10 cities by the Ministry of Labor and Social Security in May 2001, 46.2% of laid-off workers get jobs via recommendations by relatives and friends, 20.8% via an employment agency, 13.1% via newspapers and periodicals, 11.2% self-employed, 7.7% employed in other ways, and 12.8% arranged by the former employer. Therefore, we should:

(1) Strengthen the construction of the service system at the grassroots level. In a city, the training programs on re-employment are usually organized and implemented by four networks at the levels of municipality, district, street office, and community, mostly at the street office and community levels. As the number of laid-off workers increases, however, the labor service agencies at the two levels find it more difficult to fulfill their duties, for their management mechanism, staffing, personnel makeup, and quality as well as funds are not adaptable to the situation of socio-economic development. According to relevant data, there is a small staffing quota for national public employment service personnel, and each member of the staff serves about 12,000 laborers, 2–40 times that of the developed countries. So it is quite necessary to increase the input of human and material resources into the service agencies.

(2) Perfect the service functions of the existing public service agencies, with a focus on functions including policy consultation, vocational guidance, entrepreneurial guidance, employment information providing, skill training, and transfer of social insurance relations. In particular, all public service agencies should offer one-stop job services, such as register of job applicants, vocational guidance and presentation, application for training programs, qualification test, archives management, and transfer of social insurance relations.

(3) Improve efficiency of the existing public service agencies. Quite a few of the agencies are overstaffed but inefficient. According to relevant data, the number of job-introduction agencies under the labor departments is 4.39 times that of private ones, the number of staff members is 4.42 times, but the person-time of successful job introduction is only 3.17 times. It is thus imperative to improve the efficiency of the public service agencies.

(4) Permit and encourage development of private employment service agencies. These agencies, on the one hand, can supplement the public employment service agencies to help more job-seekers get employed, and on the other, can improve the service efficiency of the public employment service agencies through competition.

3 Earnestly implement all preferential policies intended for re-employment

China has introduced a series of preferential policies to encourage laid-off workers and unemployed persons to get employed, including a policy for tax reduction and exemption, a preferential policy of industrial and commercial registration, a preferential policy for administrative charges, a preferential policy for credit loans, a policy for job subsidy, and a policy for free training programs. What is important at this moment is to put them into practice. According to data provided by relevant departments, there are less than 20% of laid-off workers and unemployed persons who have enjoyed the preferential policy, only 18.4% enjoyed the preferential policy for tax reduction and exemption; and only 7.6% enjoyed the preferential policy for petty loans. According to a survey on the re-employment of laid-off workers in Shenyang, Qingdao, Changsha, and Chengdu conducted by the Ministry of Labor and Social Security of the People's Republic of China along with the UN Development Program, the major problem found during the implementation of preferential policy is the limited coverage; 27% of laid-off workers failed to enjoy the preferential policy; 18% failed to use the executive policy thoroughly; and 11% knew little about the preferential policy. From a global perspective, what matters now is to introduce a variety of new preferential policies rather than putting the existing ones into practice.

4 Promote re-employment by expanding community services in flexible and diverse forms

Ever since the mid and late 1990s, one of the main measures for local governments to help laid-off workers get employed is to promote employment within the community, because the community is viewed as a new growth point for China's urban employment and as a main channel for re-employment. According to the current circumstances in China, the development of the service industry in the community is of special importance to re-employment and also of strategic importance to alleviating the overall contradiction between the supply and demand of jobs and to promoting sustainable development of China's economy as a whole. According to statistics, the share of community employment usually is 20–30% in developed countries, 12–18% in developing countries, but only 3.9% in China. Employment in the community can be realized in various forms, but it is mostly informal employment. Relative to formal employment, the informal employment means the form of employment by which one can legally provide commodities and services but he or she has not signed a labor contract with the employer, or is unable or unqualified to establish stable labor relations. Definitions of the informal sector may vary from one country to another, but the informal sector has a very strong absorptive capacity of labor force in developing countries. From 1990 to 1993, the informal sector has created 83% of new jobs in Latin America. Flexible patterns of employment are ubiquitous in developed countries. In 1996, part-time jobs accounted for more than 20% of the total employment in the United Kingdom, the Netherlands, Norway, New Zealand, Australia, Denmark, and Sweden. Since the reform and opening up, informal employment has existed in China all the time, but it occupied a small proportion of the total employment. With the establishment of the market-oriented employment mechanism as well as a series of changes including a miniaturized family, unitized house, aging population, and modernized life, there are an increasing number of temporary and irregular jobs in community, and it is an irresistible trend that the proportion of informal employment will increase gradually.

For this purpose, we should: 1) make and implement policies and preferential measures to promote development of service industry in community according to its development characteristics. These policies and preferential measures include easing admission to the community service industry, encouraging entrepreneurial business as needed, and providing assistance, guidance, and support for organizations or individuals who have engaged in community services; 2) strengthen the construction and improve management of the community to set up the community management system under the centralized leadership of the government, which will attract wide social participation, enable each sector to fulfill its own duties, and promote the function of providing services, guidance, and administration for informal labor organizations and employed persons. But we should explicitly distinguish between governmental functions and market functions, between public welfare projects and profit-oriented projects. The neighborhood committee shall neither act as the community manager nor participate in the business service as the legal person of the service enterprise; and 3) design the methods of safety guarantee that fit in with flexible forms of employment, including an endowment insurance and unemployment insurance, which can remove worries and guarantee the legal rights and interests of the service staff in the community.

5 Provide effective fund guarantee for the implementation of a proactive employment policy

In order to implement the *Notice of the CPC Central Committee and the State Council for Further Work on Re-employment of Laid-off and Unemployed Persons*, the Ministry of Finance and the Ministry of Labor and Social Security specified the sources, spending programs and management methods of re-employment funds in the *Notice of Funds Management for Promoting Re-employment of Laid-off and Unemployed Persons* issued on Dec 3, 2002, which laid a policy foundation for a guarantee of implementing the re-employment policy. On this basis, we think that we should:

(1) Increase input into re-employment funds and raise the proportion of employment expenditure in the GDP within the financial budget. Both the Central Government and local governments should actively raise funds through channels both inside and outside budgets to increase the input of funds within the budget into policy for promoting employment and re-employment. First, as China has considered creating new job opportunities as one of the main objectives of the governmental macro regulation and control, the budget funds must be increased in order to realize this objective. Second, as the reform of the economic system deepens, a large number of laid-off workers from state-owned enterprises will remain a major problem in a certain period of time. Finally, as the market-oriented employment mechanism has not been established completely, a considerable amount of initial investment is needed for the construction and perfection of the

labor force market. According to data from foreign countries, from 1990 to 1991 and from 1998 to 1999, the expenditure of employment policy funds accounted for 0.7% and 0.43% of GDP respectively in the United States, 1.54% and 1.19% in the United Kingdom, and 2.15% and 3.43% in Germany. For the three reasons above, we think that China's employment expenditure within the financial budget should not be less than 1% of the GDP in the next few years.

(2) Adjust the expenditure structure of re-employment funds and increase funding for re-employment training and labor market construction that have long-term effect. As prescribed by the Ministry of Finance and the Ministry of Labor and Social Security, the re-employment funds are mainly used to cover expenditures as a subsidy for social insurance to promote the re-employment of laid-off and unemployed persons, as a guaranteed fund for small-sum loans and interest subsidy of small-sum guaranteed loans for meager profit projects, as a subsidy for re-employment training and vocational introduction, as a subsidy for public welfare jobs, and as a subsidy for labor market construction. Among these expenditures, some of them may achieve short-term effect instantly, e.g. subsidy for public welfare jobs; but some may achieve long-term effects such as improving the structure and quality of employment while generating the effect of expanding demand in a short term, e.g. training and labor market construction. The government should put more re-employment funds into programs with long-term effects rather than in those with short-term effects.

(3) Strengthen the management of re-employment funds and improve the efficiency of fund use. We should, on the one hand, make use of the re-employment funds as earmarked and strengthen the management of the fund budget and settlement in strict accordance with a specified scope, standard, and procedure, and, on the other hand, seek necessary funding supports from industries that may promote employment. For example, the government's funding support is quite necessary in the early development period of community employment as well as in some weak fields and emerging service fields, because it can increase employment effectively.

6 Integrate implementing the proactive employment policy with perfecting the social security system

The re-employment of laid-off and unemployed persons has become more difficult due to the increasingly fierce competition for jobs. Since the year of 1998, the re-employment rate of laid-off workers from state-owned enterprises has come down year by year, e.g. 50% in 1998, 42% in 1999, 35% in 2000, 30% in 2001, and 9% in the first half of 2002. According to a survey, 51% of workers are laid off from state-owned enterprises over three years, with an average age of 40 years old, 40% below junior middle school education level, and 50% with primary technical grade or no grade. These people are not competitive in the labor market, much less able to fend for themselves, so they form a group with the most difficulty to get jobs. In other words, hardly can we make the pledge that 100% of laid-off and unemployed persons are re-employed even if we do quite a good job in training and guidance; a number of them will depend on unemployment insurance for a long time, and some even will become a group eligible for social relief. According to relevant data, by the end of 2002, the number of people who have joined unemployment insurance will be close to 100 million, and the number of people who are entitled to urban minimal living security will be 20.52 million. The objective that "all the eligible urban poor will receive the benefits to which they are entitled" has been basically achieved. It is predictable that the number of people who are entitled to unemployment insurance and social relief will increase significantly with the deepening reform of the economic system and the adjustment of the economic structure as well as the accelerating process of industrialization and urbanization. Therefore, we must perfect the social insurance system, widen coverage of unemployment insurance, raise the collection rate of insurance premiums, improve the social relief system, require financial departments at all levels to increase expenditure in this regard, and guarantee a sufficient funding source in order to provide the social security foundation for the implementation of the employment and re-employment policy. Judging from the lessons learned from western welfare countries and China's long-term development trend, however, we should pay attention to the inefficiency of the employment policy due to a high-welfare system while we are improving the unemployment insurance and relief system. For this reason, we should not simply give priority to the construction and improvement of the social security system; rather, we must make an effective combination between the social security system construction and the proactive employment policy.

(Published in *Economic Management*, Issue 5, 2003)

Part 2
On economic development

19 Several issues to strengthen the construction of irrigation and water conservancy

China is a country relatively short of water resources, with the gross amount rank-ing sixth in the world; however, China's water resource per capita only ranks 12th in the world; furthermore, the spatial distribution of water resources is uneven, with great regional and seasonal difference; the water resources in the north account for only 19% of the gross water resources in China, and 81% in the south.

On the whole, both the gross amount and per capita possession of water resources are on the decline. From 2000 to 2009, the gross amount of water resources fell from 2.77 trillion to 2.418 trillion cubic meters, down 16.3%; and the per capita possession fell from 2193.9 to 1816.2 cubic meters, down 17.2% (see Table 2.19.1).

By reasons for water shortage, there are four types of water shortage:

(1) Shortage of water resources: it means the gross amount of water resources are insufficient to sustain local economic and social development; for exam-ple, Beijing and Tianjin.
(2) Shortage of water regulating projects: for example, the southwestern areas where there is plenty of annual precipitation, usually 1000–2000mm, but flood or drought occurs frequently due to uneven distribution and an inad-equate regulating project.
(3) Shortage of high quality water: it means that the original total water resources are sufficient to sustain local economic and social development, but poor water quality leads to a shortage of water.
(4) Shortage of water management: it means that the insufficient use of water is due to the waste of water resources as a result of an extensive pattern of water consumption.

As the source of human life, water is a basic substance indispensable to peo-ple's living; however, it can at times bring about hardship or even disaster for human survival and evolution. Since the new China was founded, the Commu-nist Party of China and the Government have placed great emphasis on water conservancy construction and achieved remarkable results; certainly there are quite a few problems that need further improvement.

Table 2.19.1 Gross Amount of Water Resources and Per Capita Possession of China

Year	Water resources quantity (100 million cubic meters)	Precipitation (100 million cubic meters)	Per capita possession (cubic meters)
2000	27,701	60,092	2,193.9
2001	26,868	58,122	2,112.5
2002	28,261	62,610	2,207.2
2003	27,460	60,416	2,131.3
2004	24,130	56,876	1,856.3
2005	28,053	61,010	2,151.8
2006	25,330	57,840	1,932.1
2007	25,255	57,763	1,916.3
2008	27,434	62,000	2,071.1
2009	24,180	55,959	1,816.2

Source: National Bureau of Statistics website

1 Favorable opportunities for farmland water conservancy construction in China

Agricultural water takes up a considerable proportion in the gross amount of water resources. According to relevant data, by 2011, the proportions of various water uses are as follows: agricultural water 61.3%, industrial water 24%, domestic water 12.7%, and ecological water supplement 2%. So, strengthening farmland water conservancy construction is of important strategic significance. At present, there is favorable opportunity for us to strengthen and improve farmland water conservancy construction.

(1) Remarkable achievements made in farmland water conservancy construction

Remarkable achievements made in water conservancy construction have laid a solid foundation for strengthening and improving farmland water conservancy construction. According to statistics, over the last 60 years, China has built nearly 300,000km of river dykes and more than 87,000 reservoirs, with over 700 billion m³ water supply capacity of water conservancy works, 905 million *mu* (a unit of area, equivalent to 0.0667 hectares) of effective irrigated area, 1.1 million m³ of controlled water and soil erosion area, and 230 million kilowatts of installed hydro power capacity. China makes up 6% fresh water and 9% arable land of the world's total, and feeds 21% of the world's population, thanks to farmland water conservancy construction.

(2) Solid economic foundation for strengthening water conservancy construction

Rapid growth of China's economy and financial revenue constitutes a solid economic foundation for strengthening and improving farmland water conservancy construction. Due to these years' rapid economic growth in China, the total size of the economy has jumped into the second place in the world. Despite low per capita GDP, it reached US$5,414 in 2011 as reckoned by the International Monetary Fund (IMF), a symbol that China has become one of middle-income countries. In recent years, China has witnessed a sound situation and rapid growth of financial revenue, which reached up to RMB1 trillion in 50 years (1.14 trillion in 1999), and grew from 1 to 2 trillion in four years, from 2 to 3 trillion in two years and from 3 to 4 trillion in only one year; afterwards, it increased 1 trillion in about one year, up to 10.3 trillion in 2011. It is thus evident that China has a strong economic base.

(3) A new stage of development – the industry nurtures agriculture and the city promotes the countryside

Since the founding of new China, there are three stages for rural policy:

The first stage means the period from the founding of the People's Republic of China in 1949 to the beginning of reform and opening up. As the State policy at this stage required the agriculture to support industry and the countryside to support cities, a lot of money was collected from the countryside for industrial and urban construction. Prior to the "5th Five-Year Plan", much more money was collected from the countryside than put into agriculture. This happened mostly in the period from the "1st Five-Year Plan" to the "4th Five-Year Plan", in which about RMB110 billion Yuan were withdrawn from the countryside, about 5.5 billion per year on average; the largest amount, 93.24 billion, was collected in the "2nd Five-Year Plan" and the "4th Five-Year Plan", accounting for about 84.8% of the total money.

The second stage begins with the reform and opening up till the year of 2000. The State policy for the countryside at this stage aimed to reduce the tax burden and increase investment, i.e. "give more to, take less from and liberalize the countryside". In this period, the State, on the one hand, managed to reduce the tax burden on the countryside, and on the other, increased support for countryside, agriculture, and farmers; as a result, the amount of funds invested in the "three agricultural services" was greater than that withdrawn from the countryside. By rough calculation, the net investment of the State into the countryside within 25 years has exceeded RMB539.566 billion Yuan.

The third stage begins with the "10th Five-Year Plan" when the basic State policy for "three agricultural services" was to provide full support for the countryside, without taking any penny thereof. For example, the agricultural tax was exempted, a considerable amount of investment was put into agriculture and the countryside, and the "three agricultural services" were compensated comprehensively. According to data provided by the Ministry of Finance, the national financial spending for agriculture amounted to RMB351.7 billion in 2006, 431.8 billion and 595.55 billion in 2007 and 2008 respectively, 725.31 billion in 2009, and up to 2104.36 billion in the first four years of the "11th

Five-Year Plan", surpassing the total sum in the previous 50 years; and it broke through one trillion in 2011.

(4) New requirements for strengthening and improving farmland water conservancy construction

The current policy to expand domestic demand and maintain a steady and rapid economic growth has raised new requirements for strengthening and improving farmland water conservancy construction.

First, maintaining agricultural harvest and increase in grain yield is an important means to fight inflation. According to practical economic operation over the years, the rising CPI is directly related to grain, vegetables, meat, and its products and other foods. So the rising CPI can be harnessed by strengthening and improving farmland water conservancy construction as well as by maintaining the agricultural harvest and increase in grain yield.

Then, strengthening and improving farmland water conservancy construction is also important to increasing demand of investment. In recent years, China's rapid economic growth is driven heavily by investment. As export's role to stimulate economic growth decreases due to the unstable, international economic and financial environment, we must expand domestic demand to stimulate economic growth, especially the consumer demand. Nevertheless, it is hard to achieve substantial results in a short time by expanding consumer demand, for it involves a series of problems concerning the reform of the distribution system.

For this purpose, we must also maintain a certain growth rate of investment. But we need to improve the structure of investment in order to not focus investment on increasing industrial production capacity or on "iron roosters", i.e. railways, highways, and urban infrastructure construction. Strengthening and improving farmland water conservancy construction is both an urgent need and one of the important measures to improve the structure of investment.

(5) Great emphasis is placed on farmland water conservancy construction by the CPC central committee and the state council

In 2011, the CPC Central Committee issued the No.1 Document, which convened the first national work conference on water conservancy, constantly improved the policy system, strengthened efforts on all work, and pushed farmland water conservancy construction into a new stage. In February 2012, the State Council issued the *Opinions on Implementation of the Most Stringent Water Management System*; on April 7, 2012, the National People's Congress held the Standing Committee meeting, listening to the report by the Minister of the Ministry of Water Resources on farmland water conservancy construction, and answering inquiries of Standing Committee members in company with leaders from other ministries and committees, which helped supervise and promote farmland water conservancy construction.

2 The currently grim situation facing farmland water conservancy construction

(1) Farmland water conservancy construction falls far behind the need of modern agriculture development

At present, nearly half of the arable land in China is nicknamed "rained paddy"; the existing irrigation and drainage systems were mostly built in the period from the 1950s to 1970s, featuring low standard, poorly supported facilities; aging or run-down conditions with decreasing benefits, and, particularly, the "last kilometer" problem during farmland irrigation. Flood control needs urgently to be strengthened in the management of medium and small rivers, seepage prevention, the reinforcement of small-sized unsafe reservoirs, and the prevention of mountain torrent disasters. Currently, there are still 242 million rural residents and 33.14 million rural teachers and students short of potable water supply.

According to a survey by the Agriculture and Rural Committee under the National People's Congress, 10% of the large, irrigation areas are not furnished with supporting facilities; 40% of the buildings are damaged; and 70% of farmland works need to be reconstructed. The existing key medium-sized irrigation areas are dependent on main canal construction for continued construction and water-saving reconstruction; the end-canal system is not furnished with supporting facilities, leading to imperfect farmland irrigation network and insignificant effect of engineering construction. In Guangxi Province, for example, the waterproof permeability of canals in end-canal system is only about 45%, and the serviceability rate about 50%. In Anhui Province, the serviceability of water electromechanical equipment throughout the province is only 60%, the serviceability of small reservoirs in hilly areas is merely 30%, the irrigation guarantee rate at irrigation pumping station is less than 70%, and the projects for stagnant water drainage are operating to the standard designed for a waterlog that may occur every three or seven years.

(2) Huge fund gap due to insufficient investment

In the period of the "11th Five-Year Plan", the Central Government earmarked RMB46.554 billion Yuan for farmland water conservancy construction via the department of water resources; about 88.98 billion of the Central Government's other special funds were also appropriated for this purpose, about 160 billion of local government's funds were put into farmland water conservancy construction, and about 20 billion of bank loans and social funds were utilized for the same purpose; therefore, the total investment in this regard amounted to 315.52 billion, averaging 63.104 billion per year. According to statistics, after the "rural compulsory labor and accumulated labor" are cancelled in the countryside, the labor hour of annual national investment reduced from the peak level of 13 billion labor hours to the current level of 3 billion labor hours, decreasing by 10 billion per year. Given 10 Yuan per labor hour, the amount of investment reduced will be 100 billion Yuan – but given 20 Yuan per labor hour, the amount will be 200 billion – this indicates that all investment made so far in the farmland water conservancy construction can hardly make up the shortfall incurred since the "two types of labor" investment channels were terminated.

(3) Extensive pattern of agriculture water use and inefficient utilization of water resources

The current total water consumption of China is about 600 billion cubic meters while the total consumption of agriculture water reaches up to 372 billion cubic meters. In addition, flooding irrigation in many regions has led to the inefficient utilization and considerable waste of water resources. According to statistics, the efficient utilization coefficient of China's farmland irrigation water is 0.51, much lower than the world advanced level of 0.7–0.8; if it reaches the world advanced level, about 1/3 of water consumption will be saved, i.e. about 120 billion cubic meters, equivalent to twice the water volume of the Yellow River. The water productivity (grain yield per unit consumption of water, i.e. kg/m^3) is less than $1.2kg/m^3$ while the world advanced level is about $2kg/m^3$; if it reaches the world advanced level, water consumption will be reduced by about 40%, which can be saved.

(4) Lagging reform of system and mechanism

The reform has advanced slowly in the large- and medium-scale irrigation areas and the pumping stations, and the basic expenditures for the public welfare personnel and the maintain funds are not put in place. The reform of the property right system of small-sized irrigation works has lagged behind, leading to problems such as ambiguous property rights, unclearly defined main body of management and maintenance, unfulfilled duties, and few channels of funds. The difficulties in promoting the comprehensive reform of the agricultural water price and the low actual collection rate of water charges have exerted adverse effects on the normal operation and maintenance of water conservancy works. As a result, some irrigation stations are merged; some professional service organizations are beset with difficulties, such as drought relief service team, water conservancy science and technology team, and irrigation experimental station; and the cooperative organization of agriculture water is lacking necessary assistance.

3 Several noteworthy problems in the process of strengthening and improving farmland water conservancy construction

The CPC Central Committee and the State Council have set clear objectives for strengthening and improving farmland water conservancy construction: the continued construction of supporting facilities and water-saving reconstruction in large-scale irrigation areas and key medium-scale irrigation areas will have completed by the year of 2020. In combination with the implementation of the national program to increase grain production capacity by 50 billion kilograms, a number of new irrigation areas will be built in areas with mature conditions of water-related resources; the effective irrigation area of farmland will also be widened; furthermore, the large- and medium-scale irrigation and drainage stations will be upgraded and modified to strengthen the control of key water logging areas and improve the irrigation system. To achieve these ambitious objectives, we should take into account the following suggestions:

(1) Enhance integrated planning and make scientific development strategies

The Ministry of Water Resources has developed a county–territory program for farmland water conservancy construction; however, this program alone is not enough – we should work out a program and development strategy at a higher level, and properly deal with the following relationships:

a. The relationship between the national water conservancy construction and the farmland water conservancy construction. They are related to each other, but differ from each other. Water conservancy construction is a broad concept that includes farmland water conservancy construction. The former is sometimes not directly related to the latter; for example, the Three Gorges project is designed mainly to control flood and generate electricity, and the south-to-north water diversion project is intended to address water shortage in the north, especially in Beijing. These projects are essential; at present, however, we should transfer the focus of water conservancy construction to farmland water conservancy construction, and put more investment and effort into it.

b. The relationship between large-scale projects and medium- and small-scale ones. In the past years, we place much more emphasis on large-scale projects than on medium- and small-scale ones. For example, the main body of the Three Gorges project has basically been completed, but the comprehensive harnessing project of 14 tributaries of the Yangtze River in the Three Gorges reservoir region, which should have been completed by the end of 2010, is not included in the investment plan, and neither is the farmland water conservancy construction. It is necessary to build some large- and medium-scale projects, but the project benefits will not be achieved until a number of small, supporting projects are built, especially until the "last kilometer" problem is tackled.

c. The coordinating relationship between regions. There are more water resources in the south than in the north of China. The amount of water resources in the north is only a quarter of that in the south, so the south-to-north grain diversion pattern was formed in history, 3.3 million tons of grain diverted per year on average from 1953 to 1959, 1.7 million tons from 1960 to 1969, and 1.9 million tons from 1970 to 1975; the pattern was changed to north-to-south grain diversion in the 1980s, and 14 million tons of grain were diverted to the south per year by the end of the 20th century. This is correlated to the fact that the south took the lead in industrialization and urbanization, which led to the occupation of some arable land, the increasing industrial use of grain, and the population migrating towards the south. However, there is one problem that is usually neglected, i.e. the farmland water conservancy construction in the south was lagging far behind that in the north.

According to relevant data, the effective irrigation area in the south only increased 17 million *mu* in 1988 as compared with that in 1980, and that in the southeastern coastal region decreased 9 million *mu*; and in the same period, the effective irrigation area in the south surged to 406 million *mu*, increasing 96 million *mu*. Ultimately, great changes occurred in the supply and demand pattern. The reason for this lies in the fact that we have enlarged the planting area to produce grain in the north that is not rich in water resources. According to the new round of national investigation and evaluation of underground water resources, the multi-year average of national underground water resources is 920 billion cubic meters, including more than 880 billion cubic meters of underground fresh water resources, with more than 600 billion cubic meters in the south, accounting for about 69%, and about 270 billion cubic meters in the north, accounting for about 31%. In many places in the north, the groundwater is excessively exploited to grow grain, leading to a number of eco-environmental problems, such as "funnels" in the groundwater level and surface subsidence. In the North China Plains, for example, the shallow groundwater level has fallen 10–20m accumulatively on average by the end of 2009, with the maximum surpassing 40m, and it is even more serious in some places. Considering the present "water productivity" of China, the diversion of 14 million tons of grain towards the south amounts to the diversion of 12 billion cubic meters of water, almost equivalent to the water quantity newly diverted in the eastern and central lines of south-to-north water diversion project (Phase I), or to 70% of the total water quantity diverted; virtually, the water diverted to the north is carried back to the south. The pressure on transportation is also intensified by the north-to-south diversion of coal and grain.

(2) Improve the mechanism of fund input and utilization, and promote the utilization benefit of funds

a. Increase the gross amount of fund inputs. As required by the Central Government, funds should be raised through multiple channels to make it possible that the annual average of total social input into water conservancy works in the period from 2011 to 2020 will be twice that in 2010, i.e. the gross amount up to 4 trillion Yuan, 400 billion per year, with most of them to be put into the farmland water conservancy construction. In 2011, the fund spent this way by the Central Government and local governments exceeded 126.7 billion Yuan, and the local governments also withdrew 27 billion from land transfer income for the sample purpose. These two items amount to 153.7 billion Yuan, but it is still far from the amount of funds required. So we should establish and improve the diversified investment mechanism based on public finance; continue increasing the investment of the central and local finances into the farmland water conservancy construction, ensure input of various special funds into such construction, work out as soon as possible the specific methods to implement the policy of withdrawing 10% from land transfer income for this purpose, improve the financial support policy, encourage and support the eligible local government financing plat-forms to expand direct or indirect financing channels for the construction of water conservancy works, and perfect the agriculture subsidy policy and further carry out the subsidy policy for drought control and water-saving irrigation.

b.   Integrate funds from various sources and make overall arrangements for the use of these funds. The farmland water conservancy construct used to be criticized as "rivers harnessed by nine dragons" (a metaphor of manage-ment that means ambiguity of power and duties when the water conser-vancy is under the surveillance of more than one authority). This criticism can be reasonable if we take a look at the funding channels. Under the current system, there are eight funding channels for farmland water con-servancy construction: (i) the Central Government's subsidies, including construction funds for key counties; (ii) the Central Government's inputs of fixed asset investment for water conservancy construction, including funds for the national program to increase grain production capacity by 50 billion kilograms; (iii) funds for national comprehensive agricultural development; (iv) funds for rural land remediation; (v) funds for "one case, one meeting" and "substituting rewards for subsidies" aimed at stimulating farmer's initiative in investing with their labor; (vi) funds for modern agri-cultural development and incentive funds for top grain-producing counties; (vii) funds for poverty relief and development; and (viii) funds for tobacco and sugar industry. Administrative departments of these funds involve the National Development and Reform Commission, the Ministry of Finance, the Ministry of Water Resources, the Ministry of Agriculture, the Ministry of Land and Natural Resources, and the Poverty Relief Office. For this rea-son, we should find ways to consolidate and make an overall arrangement for these funds specific to the farmland water conservancy construction on the principle of "unchanged channels and usage, complementary advan-tages, rewarding by merits and resultant force" so as to improve the utiliza-tion benefit of the funds.

c.   Take into serious consideration the utilization benefit and security of the funds. A large majority of the 4 trillion funds will be dedicated to water conservancy construction. How to manage and utilize these funds is indeed worthy of serious consideration. Every project of the water conservancy works should be subject to thorough appraisal so that the money will be truly invested in works that can generate substantial social benefit and economic benefit. For this purpose, we will try to avoid any severe error or waste; select contractor and call for bids in strict accordance with legal procedures to prevent corruption; increase transparency of fund utilization, and strengthen supervisions from both the government sectors and social organizations, especially the supervision by public opinions.

(3) Save water and improve water-use efficiency

At the beginning of 2012, the State Council introduced the idea to implement the most stringent water resources management system, thus setting three "red lines" (permissible minimum limit) for control of the development and utilization of water resources. The first red line is set for the control of total water use. By the year of 2030, the total national water use will be controlled below 700 billion cubic meters (no more than 635 billion cubic meters in 2015 and 670 billion cubic meters in 2020). The second red line is intended to control water-use efficiency. By the year of 2030, the water-use efficiency will reach up to or near the world's advanced level; the water consumption per 10 thousand Yuan of industrial value added (based on the constant price in 2000) will fall below 40 cubic meters (down 30% in 2015 and below 65 cubic meters in 2020); the effective utilization coefficient of farmland irrigation water will be raised beyond 0.6 (over 0.53 in 2015 and 0.55 in 2020). The third red line aims to ensure water quality in water functional area up to standard. By the year of 2030, the water qualification rate will be above 95% (over 60% in 2015 and over 80% in 2020).

It requires systematic engineering to control the three red lines, which in turn requires comprehensively promoting construction of the conservation-minded society, increasing income and reducing expenditure. As for the farmland water conservancy construction, great emphasis should be placed on the development of high-efficient water-saving irrigation farming. Agriculture consumes the most water resources, but the water-saving irrigation only covers an area of 430 million *mu* of the existing 905 million *mu* of effective irrigation area, less than 50%. In addition, the high-efficient water-saving irrigation technologies, such as quota sprinkling irrigation, micro irrigation, and pipe irrigation, are applied in less than 200 million *mu* of the total water-saving irrigation area. There is huge potentiality in this regard.

(4) Reform the system and mechanism

At present, the reform on farmland water conservancy construction should focus on seven key points: (1) property rights system of small-scale rural water conservancy works, (2) water project management system, (3) water resources management system, (4) investment and financing system of water conservancy works, (5) water conservancy construction management system, (6) comprehensive reform of agricultural water price, and (7) construction and reform of water conservancy service system at the grass-root level.

So far, nearly a third of more than 20 million small-scale rural water conservancy projects in China have been subjected to the reform of the property rights system. However, we should speed up the reform and vitalize the stock of water conservancy assets, clarify the title of property and encourage the transfer and auction of ownership, make flexible use of the rights of management and specify the competent organization and its responsibilities for management and protection to achieve positive operation and rolling development of water conservancy facilities, and particularly facilitate the development of farmer's water-use cooperative organization based on Rural Water Users Association. Currently there are 78,000 organizations of this type in China. They should be expanded to play more important roles in the management and application of small-scale farmland water conservancy works.

With regard to the comprehensive reform of the agricultural water price, we should: (1) unify and raise the awareness that agricultural irrigation water will not be available free of charge; (2) determine reasonable water price by setting up a reasonable pricing mechanism to promote saving water and increase the utilization benefit and efficiency of water resources; and (3) grant a certain amount of subsidy from governmental finance by perfecting the financial policy for subsidizing operation and management of agricultural irrigation works so as to promote saving water, reduce farmers' water use cost, and ensure positive operation of irrigation and drainage facilities.

References

1. The P.R.C. National Bureau of Statistics, *China Statistical Yearbook*, Beijing, China: China Statistics Press, 2011 edition, 2011.
2. *A Decision of the CPC Central Committee and the State Council on Accelerating Reform of Water Conservancy Development*, the CPC Central Committee Document No. 1, 2010.
3. *Opinions of the State Council on Implementation of the Most Stringent Water Resources Management*, the State Council Document No. 3, 2012.
4. Chen Jiagui, Industrialization Process and Changes in Revenue and Expenditure Structure, *China Industrial Economics*, Volume 264, Issue 3, 2010.

(Published in *Southwest Finance*, Issue 8, 2012)

20 Thinking of the development of new but strategic industries in China

The new but strategic industries are characterized by intensive knowledge technology, low consumption of material resources, great growth potential, strong driving forces as well as good comprehensive benefit, and can reflect national competitiveness in the future. The development of these industries is of strategic importance to the change of the economic development pattern, promotion of industrial transformation and upgrading, and enhancement of China's industrial competitiveness on the international market in the future.

After the financial crisis, major countries in the world are racing to control the strategic commanding height for a new round of development. Strategic emerging industries are incubated and developed around the globe. Some major countries begin to compete with each other for the future leading industries by making strategic plans to promote rapid growth of emerging industries such as energy-saving and environment-friendly industry, new energy resources, information, and biology.

Despite financial difficulties, the Obama administration has placed great emphasis on technology research and the industrial development of new energy, aerospace, and broadband network, and actively promoted the "green economic recovery program" and "green technology" revolution. The Japanese government has focused on new industries including IT applications, new models of automobiles, low-carbon industry, and new energy (solar). The European Union has aimed to improve "green economy" and other high technologies, and has decided to invest 105 billion Euros into "green economy" by the year of 2013.

1 Historical opportunities and realistic conditions for development of new but strategic industries in China

Quite a few times in history, China's technological development has missed out on opportunities for the steam engine era as well as the electrical and electronic era. With the advent of a new round of technological and industrial revolution at present, the emergence of new technologies will provide a huge space for industrial development and create better opportunities for economic development. The changes in the current global economic competition pattern have provided a historical opportunity for China to occupy the commanding height in the future economic competition.

First, the economic recovery in developed countries is confronted with a number of difficulties. The development pattern the American economy faces serious challenges and its economic recovery lacks momentum, for the twin deficits have aggravated its debt burden and the financial crisis has weakened its economic strength; the European countries are too far away to care about making investments in strategic emerging industries due to the economic downturn caused by the intensifying European sovereign debt crisis; and Japan also has great trouble making investments in strategic emerging industries due to a gloomy outlook of the recovering economic growth, plus the accident at a nuclear power station, much less the fact that its economy has long stayed at a low growth stage.

Then, the current situation shows that the competitive edge of developed countries has not dominated the field of the strategic emerging industries.

We should seize this favorable but fleeting window of opportunity and take advantage of the narrow gap between China and developed countries in emerging industries to make a leapfrog progress in the development of this field.

Over several decades' development at a high rate especially since the reform and opening up, China's economy now has been provided with the preliminary, realistic foundation for incubation and development of strategic emerging industries.

(1) Solid economic foundation. China's economy has developed rapidly over these years; the economic scale has jumped into the second place in the world; despite the low per capita GDP, i.e. only US$4,260 in 2010 as reckoned by the World Bank, China has become one of the middle-income countries; and, in recent years, China has witnessed a fairly good financial revenue that keeps growing rapidly, i.e. over RMB8.3 trillion Yuan in 2010 and possibly exceeding 10 trillion in 2011. So there is no doubt that China has solid economic bases.

(2) Solid industrial basis. China has set up the complete national economic system and industrial system with strong supporting capacity. Of about 500 industrial products around the globe, 220 products are manufactured in China, with the production output ranking first. According to UN statistics, three out of the eight categories of industrial manufactured products in global trading are made in China, with the export occupying over one in four shares in the global market. China has become one of the world's industrial powers. Not only has the large-scale production generated demands of strategic emerging industries, but also has prepared the ground for the development of these industries.

(3) Technological innovation basis. China's hi-tech industry has developed rapidly in recent years; in 2010, there were about 30,000 enterprises engaged in production of hi-tech products in China, involving more than 10 million employees. The industrial value added of hi-tech enterprises has accounted

for about 9% of the total industrial value added generated by industrial enterprises above a designated size. China's technology in quite a few strategic emerging industries can almost equal the developed countries, or has the advantage of synchronous development with the developed countries in some new industries, and even has the leading advantage over developed countries in several new industries. All this has paved the way for the incubation and development of strategic emerging industries.

(4) Basis of outstanding human resources. Ever since the reform and opening up, China has produced a large number of scientific researchers and engineering technicians, many of whom have rich practical experiences and know much about the world trend of science and technology development after they have finished their overseas education or continued education.

(5) Basis of rich material resources. China abounds in resources for the development of the strategic information industry, e.g. nonferrous metals and rare earth, and has relative advantages in such resources as biology, solar energy, wind energy, and key raw materials.

(6) Superior institutional basis and policy basis. China's institutional advantage lies in the fact that various resources can be pooled together to do big things. Since the outbreak of the international financial crisis, the CPC Central Committee has stressed repeatedly and made relevant plans and supporting policies for independent innovation and the development of strategic emerging industries.

By the year 2020, China plans to increase its spending on scientific research and development from the present 1.35% to 2.5% of the GDP, increase the contribution rate of scientific and technological progress to the GDP from present 39% to 60%, and increase the number of patents and papers cited from the 20th place at present to the fifth place in the world.

In addition, China has a vast market attractive to strategic emerging industries.

2 Problems facing the development of strategic emerging industries in China

In the light of the State Council's planning, investment will be increased in seven major industries that are seen as strategic emerging industries in a long period starting from the "12th Five-Year Plan", such as energy efficiency and environmental protection, biology, high-end equipment manufacturing, new energy resources, new materials, and new energy vehicles; meanwhile, the reform of the science and technology system will be deepened and the transformation of scientific research achievements will be accelerated so as to both promote industrialization and establish an industrial chain. By the year 2015, the basic pattern facilitating healthy development and coordinated advancement of strategic emerging industries will have taken shape, which can promote the upgrading of industrial structure and increase the proportion of industrial value added to around 8% in GDP.

By the year of 2020, the value added of strategic emerging industries will account for about 15% of the GDP, thus remarkably enhancing the capacity to absorb and enlarge employment; energy efficiency and environmental protection, new generation information technology, biology, and high-end equipment will become the pillar industries of national economy; new energy resources, new materials, and new energy vehicles will become the forerunner industries of national economy; the innovation capacity will be enhanced, and a great number of key core technologies will reach the world advanced level in several industries; a great number of internationally influential large enterprises, as well as a great number of innovatively vibrant small and medium-sized, will be established; and an industrial cluster will be built, composed of strategic emerging enterprises that have a complete industrial chain, strong innovativeness, and distinct characteristics.

By efforts in the next 10 years or so, the overall innovative capacity and development of the strategic emerging industries will come up with the world advanced level and provide strong support for the sustainability of economic and social development.

In recent years, we have done a great deal in promoting the development of strategic emerging industries. In 2011, for example, 18 provinces and cities issued their guiding opinions, six worked out their action plans, and nine set up special funds for promoting the development of strategic emerging industries. One more example: in December 2011, the split catalogue of strategic emerging industries was compiled under the leadership of the Ministry of Industry and Information Technology, which consists of seven main categories, 100-odd subcategories, 400-odd small categories, and 24 key directions, and will be put into trial operation after further demonstration. By the year of 2012, the Ministry of Industry and Information Technology will carry out four special programs on new generation information technology, high-end equipment manufacturing, new materials, and new-energy vehicles, and 15 programs for subdivided fields including the Internet of Things and intelligent equipment manufacturing. In addition, the National Development and Reform Commission and the Ministry of Commerce promulgated *the Catalogue for the Guidance of Industries for Foreign Investment (revised in 2011)* as of January 30, 2012 to encourage foreign investment in strategic emerging industries, including high-end manufacturing and new but strategic industries; cancel the foreign shares limit in such fields as new energy power generation equipment so that the number of entries with shares limit was reduced by 11 entries; and increase entries including key components and parts of new energy vehicle, Ipv6-based next generation internet system equipment, etc.

Notwithstanding much progress in the development of strategic emerging industries, there are some noteworthy problems:

(1) Following suit. Without taking into account their local reality, development foundation, and relative advantages, some local governments initiated haphazard investment. Take wind energy power industry as an example,

the national wind energy power installed capacity exceeded 30 million kilowatts in 2010, reaching the planned targets for the year of 2020, and was predicted to be 45 million kilowatts at the end of 2011; however, about a third of generator sets are currently not combined to the grid. Take optoelectronics industry for another example, quite a few enterprises have slipped into loss since the year of 2011 due to a 40–50% fall in prices of photovoltaic products, including polycrystalline silicon and silicon slice, as the domestic demand shrinks.

(2) Similar development pattern in different regions. According to the national planning, seven major strategic emerging industries will be developed, but many provincial and municipal governments simply play the sedulous ape, leading to industrial structure convergence.

(3) Inadequate attention and insufficient investment into key technology and the key link of industrial development. New industries differ from strategic emerging industries. A new industry means one that is mature and registers robust development while a strategic emerging industry is immature so much so that it cannot be a leading industry until breakthroughs are made in some key technology and key links, e.g. electric car, wind energy, etc. In addressing these key technologies and key links, however, the manufacturers are less motivated and the State has made less investment than it has pressed for mass production and industrialization that can guarantee more financial subsidies for the manufacturers and more political achievements for government officials. If this practice continues, it will bring about great risks and wastes, for we will lose grip on key technologies even if some products are already industrialized; consequently, we will have to purchase these key technologies, unworthy of our original intention to develop strategic emerging industries.

(4) Less knowledge about the risks and side-effects in the development of strategic emerging industries. Now that it is immature, the strategic emerging industry is inevitably faced with risks. Nevertheless, most enterprises are now thinking more about opportunities but less about risks, and they will feel all at sea at the advent of risks; in the meantime, the government sectors are thinking much more about the development of individual products, but much less about new problems to be incurred by the development of an industrial chain.

3 Problems needing overall planning and coordination during the advancement of strategic emerging industries

Confronted with the complexity and high risks in the development of strategic emerging industries, we need to make an overall plan and coordination of the following five relations:

(1) Relation between market regulation and government guidance. We should bring into full play the relative advantages of China's market resources,

speed up the incubation of the emerging market through innovating and changing the consumption pattern, arouse enthusiasm of enterprises, and promote integration of production, learning, scientific research, and practical application. In addition, we should lay emphasis on the roles of government guidance, especially the role of government as industrial guide and public products provider in key fields and key links concerning development of strategic emerging industries; create the atmosphere that stimulates the innovative development of industries; and reduce risks and uncertainties in the development of strategic emerging industries.

(2) Relation between the Central Government and local government. The incubation and development of strategic emerging industries depend heavily on joint effort and close cooperation between the Central Government and local governments. Not only shall we give full play to the Central Government's macro regulation and overall planning roles, but also arouse the local government's enthusiasm, initiative, and creativity. Not only shall we carry out the Central Government's strategic plan, but also take local reality into consideration to avoid haphazard development and local structure convergence. Not only shall we prevent the redundant construction of traditional industries, but also prevent the redundant construction of strategic emerging industries.

(3) Relation between strategic emerging industries and traditional industries. The strategic emerging industry is inseparable from the traditional industry. On the one hand, the development of a strategic emerging industry is based both on a traditional industry that provides support and new industrial demand; and on the other hand, the technical transformation and upgrading of traditional industry will be initiated by the development of a strategic emerging industry so as to raise the technical level of said traditional industry. During the incubation and development of strategic emerging industries, the interaction and integration between these two types of industries need to be enhanced following the concept of industrial convergence.

(4) Relation between technological innovation and industrialization. The development of strategic emerging industries cannot do without the impetus from technological innovation and the traction from industrialization, both of which need to work together. On the one hand, technological innovation directs and provides knowledge and technical achievement support for industrialization; on the other hand, industrialization will help transform innovative products into practical productivity and provide specific requirements and clear direction for technological innovation.

It needs some time to generate and industrialize achievements of technological innovation. When a technology remains immature, it should not be industrialized in a hurry until key technical problems are tackled. At no time shall we initiate large-scale industrialization, or we will pay a heavy price for it.

(5) Relation between national and international innovative resources. The incubation and development of strategic emerging industries are implemented

in an open environment. With both national and international innovation resources, we should, on the one hand, raise the capabilities of technical import, assimilation, and absorption as well as re-innovation and integrated innovation, and make an integrated use of innovation resources both at home and abroad; and on the other hand, we should be fully aware that the original innovation and core technologies in future competition for the commanding height of strategic emerging industries must be addressed through enhancing the capability of independent innovation.

(Published in *China Business Journal*, January 9, 2012, entitled *Grasp the Time Window of Strategic Emerging Industries*, revised upon selection)

21 The comparison of the BRIC countries' economic development characteristics

As the leading representatives of emerging market economy, BRIC countries have come into play in the international arena. What's more, they performed far better than other developed economies in coping with the once-in-a-century international financial crisis, and become an indispensable force to promote global economic recovery.

According to IMF's prediction, the proportion of emerging market economies in the global output, measured per purchasing power parity (PPP) rose from 36% in the 1980s to 46% in 2009, increasing 10 percentage points, and will reach up to 51% in the year of 2014, surpassing developed economies for the first time. The BRIC countries' proportion of global output rose from 14.4% in the early 1990s (1992) to 22.3% in 2009, nearly a quarter of global output.[1] In addition, BRIC countries make up 40% of the world's population and one third of the world's land resources; this is why they could come out strong and take the spotlight in the global arena.

In a relative sense, the financial crisis caused a re-distribution of power around the globe; namely, the power of emerging market economies represented by BRIC countries is increasing while that of developed economies is decreasing. This is of vital importance to the global development pattern and global governance in the future. Nevertheless, how influential the BRIC countries will be in global development is contingent on their sustainability. Although they are classed as emerging market economies, BRIC countries are varying in developmental patterns; in particular, they are immature as compared to developed economies. Therefore, this paper is intended to make a comparison of characteristics of BRIC countries' development, and discuss their potentialities and drawbacks as well as how to promote sustainable development.

1 Engines that drive BRIC countries' economic growth

While consumption, investment, and net export are three engines that drive GDP growth, the case is different in BRIC countries.

Table 2.21.1 Brazil: Contribution Rates of Three Demands to GDP Growth (%)

Items \ Years	2001	2002	2003	2004	2005	2006	2007	2008
Consumption	—	74.00	75.00	80.70	81.30	81.50	81.50	—
Investment	18.90	17.20	15.80	17.10	16.00	16.80	17.20	—
Net export	—	1.90	3.20	2.90	3.10	1.70	0.01	—

Source: UN, CEPAL, Amuario cstadistico de America Latinayel Caribe

(1) Brazil: Domestic demand contributes more to GDP growth than overseas market demand does, domestic demand is fueled largely by consumption, and investment rate remains low

Brazil's GDP growth is stimulated mainly by domestic demands, e.g. consumer demand contributed about 80% while overseas market demand (i.e. net export) did only 2–3%, which was much lower and even negative in some years. As compared with other emerging countries, Brazil's investment rate has been on the low side, less than 20% (see Table 2.21.1). This is due to the "crowding-out effect" generated by the high cost of investment as a result of Brazil's high rate of real interest and tax (see Table 2.21.2). In 2007, President Luiz Inácio Lula da Silva's government began to implement the "Program for Acceleration of Economic Growth" (PAC, la Program de Aceleracao do Crescimento), with an attempt to raise investment rate to 25%.

(2) Russia: GDP growth depends largely on domestic demand but overseas market demand also plays important roles, with growth performance relying heavily on the export of energy resources

Russia's GDP growth depended largely on domestic demand, but overseas market demand also played an important role; consumption accounted for 60–70% of the GDP, investment did above 20%, and net export around 10% (see Table 2.21.3). What is more important is that Russia's growth performance depended heavily on the export of energy resources. Russia tends to witness fairly good financial and growth performance when the price of energy resources remains high on the international market.

Table 2.21.2 List of Brazil's Real Interest Rate (%)

Items \ Years	2002	2003	2004	2005	2006	2007	2008
Real interest rate	10.30	9.90	10.00	12.48	9.30	8.62	6.73
Taxes in GDP	35.86	35.54	36.80	37.61	34.20	35.60	36.56

Source: http://br.mofcom.gov.cn

Table 2.21.3 Russia: Contribution of Three Demands to GDP Growth (%)

Items \ Years	2001	2002	2003	2004	2005	2006	2007	2008
Total GDP	100.0	100.0	100.0	100.0	100.0	100.0	100.0	100.0
Final consumer spending	65.8	68.9	68.1	66.9	66.4	66.6	66.0	66.0
Investment	21.9	20.1	20.8	20.9	20.1	20.3	24.3	26.2
Net export of commodities and labor	12.7	10.8	11.3	12.2	13.6	12.7	8.6	8.9

Source: Российская экономика в 2006 году: тенденции и перспективы (выпуск № 28), Институт экономики переходного периода.

From a financial perspective, the substantial increase in Russia's tax revenue in recent years is due to an uptrend in the international resource market. First, the prices of petroleum, natural gas, and metal materials keep rising in the international market, which leads to the Russian budget system increasingly dependent on the export of energy resources. If the Russian economy is divided into two sectors, i.e. petroleum and natural gas sector and non-petroleum and natural gas sector, the former will account for 23% of Russia's GDP in 2003 and about 30% in 2014, predicted the World Bank and Russian Ministry of Industry and Energy Resources. According to the prediction by Bash Markov, executive director of Russian Center for Efficient Utilization of Energy Resources, the proportion is 24.7% in 2003, 32.7% in 2004, 37.2% in 2005, and will be much higher in 2006.[2] The World Bank also divided the Russian federal budget into petroleum and natural gas budget and non-petroleum and natural gas budget. According to calculated results, Russian federal budget has kept surpluses since the year of 2000, but it may turn into a deficit that persists for consecutive years if the financial revenues from petroleum and natural gas sector are counted out; in addition, financial deficit was on the rise in the period from 2005 to 2006. If financial revenues from petroleum and natural gas sector are counted out, the Russian federal financial deficit will make up 5.9% of the GDP in 2005, and further up to 7.4% in 2006.[3]

The export structure of Russia shows that the export of energy products accounts for 80% of total export growth. While the export of petroleum, petroleum products, and natural gas made up 28.4% of total exports in 1992, it will rise to 60.3% in 2006 (see Table 2.21.4).

On this ground, President Putin acknowledged, "Russian economic growth owes first to the favorable market movements in recent years. Due to unprecedented improvement of foreign trading conditions, Russia has obtained considerable economic advantage and extra earnings. . . . Obviously, without these funds, i.e. favorable market movements, our achievements in social and economic development would be insignificant in many aspects".[4]

Table 2.21.4 Export Value of Russian Petroleum and Natural Gas during 1992–2006 and Its Proportion in Total Export Values

Years	Petroleum		Petroleum products		Natural gas	
	Million US dollars	Proportion (%)	Million US dollars	Proportion (%)	Million US dollars	Proportion (%)
1992	6,662	12.4	2,202	4.1	6,398	11.9
1993	8,061	13.5	3,061	5.1	6,964	11.7
1994	8,948	13.3	3,398	5.0	7,939	11.8
1995	12,297	15.2	4,108	5.1	13,381	16.5
1996	15,578	17.6	7,442	8.4	14,683	16.6
1997	14,346	16.2	7,145	8.1	16,420	18.6
1998	10,254	13.7	4,262	5.7	—	—
1999	14,101	18.8	4,713	6.3	—	—
2000	25,284	24.1	10,938	10.6	16,644	16.1
2001	24,576	24.1	9,402	9.4	18,303	18.3
2002	28,950	27.0	11,227	10.5	15,897	14.9
2003	38,816	28.6	14,064	10.5	19,981	15.0
2004	55,024	30.0	18,998	10.5	20,981	11.5
2005	79,216	32.5	33,650	13.6	30,424	12.9
2006	96,675	31.7	44,217	14.5	42,160	14.1

Source: Российская экономика в 2006 году: тенденции и перспективы (выпуск № 28), Институт экономики переходного периода.

(3) India: Economic growth is stimulated largely by consumption and investment, with obvious advantages in service export

On the whole, there is a drastic fluctuation in Indian macroeconomic data, suggesting no clear regularity. Table 2.21.5 suggests that India's GDP growth also depends largely on domestic demands. But consumption makes up a large proportion in domestic demands; private consumption plus governmental consumption contributes above 50% to GDP growth. As compared with other BRIC countries, India's relatively developed financial system serves as an important supporting factor for Indian economic growth. Another factor that cannot be neglected is the adjustment of the internal economic structure, especially the modernization of consumer sector.

In recent years, India has witnessed rapid investment growth and considerable contribution of investment to GDP growth, including 40–50% contribution rate of capital formation to GDP growth. There is drastic fluctuation in the net export of India, usually contributing negative to GDP growth. It is noteworthy that India has an obvious advantage in service export. According to IDG statistical data, the scale of the global software outsourcing market reached US$100 billion. On the international service outsourcing market, India has become the largest country that accepts software outsource businesses around the globe due to its unique advantages, and has cornered the American market. According

Table 2.21.5 India: Contribution of Three Demands to GDP Growth (%)

Items \ Years	2002–2003	2003–2004	2004–2005	2005–2006	2006–2007	2007–2008
Consumption (private)	45.5	44.2	39.0	56.6	43.9	45.8
Consumption (government)	−1.1	3.6	3.5	6.2	6.5	6.2
Capital formation	—	59.5	65.4	64.3	37.5	NA
Fixed asset formation	40.5	38.5	56.3	51.2	45.5	55.2
Net export	40.5	−17.5	22.3	−51.7	−18.2	−3.2

Source: Economic Survey 2008, http://indiabudgel.nic.in/es2007–2008/esmain.htm

to the latest data provided by the Indian Association of National Software and Service Businesses, the outsourcing business generated US$17.2 billion sales revenues for India in 2004, accounting for up to 44% of total sales revenues on similar global market. It is predicted that India's share of global software and back-end service outsourcing market will reach up to 51%.

(4) China: Economic growth is fueled mainly by investment and export, and it is difficult to expand consumer spending

China's economic growth is stimulated apparently by investment and exports. According to Table 2.21.6, investment contributes most to GDP growth; capital formation usually contributes more to GDP than consumption does. Fig. 2.21.1 suggests that among the BRIC countries, China has the highest investment rate of 40% as averaged between 1996 and 2006. If economic growth is generally stimulated by capital accumulation in Asia, China may be a typical representative of BRIC countries.

The rising investment rate has lowered the consumption rate; therefore, an important research subject for the promotion of China's economic growth has arisen: How should household consumption be expanded?

Table 2.21.6 China: Contribution of Three Demands to GDP Growth (%)

Items \ Years	2001	2002	2003	2004	2005	2006	2007	2008
Final consumption	50	43.6	35.3	38.7	38.2	38.7	40.6	45.7
Gross capital formation	50.1	48.8	63.7	55.3	37.7	42	39.7	45.1
Net export of goods and services	−0.1	7.6	1	6	24.1	19.3	19.7	9.2

Source: *China Statistical Yearbook*

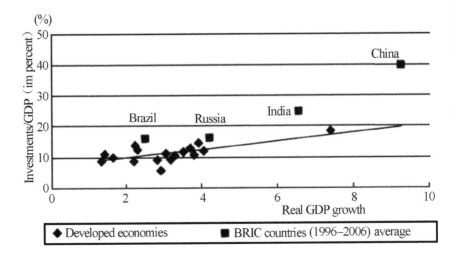

Fig. 2.21.1 Contribution Rates of BRIC Countries: Comparison with Developed Economies

Source: Feyzioglu, Tarhan, "Some Growth Trends in China", China Limited Partner Forum – Beijing September 23, 2007

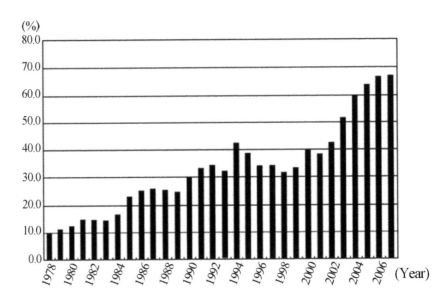

Fig. 2.21.2 Foreign Trade Dependence Ratio of China

Source: *China Statistical Yearbook*

In the terms of overseas market demand, the contribution of China's net export to GDP growth has increased considerably in recent years. From 2005 to 2007, the rate of the contribution of the net export to GDP averaged out to 21%. In addition, the foreign trade dependence of China has ascended in recent years, e.g. over 50% in 2003 and up to 66.8% in 2007.

Relative to other BRIC countries, China has the lowest proportion of final consumer demand, but the largest proportion of investment demand.

2 Development of industrialization and urbanization in BRIC countries

Generally speaking, industrialization and urbanization are considered important engines to stimulate the economic growth of a developing country. From this perspective, BRIC countries are at different stages of economic development. In Brazil and Russia, the process of industrialization is lagging behind urbanization, which remains at a high level; in China, industrialization remains at a high level, but there is still broad space for the development of urbanization; in India, both industrialization and urbanization are relatively backward. From the perspective of economic engines, therefore, in the next stage, urbanization will remain an important engine to stimulate the economic growth of China; industrialization and urbanization will play equal roles in promoting the economic growth of India; for Brazil and Russia, industrialization (or re-industrialization) will serve as the main engine to boost economic growth while the development of urbanization is supposed to focus on improving the infrastructure construction and upgrading the service industry.

(1) Industrialization in BRIC countries

From contribution of three industries to GDP growth, India manifests as a big agricultural country with agricultural value added contributing 17.8% to GDP growth; by contrast, the rate is below 5% in other countries. India is relatively backward in industrialization – the industrial value added has never contributed over 30% to GDP growth – in addition, India's rate of manufacturing contribution to GDP is 16%, the lowest among BRIC countries.

However, not only have both the reform of economic liberalization and widespread applications of information technology since 1990 facilitated establishment and development of modern service industry in India, but they also promoted the modernization process of the domestic traditional service industry so much so that the service industry has become the locomotive engine to drive India's economic growth over the past two decades. This generates another distinctive characteristic of India's economy: the service industry weighing greatly in economic growth, which seems disproportionate to the current stage of India's economic development (measured per capita GDP). The proportion of service industry is 52.83% in India, about 10 percentage points higher than China's 42.4%. The rate of contribution of India's service industry to GDP

Table 2.21.7 Comparison of Contribution Rates of Three Industries (2007) (%)

	China	Brazil	India	Russia
Agriculture	3.3	4.95	17.75	4.76
Industry	54.2	30.58	29.42	38.57
Manufacturing	48.7	17.52	16.38	19.10
Service industry	42.4	64.47	52.83	56.67

Source: Chinese data from National Bureau of Statistics (data on "the secondary industry and the industry"); other data from the World Development Index (WDI)

is not as high as Brazil and Russia, but per capita GDP is much higher. This is what we are concerned about.

The industrial value added in Russia accounted for 48% of GDP in 1990, but the rate began to descend thereafter, down to 39% in 2007. So Russia is now faced with a process of re-industrialization.

The case is almost the same in Brazil. The industrial value added made up 44% of Russia's GDP in 1980, but only 31% in 2007; this is so called the "regression of industrialization", which is related to the Latin American debt crisis that erupted in the 1980s. Ever since the 1990s, the share of Brazil's industrial output to the GDP has been on the decline; the most drastic decline occurred in manufacturing's share in the GDP, which impaired the international competitiveness of Brazil's economy.

Brazil's industry began to recover in the period between 2002 and 2004 but remained much lower as compared to the 1980s. Since the year of 2005, however, this process has been discontinued. From 2005 to 2007, Brazil's manufacturing share in the GDP decreased about 15% (see Table 2.21.8) due to a boom in Brazil's primary products sector and a recession in Brazil's industry and manufacturing sector, which was caused by an increasing demand of Brazil's primary products in developing countries, including China.

In China, the industrial value added makes up 54.2% of GDP; the manufacturing makes up 48.7%, the highest as against less than 20% in other countries.

Table 2.21.8 Proportions of Brazil's Industry and Manufacturing in GDP (%)

Years / Industries	1985	1990	1995	2000	2001	2002	2003	2004	2005	2006	2007
Industry	42.3	33.0	34.5	36.1	35.9	36.0	36.8	37.2	29.3	30.1	28.7
Manufacturing	31.6	22.7	22.5	21.6	21.5	21.9	22.9	23.0	15.5	15	14.9

Source: UN, CEPAL, Anuario estadistico de America Latina y el Caribe 2008

Note: Industrial and manufacturing data in 2007 are slightly different from WDI data in Table 2.21.7.

Table 2.21.9 Comparison of Urbanization Levels (%)

Countries \ Years	1960	1970	1980	1990	2000	2001	2002	2003	2004	2005	2006	2007
China	16	17	20	27	36	37	38	39	39	40	41	42
Brazil	45	56	67	75	81	82	82	83	84	84	85	85
India	18	20	23	26	28	28	28	28	28	29	29	29
Russia	54	62	70	73	73	73	73	73	73	73	73	73
World average	33	36	39	43	47	47	47	48	48	49	49	50

Source: World Bank WDI database

In the future, China's industrialization should focus on improving the industrial structure and boosting the development of the service industry, rather than raising the industrial share in the GDP so as to improve the industrial structure, enlarge employment, facilitate energy conservation and emission reduction, and develop low-carbon economy.

(2) Urbanization in BRIC countries

From the international comparison of the urbanization level and per capita GDP (see Fig. 2.21.3), few countries have realized per capita GDP of US$10,000 until the urbanization rate reaches 60%. For this reason, the urbanization level is in reality an important approach to increasing economic growth and per capita income in a country.

According to data in 2007, the urbanization rate is only 30% in India, a bit more than 40% in China, 85% in Brazil, and 73% in Russia. From these data

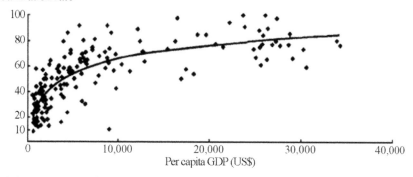

Urbanization rate

Per capita GDP (US$)

Fig. 2.21.3 International Comparison of Urbanization Level and Per Capita GDP
Source: World Bank WDI database

alone, there is a huge space for the development of urbanization in both China and India, and urbanization will be an important engine to drive the economic growth of both countries in the future. In Brazil, however, urbanization seems excessive and very much discordant with lagging industrialization. The problem incurred by excessive urbanization and lagging industrialization is a great deal of urban poverty as peoples' income level can hardly be raised by job opportunities created during industrialization. For Brazil's future development, therefore, the realistic choice will be speeding up the development of industrialization while "curbing urbanization" to some extent.

The urbanization level is already very high in Russia. As compared with China and India, Russia and Brazil should focus urbanization on infrastructure construction and the modern urban service industry so that the level of the service industry can be raised and the share of the service industry in GDP can be increased constantly.

3 Roles of government and market in BRIC countries' economic development

Considering the different characteristics of economic development in BRIC countries, the government and market play different roles in economic activities. Since the outbreak of the sub-prime mortgage crisis, people have reflected profoundly on the economic roles of government and market. The following is an analysis of government and market roles in BRIC countries, intending to depict impetuses that boost economic growth at the institutional level and to promote sustainable development of the national economy via institutional reform.

(1) *As transitional economies, Russia and China are so strong in government power that the government intervenes heavily in economic activities*

BRIC countries are developing economies, so they are faced with the problem of economic development. The point is that Russia and China are confronted with the problem of transitioning from a planned economic system to a market economic system. Russia adopts shock therapy in the system transition, leading to stagnant growth for a long time and even to negative growth.

China adopts a progressive strategy in system transition to strike the balance between reform growth and stability so that it has achieved a rapid economic growth and a stable society. Just because Russia and China are transitional economies, it is evident that the government intervenes heavily in economic activities. In these two countries, government interventions are obviously stronger than those in Brazil and India.

Since President Putin took office, the state-owned elements have increased significantly in Russia's economy. It is predicted that the state-owned elements made up 34% of the GDP before 2003, up to 50% in recent years, and will be on the rise. Of the top 10 companies in Russia, there are six state-owned or state-controlled companies. The sales volume of Russian top 10 companies has

Table 2.21.10 Russian State-owned Economic Elements Expanded since 2004 (%)

State-owned elements in joint-stock companies	Proportions in joint-stock company				
	2004	2005	2006	2007	2008
Enterprises with 100% state-owned shares in legal capital	4	10	30	45	54
Enterprises with 50–100% state-owned shares in enterprise legal capital	15	13	12	10	7
Enterprises with less than 50% of state-owned shares in legal capital	81	77	58	45	39

Source: Institute of Russian, Eastern European, & Central Asian Studies, Chinese Academy of Social Sciences

surpassed 20% of the GDP, especially the Gazprom, which contributes 8% to the Russian Federal budgetary revenue. According to data from OECD, the state-owned oil and gas companies of Russia have currently controlled 33% of oil production and 80% of natural gas production. In the Russian financial industry, the state-owned banks have possessed 40% of the total banking system assets, and the household deposit in saving banks has accounted for 54% of gross savings.

As far as China is concerned, the number of state-owned enterprises throughout the country was reduced from 238,000 to 126,000, down 47.1%. However, the decreasing number of state-owned enterprises does not necessarily mean the dominant position of state-owned economy weakens in national economy; rather, China's state-owned enterprises become much stronger after a comprehensive strategic reorganization. In the period between 1998 and 2005, the total assets of state-owned enterprises have increased year by year, and even the local state-owned enterprises show a robust uptrend in total assets, despite a drastic decrease in the number of these enterprises. According to UBS's prediction, institutions under the State administration, such as municipal services, medical care, and science education, made up 11% of the GDP in 2006, and the state-owned and state-controlled enterprises contributed 26% to the GDP in the current year. The reasons are that the government has voluntarily abandoned its leading role in labor-intensive industries but kept a firm hand on capital-intensive ones by holding a big stake in these key industries. In general, the government remains influential in a state-owned economy.

(2) Inadequate government economic intervention in India and Brazil

In India and Brazil, the reforms continue to deepen primarily within the framework of market economy. The government force and intervention may get strong at times and weak at other times due to disagreeing voices about government economic interventions in different periods; on the whole, however, the government force is not as strong as expected in economic activities of India and Brazil.

In India, for instance, the Central Government currently possesses 214 state-owned enterprises (except financial bodies) engaged in key fields of the national economy such as grain, electricity generation, energy resources, and transportation. The total assets amount to close to US$150 billion, and gross production value accounts for 11% of India's GDP, including 27% contributed by industrial manufacturing enterprises that produce 95% coal, 66% petroleum products, 83% natural gas, 32% finished steel, 35% aluminum, and 27% nitrogen fertilizer of India. Of the 240 Central Government-owned enterprises, the Indian Railway Company alone has employed 1.6 million workers, the largest commercial employer in the world. In Brazil, the process of privatization has progressed rapidly under the influence of the Washington Consensus, something of a "reactionary" to government intervention advocated by the early structuralism development economists; as a result, government intervention has weakened in economic activities. At the beginning of 1980, there were more than 800 state-owned enterprises; in the period between 1998 and 2002, the number averaged out at 108.

(3) Low level of social security in BRIC countries

As developing countries, BRIC countries remain at a low level of social security. Nevertheless, the level varies from one country to another.

BRIC countries differ little in education spending. In the year of 2005, the government education spending made up 4.6% of the GDP in China, while the proportion was less than 4% over the same period in the other three countries (see Table 2.21.11). But they differ much in medical and health spending. In 2005, the government medical and health spending accounted for 3.48% and 3.22% of the GDP respectively in Brazil and Russia, less than 2% in China, and much less than 1% in India (see Table 2.21.12).

It should be noted that the government spending (measured only per gross spending on education and health) on social security is slightly higher in Brazil and Russia than in China and India due to the difference in development level (per capita GDP is higher in Brazil and Russia than in India and China).

Table 2.21.11 GDP Proportions of Government Education Spending in BRIC Countries (%)

Countries \ Years	2001	2002	2003	2004	2005
China	4.23	4.55	4.75	4.53	4.60
Brazil	3.88	3.78	—	4.01	—
Russia	3.11	3.84	3.67	3.54	3.77
India	—	—	3.66	3.75	3.25

Source: China's education spending data from China Statistical Yearbook, and other data from WDI

Table 2.21.12 GDP Proportions of Government Medical and Health Spending in BRIC Countries (%)

Years / Countries	2001	2002	2003	2004	2005
China	1.64	1.72	1.74	1.79	1.82
Brazil	3.08	3.23	3.10	3.33	3.48
Russia	3.35	3.54	3.29	3.10	3.22
India	0.94	0.92	0.89	0.87	0.95

Source: WDI

(4) From the perspective of economic freedom, BRIC countries' marketization levels need improving

An international comparison of economic freedom is given in Table 2.21.13. This table shows that the economic freedom is lower in China and Russia than in India and Brazil. In general, however, the economic freedom remains low in all BRIC countries. Most of the item indexes of the four countries are below the world average. It is thus clear that the marketization level of BRIC countries needs to be improved, notwithstanding the different roles of the government or state-owned economic force in economic activities. Further promotion of market reform will be the development trend as well as an important source of economic growth for BRIC countries in the future.

4 Challenges facing BRIC countries' future economic growth

From the perspective of production functions, the economic growth of a country depends on three major factors, such as capital, labor, and technology. If technology is interpreted as total factor productivity (TFP), then the institutional factor can also be included. Discussing the potentials and challenges facing BRIC countries in terms of capital, labor, technology (in narrow sense, it means labor productivity), and system will relate directly to the sustainability of BRIC countries' future economic growth.

It is generally believed that BRIC countries have potential advantages in aspects of the following list.

(i) Broad space for development and rapid growth rate, as late-developed countries;
(ii) Abundant labor resources owing to a large population;
(iii) Large economic size favorable for industrial expansion and upgrading; and
(iv) Rising middle class provides support for expansion of consumer market.

Table 2.21.13 International Comparison of Economic Freedom (2009)

Country and region	Combined index	Enterprise freedom	Foreign trade freedom	Financial freedom	Government scale	Currency freedom	Investment freedom	Financial freedom	Property rights	Corruption free	Labor freedom
Russia	50.8	54.0	60.8	78.9	70.6	65.5	30.0	40.0	25.0	23.0	60.0
China	53.2	51.6	71.4	70.6	88.9	72.9	30.0	30.0	20.0	35.0	61.8
India	54.4	54.4	51.0	73.8	77.8	69.3	30.0	40.0	50.0	35.0	62.3
Brazil	56.7	54.4	71.6	65.8	50.3	77.2	50.0	50.0	50.0	35.0	62.7
France	63.3	87.4	80.8	50.9	14.5	71.7	60.0	70.0	70.0	73.0	54.5
Japan	72.8	85.8	82.0	67.5	61.1	93.6	60.0	50.0	70.0	75.0	82.5
Finland	74.5	95.1	85.8	64.3	28.6	87.4	70.0	80.0	95.0	94.0	44.8
UK	79.0	89.8	85.8	61.0	40.3	80.4	90.0	90.0	90.0	84.0	78.5
US	80.7	91.9	86.8	67.5	59.6	84.0	80.0	80.0	90.0	72.0	95.1
HK, China	90.0	92.7	95.0	93.4	93.1	86.2	90.0	90.0	90.0	83.0	86.3
World average	—	64.3	73.2	74.9	65.0	74.0	48.8	49.1	44.0	40.3	61.3

Source: The Heritage Foundation, 2009 INDEX of Economic Freedom

However, the future development of BRIC countries is also confronted with various challenges, such as high foreign-trade dependence, big gap between the rich and the poor and imperfect market system. These problems may certainly differ in severity from one country to another.

The following discussion will focus on problems concerning capital (measured per savings), labor (measured per population and labor resources), technology (measured per labor productivity), and system (measured per marketization level) in BRIC countries.

(1) Brazil: Low savings, weak infrastructure, and backward labor productivity

Due to low savings, Latin American countries depend largely on foreign investment and high consumption for economic growth. From the international comparison, the total savings deposit is less than 20% in Brazil, the lowest in the BRIC countries (see Table 2.21.14).

Brazil has weak infrastructures. First of all, the logistics infrastructures are backward. Due to long-term lack of funds, the transportation infrastructure facilities, including roads, ports, airports, and sea lanes, are out of repair or date and fail to measure up to efficient and prompt modern logistics. Next, Brazil has backward energy infrastructure facilities (mainly involving electricity generation, construction of power transmission and transformation lines, and development and utilization of petroleum, natural gas, and new energy resources) and urban infrastructures, which is a "bottleneck" problem restricting economic development.

Besides, the labor productivity is lagging behind, remarkably, in Brazil (see Table 2.21.15). From 2000 to 2008, Brazil's average labor productivity was only 0.9%, less than China's 10%, and much less than Russia and India. The reasons of backward labor productivity include poor quality of education, low efficiency of education spending, and out-of-date labor law.

Table 2.21.14 Comparison of Savings between BRIC Countries and World Average (Proportion of Total Savings Deposit in GNI) (%)

Countries \ Years	1970	1980	1990	2000	2001	2002	2003	2004	2005	2006
China	27	33	40	37	38	41	44	47	51	54
Brazil	19	18	19	14	14	15	16	19	17	18
India	15	17	22	26	26	27	29	32	33	34
Russia	—	—	30	37	33	29	30	31	32	31
World average	25	23	22	22	21	20	20	21	21	22

Source: World Bank, World Development Indicator (WDI) database

Table 2.21.15 Comparison of Labor Productivity Growth of BRIC Countries (%)

Countries \ Years	Brazil	Russia	India	China
1987–1995	0.2	−6.8	3.8	6.2
1995–2008	0.8	4.4	4.7	7.7
2000–2008	0.9	5.9	4.9	10.4
2005	−0.1	5.8	6.8	9.4
2006	1.5	6.7	7.0	10.7
2007	2.3	7.3	6.1	12.1
2008	3.7	6.0	4.4	7.7
2009	4.3	3.5	3.9	9.1

Source: The Conference Board, Total Economy Database, January 2009

(2) Russia: Short of labor resources, highly dependent on the export of energy resources, and heavy government intervention

In general, Russia has advantageous human capital, high labor productivity and rich saving resources, but it needs to improve institutional systems. To be specific, Russia's future economic growth will face the following challenges.

There are problems about population growth and labor force supply in Russia. While the number of employed persons with higher and secondary education currently makes up 87% of the total population employed (11.8% with higher education), Russia remains short of labor force given the total supply. It was pointed out in the *United Nations Survey on Russia's Population* that the demographic structure of Russia will deteriorate. At present, 578 children and old people are supported by 1000 laborers in Russia; by the year of 2025, however, there will be 800 children and old people dependent on 1000 laborers, for the labor force population in Russia will be reduced from 90 million to 76 million, while the number of pensioners will rise from 38 million to 43 million.

Russia's economic growth is noticeable, but it depends largely on the export of energy resources so much so that Russia's growth performance is subject heavily to changes of the international energy market and even the oil price. With the support of a high oil price in the international market, the enormous export of energy resources has facilitated the recovery and pickup of Russian economic and social conditions so as to increase wages and expand consumption, but it has done little to promote the development of both the manufacturing industry and technological progress. Now, Russia's economy, reliant heavily on the export of energy resources, begins to flag at the time of a steep fall in oil price after the international financial crisis.

Just because the economic growth relies heavily on the export of energy resources, the Russian government has always intervened in the key industry. Apart from energy resources, the Russian government has obviously strengthened control over key industries including aviation, electric power, automobiles, and finance. From the perspective of long-term development, this practice should be evaluated carefully to confirm if it conforms to market reform and if it is helpful to the transformation of the Russian economic development pattern.

(3) India: Unemployment and income gap, backward infrastructure, and underdeveloped manufacturing industry

India's economic growth is fueled primarily by a relatively prudent and efficient financial sector and rich human resources. India has more potential for capital supply (i.e. savings level) and labor productivity, but less for human capital accumulation (e.g. education level). Besides, India's economic development will face other challenges in the future.

(i)   Excessive population, serious unemployment, and big income gap. From the analysis above, household consumption is an important factor to stimulate economic growth in India, owing to the huge population base and additional population per year, as well as the enhanced purchase power as a result of the sustainable development of India's economy. A mass of new wealth is consumed during the rapid expansion of India's population. According to statistics by the World Bank, two thirds of India's investments in a year are spent on additional population, for the rapid expansion of India's population in large quantities has led to universal and long-term social poverty. Furthermore, there is also the problem of unemployment that has long troubled the government in India. It is estimated that India's unemployment rate is 9.21%. But the secondary industry that has the strongest capability to absorb employment accounts for only 24% of the national economy, which is not conducive to the unemployment problem. In addition, there is a big gap between the rich and the poor in India, e.g. 20% of those with a maximum income earn 41.8% of the total income while 20% of those with minimum income earn only 8.7% of total income. Not only will an excessive gap between the rich and the poor give rise to the decline in resident's purchasing power, but it will also lead to social instability. Therefore, the problem brought about by overpopulation should be tackled with an approach conforming to Indian national circumstances.

(ii) Backward infrastructures hindering India's economic development. India has insufficient commercial energy resources, a severe transportation bottleneck, and a short supply of electrical power. According to the World Bank's report, one third of business owners in India complained that the major barriers in corporate development came from backward infrastructures, including airport and seaport. Indeed, the backward infrastructures not only brought down the return on investment, but also kept off the foreign direct investment.

(iii) Backward manufacturing industry. As mentioned above, the manufacturing industry made up only 16% of the GDP in India, the lowest among BRIC countries. The Indian government has virtually recognized that sustainable development economy in the future will depend more on the manufacturing industry than on the service industry, for the development of the manufacturing industry will be indispensable to job creation, technological innovation, and the development of the service industry.

(4) China: Imbalance between investment and consumption, disproportion of income distribution, and underdevelopment of the service industry

By analysis of standard production functions, China's economic growth in the future will be faced with the following challenges: (i) in terms of capital accumulation, the high savings rate will not change in a short term, but it will be lower than it was as the development pattern is changed and priority is given to expanding consumption, especially as the age structure is changed (population aging); (ii) despite very rich labor resources, the transfer and urbanization of rural labor forces continue to be main engines that stimulate economic growth; however, the positive effect of "demographic bonus" of economic growth will be on the wane and even vanish; (iii) the rising cost of various factors, the adjustment of energy resource prices, the appreciation of Renminbi, and the rising environment cost and social cost have aggravated the burden on enterprises and impaired labor productivity; and (iv) the marginal benefit of reforms is on the decrease.

In addition, there is the problem of imbalanced development in China.

(1) Imbalance between investment and consumption. China's economic growth is obviously driven by investment. For consecutive years, the investment rate (percentage of investment volume in the GDP) is more than 40%, even close to 50%; whereas, the investment rate of some rapidly growing economies is a little more than 40% during the investment boom. This imbalance is a structural problem highlighting the Chinese economy.

(2) Disproportion of income distribution. One of the reasons for the low consumption rate in China is the problem caused by income disparity. Currently, China's Gini coefficient is about 0.45. It is getting more difficult to expand consumption due to income disparity, for the general demands of the rich (major possessions including house and automobile) are already satisfied, but the demand for high-grade consumer goods (e.g. diversified services) are not due to a shortage of supply. By contrast, the poor are not as strong in real purchasing power, but they are considered the most potential consumers.

(3) Apparent underdevelopment of the service industry. China's economic development in the future should focus on expanding domestic demand, especially the consumer demand. But this has much to do with changes in industrial structure, e.g. development of the service industry; on the one hand, the development of the service industry can help expand consumption by increasing employment and income, and on the other, the development of the urban service industry with the advancement of urbanization can also satisfy the increasing demands for services. As a matter of fact, the

consumption of services will take the largest share of all consumer items in the future. There is no lack of precedents in developed countries.

(Published in *Economic Research Report (2010–2011)*, Economic Management Press, May 2011)

Notes

1 Measured per present price of US dollars, the proportion of emerging market economies in the global output has descended at first and then ascended since the year of 1980 till present (this may have more to do with changes in US dollar exchange rates): descending first from 30.36% in 1980 to 16.43% in 1992, then ascending to 30.74% in 2009, and will ascend to 36.35% in 2014; whereas measured per US dollars, the proportion ascended from 5.28% in 1992 (Russian data missing) to 15.27% in 2009, and will ascend to 19.39% in 2014.

2 Бащмаков: И, Ненефтегазовый ВВП как индикатор динамики российской экономики, Вопросы экономики, № 5, 2006г.

3 Институт экономики переходного периода, Российская экономика в 2006 году: тенденции и перспективы (выпуск № 28).

4 В. Путин, Послание президента России Владимира Путина Федеральному собранию Российской Федерации, Деньги и кредиты. № 5, 2003г.

22 Cope with world economic changes and challenges

The international financial crisis has exerted a far-reaching impact on the global economy and given rise to profound changes in the world economic and political pattern, but the general trend of economic globalization remains unchanged. Meanwhile, some new characteristics are presented in the world economy: the accelerating adjustment of world economic development patterns, the quickening pace of major countries racing to seize strategic commanding height for future development, and the increasing pressure of global climatic change. We should take into consideration both the external and domestic situations from an international perspective and through strategic thinking, recognizing opportunities and challenges in the future development, scientifically grasping laws of development, and striving to push China's economic and social development, as well as the overall national strength, to a new level.

1 A long and winding road for economic globalization

Respond actively to new challenges of economic globalization. The international financial crisis has brought about an economic impact for all countries and also exerted a negative impact on the evolution of globalization. The increasing tendency of trade protectionism leads to new obstacles to economic globalization, especially when some developed countries have reinforced their trade protectionist measures, including anti-dumping, anti-subsidy, and depreciation of domestic currency, to protect the domestic market and employment and pose barriers to cross-border mergers and acquisitions of energy enterprises and key industries. Besides, the liberalization of trade and investment worldwide might be compromised by the exclusiveness of bilateral or regional cooperation which is sought by all countries under the influence of economic recession and employment pressure. It is thus clear that there will be a zigzag road for economic globalization under the pressure of the international financial crisis.

The general trend of in-depth development of economic globalization remains unchanged. As objections to the trade protectionist measures adopted by some countries are voiced among international organizations and other countries, the main theme of the world community remains obedient to multilateral economic and trade rules and seeking international economic cooperation, whereas the essential all-round and multi-level feature of international economic cooperation remains fundamentally unchanged. With economic globalization extending into quite a number of fields including production, marketplace, trade, investment, finance, and technology, each economy has integrated with the other, namely, they are interdependent. The momentum of economic globalization still exists, the evidences of which involve global capital flow, technological progress, and market opening up. Each country in the world, developed or developing, has benefited from its participation in economic globalization. Given economic recovery after the international financial crisis, an important strategic choice for all countries to achieve economic growth and prosperity is to promote the liberalization of trade and investment and the construction of a multilateral trading system. Therefore, the general trend of economic globalization will be in no case reversible.

The pace of economic internationalization has accelerated in China. As one of the major trading countries, China leads the world in the utilization of foreign investment and pushes the process of economic internationalization into two stages: "bringing in" foreign funds and technology, and Chinese commodities "going out". In recent years, China's economic internationalization has manifested a new tendency that outward foreign investment has increased as more and more domestic enterprises begin to expand overseas markets.

During the "12th Five-Year Plan", the "bringing in" and "going out" policy of China's economic development will ascend to new levels and new heights. In regard to the "bring in", priority should be given to improving the quality of foreign investment utilization. Considering the reality of the Chinese economy, foreign investment is supposed to play positive roles in transforming economic development pattern, adjusting industrial structure, and promoting industrial transformation and upgrading. As for the "going out", it will be a key step in China's economic internationalization in the future but also more important and difficult relative to "bringing in", for there will be an increasing number of enterprises "going out" for trans-border business as China becomes one of the major countries that makes investments abroad. However, the "going out" of Chinese economy will be inevitably confronted with huge challenges due to interference and obstacles from investment protectionist measures. It is thus clear that there will be a zigzag road for China's economic internationalization, i.e. first "going out" of the domestic market, then "going into" the overseas market, and finally "going up" in the international market.

Constantly improve the openness of Chinese economic on both domestic and overseas markets. In the period of the "12th Five-Year Plan", we should make good use of resources and market both at home and abroad to open up both internally and externally and create new advantages for participation in international cooperation and competition under the context of economic globalization.

First, speed up forming the pattern of opening up to both the inside and outside world. Based on an optimizing structure, emphasizing quality and improving economic performance, we should open wider to the outside world; encourage foreign investment into hi-tech industries, energy-saving and environment-friendly industries, and the service industry; improve the quality of foreign capital attracted; and optimize the structure of industries utilizing foreign investment. Meanwhile, we should encourage and guide foreign investment into mid-west regions and economically less-developed regions.

Second, speed up forming the economic and trade relations featuring mutual benefit and win-win results. Considering the strong competitive advantages of China, we should build economic and trade relationships with developed and developing countries which feature complementary advantages as well as mutual benefits and win-win results, and create a broader market space together with other countries around the globe. When domestic enterprises are "going out", they should take into consideration the common interests of their and the host country and seek long-term development featuring mutual benefit and win-win results when they decide to set up factories by outward foreign direct investment (OFDI), contract overseas engineering projects, export labor services, merge and acquire overseas businesses, or participate in cooperative development of overseas resources.

Finally, raise the level of participation in financial globalization.

2 Coping with the world economic changes

The developed countries in the world are also reflecting seriously upon the economic development pattern. The international financial crisis broke out in the virtual economy, but the underlying problems still lie in real economy. Considering the over-expansion of social credit, the virtual economy that scales up will lead to an extremely severe "economic bubble". It was the great disparity between the virtual economy and the real economy, between consumption and export, and between liability and equity that gave rise to the widespread outbreak of the international financial crisis. The root causes for this crisis involve the development of the real economy and the transformation of the economic development pattern. Currently, there are some uncertainties in real economy or some uncertainty in the choice of the leading industry in the future, which suggests a very slow process of economic recovery since the international financial crisis.

Confronted with the severe impacts caused by the international financial crisis, developed countries like the United States begin to rethink such economic development patterns as "excessive debt-fueled consumption and excessive dependence on virtual economy". To focus back on the real economy, developed countries have worked out re-industrialization and export expansion policies; as a result, changes are taking place in the structure of global supply and demand. The *United States Manufacturing Enhancement Act* signed into law by President Obama in August 2010 is aimed to help manufacturers reduce costs, restore competitiveness, and create more jobs. As a necessary action for American "economic rebalancing", the Act is designed to realize the transformation of the economic development pattern and facilitate the transition of economic growth from depending too much on consumption to depending on exports, which in turn depends on the manufacturing industry.

"Re-industrialization" will urge other countries to change their patterns of economic development. For developed countries in the world, the transformation of the economic development pattern that features "re-industrialization" means, on the one hand, a "regression" strategy specific to the lowering position of industry in the national economy, the declining international competitiveness of industrial products, and the outward diversion of industrial investment in a huge quantity, and on the other hand, a "layout" strategy in search of a new industrial base for economic–social development. Since the beginning of the 21st century, the global pattern of imbalanced economy has come into shape, demonstrating that the world economic growth depends in some ways on the consumption of developed countries like the United States, while other countries are dependent too much on export economic growth. The transformation of economic growth from being driven by "debt-fueled consumption" to an "export-driven" pattern certainly will lead to changes in the global supply–demand structure, and thus urge other countries to have a proper understanding of the sustainability of traditional economic growth patterns and to accelerate the adjustment of their "export-driven" economic structure and transformation of their economic development patterns.

It is predictable that developed countries in the world will seek a balance in their trade policy between protecting the domestic market and exploring the overseas market in order to realize the goal of "re-industrialization". In the incipient period when the "re-industrialization" policy is put into practice, the trade protectionism policy will be reinforced; however, as re-industrialization deepens, the trade policy for expanding exports will intensify. If so, other countries are required to take actions to cope with the negative effects incurred by trade protectionism. Some new changes may also take place in the aspect of international industrial transfer. In a short term, the United States government will possibly set out some preferential policies to achieve an inbound transfer of some industries; in particular, some state governments will strengthen preferential policy to attract inbound transfer of some high-end manufacturing industries. If so, other countries are required not to place their hopes on the international industrial transfer during the development of high-end manufacturing industry.

Now it is extremely urgent for China to adjust the economic structure and transform the economic development pattern. Accelerating economic restructuring is both an important measure in response to the international financial crisis and a main direction of accelerating the transformation of the economic development pattern. The "12th Five-Year Plan" will be a crucial period for the transformation of the economic development pattern, in which we will find it difficult to address a great diversity of intertwining structural problems. We need to properly deal with the relationships between economic growth and economic restructuring, between local and global economic development, between market and government interventions, between short-term and long-term economic growth, and between domestic and international economic tendency.

With regard to adjusting the demand structure, we should give priority to boosting domestic demands, especially consumer demands that directly stimulate economic growth, while maintaining a moderate growth of investment and stabilizing foreign demands. With regard to restructuring three industries, we should give priority to raising the proportion of the service industry in the GDP while strengthening the position of agriculture as the foundation of the national economy and making large industries stronger. With regard to adjusting the urban and rural structure, we should give priority to the urbanization and integration of urban and rural development while strengthening the rural construction. With regard to adjusting the regional economic structure, we should give priority to promoting benign interaction and coordinated development between regions while implementing the overall strategy for regional development.

3 Racing to control the strategic commanding height for future development

All the major countries in the world are racing to control the strategic commanding heights for a new round of economic development. Incubation and development of strategic emerging industries are under progress across the world. Competition among major countries for the leading industry in the future economic arena impels them to make strategic arrangements promoting rapid development of emerging industries – such as energy conservation and environmental protection, new energy resources, information, and biology – so as to occupy strategic commanding heights for the new round of economic development. The administration of US President Barack Obama has placed much emphasis on the technological and industrial development of new energy resources, aerospace, and broadband network by means of implementing the "Green Economic Recovery Program" in anticipation of a "green technology" revolution; Japan has focused on emerging industries including IT applications, automobiles of a new model, low-carbon industries, and new energy resources (solar energy); and the European Union has intended to improve "green technology" and other high technologies, and decided to invest 105 billion euros in the development of "green technology" by the year of 2013.

Profound changes taking place in global economic competitive pattern have provided a historical opportunity for China to seize strategic commanding height and realize leap-forward development in the future economic competition. With the advent of a new round of technological and industrial revolution, new technologies will provide business opportunities and a huge space for industrial development. In the new arena of industrial competition, the major countries in the world have not established their competitive dominance, so China should seize this transient "window of opportunity" to realize leap-forward development by virtue of the narrow gap in emerging industries between China and developed countries.

China is primarily furnished with the realistic foundations for the incubation and development of strategic emerging industries. With regard to the foundation for technological innovation, there is little difference between China and developed countries in the technology level of many strategic emerging industries; what's more, China has the joint development advantages in some of these industries and even has pioneering advantages in a few parts of them. With regard to the industrial foundation, the complete industrial supporting system and the fast-growing hi-tech industries have laid a solid foundation for the incubation and development of strategic emerging industries in China. With regard to the resource foundation, China has relative advantages in market and human resources in addition to relative advantages in such resources as biology, solar energy, wind energy, and key raw materials. With regard to the policy foundation, the CPC Central Committee has repeatedly stressed the development of strategic emerging industries since the outbreak of the global financial crisis; relevant programs and supporting policies are under way at present.

Strategic emerging industries will be in-depth hybrids of new technologies and new industries. Technological innovation plays both leading and supporting roles in industrial development; on the one hand, it serves as the basic momentum to drive the development of strategic emerging industries, and on the other, it is directed by the development of strategic emerging industries. In the 19th century, the electromagnetic science developed into the electrical revolution that impelled the evolution of electric power and chemical industry. In the early 20th century, the semiconductor physics and material science, as well as the modern computer theory and model, developed into the electronic revolution that facilitated the rapid development of new industries including electronics and information technology. In the future, the scientific and technological innovation will open up new space for the development of productive forces, initiate new industrial revolution, promote the development of strategic emerging industries into the leading and pillar industries, and usher in a new era of green, low-carbon, and intelligent human life.

We should speed up the incubation and development of strategic emerging industries. Featured by intensive knowledge and technology, low consumption of material resources, huge growth potential, strong connection with other industries, and good comprehensive benefits, the strategic emerging industries are of important strategic significance to transforming the economic development pattern, promoting industrial optimization and upgrading, increasing industrial competitiveness in the international market, expanding domestic demand, and enlarging employment. In the complex and uncertain context of economic development, the following relationships should be taken into consideration during the incubation and development of strategic emerging industries in China.

(1) Relationship between market regulation and government guidance. We should make full use of China's relative advantage of market resources, accelerate the incubation of the emerging market, stimulate enterprises'

initiative, and promote the combination of production, learning, research, and application through the innovation and transformation of the consumption pattern. In addition, we should bring into full play government guidance, especially in important fields and key links related to the development of strategic emerging industries; allow government to play roles as industrial guide and public product provider; create the atmosphere for industrial innovation; and minimize the risks and uncertainties in development of strategic emerging industries.

(2) Relationship between strategic emerging industries and traditional industries. These two types of industries are interrelated and inseparable. On the one hand, traditional industries serve as the foundation for the development of strategic emerging industries and also provide certain support and new industrial demand for them; on the other hand, the development of strategic emerging industries will facilitate technical reform and an upgrading of traditional industries so as to raise the technical level of traditional industries. In the process of incubating and expanding strategic emerging industries, we should strengthen the interaction and integration of two types of industries under the concept of industrial convergence.

(3) Relationship between technological innovation and industrialization. The development of strategic emerging industries will not do without technological innovation or industrialization. On the one hand, technological innovation directs industrial development and provides support of knowledge and technical achievements; and on the other hand, industrialization will help transform technological and innovative results into practical productive forces, put forward concrete demand, and chart the course for technological innovation.

(4) Relationship between domestic and international innovative resources. The incubation and development of strategic emerging industries are implemented in an open environment. Given both domestic and international innovative resources, we should, on the one hand, raise our capabilities of technological import, assimilation, and absorption as well as re-innovation and integrated innovation, and make integrated use of innovational resources both at home and abroad. On the other hand, we should be fully aware that the original innovation and core technologies in future competition for the commanding height of strategic emerging industries must be addressed through enhancing the capability of independent innovation.

4 Exploring methods to cope with global climate change

Global climate change is increasing its pressure on the world economic development. As one of the most serious challenges facing mankind in the 21st century, global climate change makes a difference to human survival and evolution. Since the industrial revolution, human behaviors, including the massive consumption of fossil energy resources and cutting down forests, cause a massive emission of greenhouse gases and thus constitute the main reason for the current global climate change. Under the pressure of global climate change, the world economic development is trapped and all countries in the world are exposed to challenges for the transformation of the development pattern and the realization of sustainable development.

Each country has accelerated transformation into a low-carbon economic development pattern. Confronted with the adverse impact of climate change, all countries around the globe are in search of solutions to the emission of greenhouse gases and climate change. They have made headway in this regard, and also are promoting the transformation of economic development in a low-carbon direction.

An active response to global climate change is an intrinsic requirement for China to accelerate transformation of economic development pattern. As the largest developing country in the world, China is on course to accomplish the largest undertaking in scale in human history – industrialization and urbanization; currently, China lies in the second phase of mid-term industrialization, with heavy chemical industry occupying a considerable proportion of industry. The "12th Five-Year Plan" is a crucial period to expedite the development of industrialization and urbanization. No longer will there be unrestricted emission of greenhouse gases in China as was in developed countries at the era of industrial revolution. We are thus supposed to seize the chance of global climate change to turn challenge into opportunity, accelerate the transformation of the economic development pattern, and improve the sustainability level of China.

Explore a low-carbon economic development pattern that conforms to China's national conditions. The choice of the low-carbon pattern for China's future economic development must be based on the fundamental realities of China and the overall consideration of energy conservation and emission reduction, the adjustment of the energy structure, the development of low-carbon technologies, the cultivation of low-carbon consumption pattern, and the increase of carbon sequestration. This is done by, first, placing emphasis on energy conservation and emission reduction by means of optimizing industrial structure, reducing proportion of high energy-consuming enterprises, carrying forward the energy-saving technology transformation of key businesses and major energy-consuming enterprises, and strengthening the administration of energy conservation. Second, by optimizing the structure of energy resources by virtue of policy guidance, capital investment, development of hydropower, nuclear power and wind power, commercialization of solar photovoltaic power, development and utilization of biomass energy in the light of local circumstances, and an increased proportion of non-fossil energy in primary energy consumption. Third, by speeding up the development of low-carbon technologies and setting up industrial, building, and traffic systems featuring low-carbon emission by means of substantially developing both hi-tech and modern service industries, and the active promotion of the industrialization of low-carbon technologies. Fourth, by developing low-carbon products and advocating a low-carbon consumption pattern. And, finally, by strengthening forestry construction and increasing forest carbon sequestration.

(Published in *Economic Daily*, February 22, 2011)

23 Adjust and optimize the industrial structure; promote economically sustainable development

As an important part of economic structure, industrial structure shall be adjusted and optimized in order to thoroughly carry out a scientific outlook on the development and transformation of the economic development pattern, to cope with the post-financial crisis and global climatic change, and to make China's enterprises more competitive in a fierce, international economic competition and facilitate long-term sustainability of China's economy. In this regard, we should, on the one hand, feel urgent to make breakthroughs in a short time, and on the other, make long-term preparations for a tougher situation in the future.

1 A long-term and arduous strategy to adjust and optimize the industrial structure and promote economic sustainable development

In 2009, the production values structure of three industries in China were 10.3:46.3:43.4, and the employment structure of three industries were 39.6:27.2:33.2 in 2008.[1] Main problems in industrial structure include the following:

(1) Uncoordinated development of three industries (primary, secondary, and tertiary)

The primary industry is not stable. During the development of the primary industry, there is still no fundamental solution to peasants' heavy dependence on rainfall for crop harvest due to inadequate investment in agricultural infrastructure, especially in water conservancy infrastructure; the science and technology service system remains imperfect and weak due to an inadequate investment in science and technology; modern husbandry has little share in the gross domestic product and remains at low level due to small and decentralized business units; and the labor force, amounting to about 40% of the total population, makes up only 10% of China's GDP due to low agricultural labor productivity.

The secondary industry is not strong. Thanks to enormous industrial production capacity, China is deemed as an industrially large but not industrially powerful country. The output of the major industrial products of China is among the highest in the world, with the output of nearly 200 products ranking the first in the world, such as steel products, cement, raw coal, fertilizer, electric energy production, cotton yarn, and household electrical appliances. The yield of toys manufactured in China accounted for about 70% of the global yield, shoes did about 50%, color TV sets about 45%, air conditioners about 30%, and textile and garment trade about 24%. However, the industrial modernization level of China remains very low, only 30–40% according to prediction. See Table 2.23.1 for details.

The tertiary industry is underdeveloped. The proportion of China's tertiary industry in the gross domestic product has been around 40% for many years; the

Table 2.23.1 Evaluation of China's Industrial Modernization Level

Indicators	Real value in 2004	Clarification of real value in 2004	Standard value	Real value/ Standard value in 2004	Weight (%)	Composite index of China's industrial modernization in 2004
Value added per employee in manufacturing (US$/year – person of overall labor productivity in 1990)	7,733.1	China Statistical Yearbook 2005	50,000	0.16	35	36.7
Ratio of main production equipment up to international level (%)	27	Calculated according to sample survey of industrial enterprises in Fujian in 2004	80	0.34	8	
Information capacity of manufacturing	10.5	Adjusted according to 2003 Index Report on Manufacture Information Engineering of China	50	0.21	8	
Ratio between industrial value added and raw material value added (%)	3.14	China Statistical Yearbook on Industry 2004	6.7	0.47	7	
Industrial goods trade competition index	0.109	China Statistical Yearbook 2005	0.5	0.22	8	

(Continued)

Table 2.23.1 (Continued)

Indicators	Real value in 2004	Clarification of real value in 2004	Standard value	Real value/ Standard value in 2004	Weight (%)	Composite index of China's industrial modernization in 2004
Ratio of hi-tech export products in manufactured products (%)	27.3	China Statistical Yearbook on High Technology Industry 2004	30	0.91	7	
R&D intensity (%)	0.71	First economic census	3	0.24	7	
GDP generated by per kg energy resources (US$ in 1995)	3.6	China Statistical Yearbook 2005	5	0.72	10	
GDP relative to per kg carbon dioxide emission (US$ in 1995)	1.6	World Bank report	2.5	0.64	10	

Source: *Studies on China's Industrial Modernization Problems*, written by Chen Jiagui and Huang Qunhui et al. China Social Sciences Press, 2004 edition

highest, 43.14%, occurred in 2009, but it declined in 2010 and failed to reach the 43.5% target expected during the "11th Five-Year Plan". There will be a huge potential for the development of the modern service industry, especially the manufacture-related service industry in the future.

(2) Unreasonable industrial internal structure, especially the inner structure of industry

First, the proportion of light industry and heavy industry is not balanced. In 1978, light industry made up only 43% of China's industry and rose to 47.14% in 1985 after several years' adjustment; more than a decade later, the proportion of light industry and heavy industry has been fluctuating around 50%, indicating the trend of coordinated development. By the end of the 20th century, China's industrial structure was predominated by the heavy chemical industry. During the decade from 1999 to 2008, the proportion of light industry output value dropped from 41.9% to 28.9%, but heavy industry grew from 58.1% to 71.1%, higher than that from before reform and the opening up.[2]

Second, there is a huge overcapacity in some industries, such as steel and iron, electrolytic aluminum, cement, shipbuilding, automobile making, and textile and garment. Due to excessively rapid development, the high energy-consuming enterprises have occupied about 80% of all industrial electricity consumed.

Third, technology in traditional industries stays at a low level. There is no proprietary technology in the majority of traditional industries. By 2005, the productivity of independent industries in China is 20% only, and above 90% of enterprises have no proprietary core technologies. In China, the core technology and leading power of some pillar industries are "hollowed out". In the automobile (car) and major equipment manufacturing industries, independent industries have a domestic market share of 20–30% only. China is a major country to produce microwave ovens, but it owns only 20 out of 200-odd patents of proprietary technology concerning microwave oven production, and pays a patent royalty of US$3–5 per microwave oven exported.

Finally, there is a slow development of high and new technology industries. The value added of high and new technology industries accounts for less than 15% of the gross domestic product and less than 20% of the manufacturing industry.

(3) Unreasonable industrial organization structure

There are serious phenomena about industrial organization structure. Enterprises, whatever the size, claim to be "jack of all trades", but larger ones are not as strong as necessary and smaller ones are not as specialized and unique as practically needed. There is also the matter of unreasonable interregional allocation that shows a tendency of assimilation. In terms of economic development, these problems regarding industrial structure have indicated that Chinese enterprises are characterized by weak capability of independent innovation, poor core competitiveness, low value added of products, and a shortage of famous brands. A majority of enterprises rely on the low income of employees, the low price of energy and raw materials, and the low input in environmental protection for their earnings, survival, and development.

First, it is revealed in the National Statistical Bureau data that the proportion of workers' remuneration in the GDP was on the decline from 1992 to 2008, averaging out at 50.8%; it was 54.6% in 1992, and then came down on a yearly basis to 47.8%, the rock bottom in the period from 1992 to 2008. This is 3 percentage points lower than the annual average in this period and 6.8 percentage points down as against the highest in 1992,[3] considerably below 54–65% in countries with a mature market economy. In the same period, however, the proportion of corporate profits in the GDP jumped from 21.9% to 29.6%, and the income of employees, especially of corporate executives in monopolized industries, became excessively high. Besides, it was reckoned by an international organization that the labor cost in China's manufacturing industry is only about 3% of that in developed countries. In the decade from 1996 to 2005, the total wages of staff and workers in China increased 9.15% per year on average, less than one third of the growth rate of corporate profits in the same period (28.62%), let alone the growth rate of rural workers' wages.

Second, there is both high consumption and a serious waste of resources. Currently, the energy consumption per unit product of China's high energy consuming enterprises is about 20% higher than the average world advanced level; the gross recovery of mineral resources is 30%, more than 20% lower than foreign advanced level; and the multipurpose utilization rate of timber is 60%, 20% lower than foreign advanced level. The proportion of renewable resources utilization in gross production is also much lower than the foreign advanced level; the annual utilization of scrap steel in iron and steel industry is less than 20% of total crude steel output, much lower than 40% of foreign advanced level; and the recycle rate of industrial water is 15–25% lower than foreign advanced level. All these problems act as a severe constraint to China's future development and need to be resolved by promoting a circular economy.

Finally, the environment is seriously destroyed and contaminated. According to monitoring data from the Ministry of Environmental Protection, the total emission of water pollutants in China stays at a high level, leading to the serious pollution of water bodies. In 2005, 27% of 411 surface water monitoring sections in seven major river systems nationwide were rated as poor water quality at Class V (severe pollution); the groundwater in the downtown area of about half the cities in China was seriously contaminated, with "rivers drying up and water being polluted" in some regions. Overexploitation of water resources in some river basins has contributed to water pollution. According to the latest *Results of Water Resources Investigation and Assessment*, the development and utilization rate of Huaihe River is 53%, Liaohe River 66%, and Haihe River 100%, indicating few ecological flows in these rivers in the dry season and significantly reducing the self-cleaning capacity of the water body in these river basins.

In the long term, the current development pattern is unsustainable due to the existence of the problems mentioned above. If they are not adjusted, various difficulties facing China's economic development will bring China into a middle-income trap and affect the process of modernization.

We have to realize, however, that adjusting the industrial structure and transforming the economic development pattern cannot be accomplished in a walk or at a stroke; instead, we need to make many difficult choices, e.g. the relationship between economic growth rate and benefits and employment. Statistical data and facts have proved that a certain rate of economic growth should be maintained in order to guarantee enterprises handsome profits, to ensure a high growth of financial revenue for the State and to alleviate difficulty in employment, as China's economy is currently an extensive economy. In the five years from 2003 to 2007, China's economy maintained a growth rate above 10%; products sold quite well, and enterprises earned more profits and received higher return on investment; financial revenue grew at a high rate; both urban and rural residents were well employed, earned more incomes and lived better lives. In such a good situation, there is no external pressure or internal impetus for adjusting the industrial structure and transforming the economic development pattern. The slowdown of economic growth rate during 2008 and 2009 should have provided a good opportunity for us to adjust and optimize the economic structure, especially the industrial organizational structure, but we took some measures to protect economic growth in order to prevent a rapid slowdown of the economic growth rate; as a result, some enterprises that should have gone bankrupt survived, and the structure of investment and consumption deteriorated. It always remains a dilemma to maintain a certain rate of economic growth and facilitate the adjustment of the industrial structure and the transformation of the economic growth pattern.

Other than the relationship between the economic growth rate and benefits, China is also faced with a difficult choice between labor-intensive industries and capital- and technology-intensive industries. Due to China's large population, abundant labor, and low wage cost, as well as enterprises' low overall technology level, poor capability of R&D, and lack of core and key technologies, it is clear that China has more advantages in developing labor-intensive industries than in developing capital- and technology-intensive industries. Nevertheless, as a big country that is increasingly international in economic development, China must develop capital- and technology-intensive industries and promote industrial upgrading so as to meet the needs of national security, national economy, and people's livelihood; to maintain economic sustainability and realize industrialization and modernization; and to enhance international competitiveness. In this regard, we are caught in a dilemma.

There are also some difficult choices facing us, e.g. expanding domestic demand and increasing exports, developing heavy chemical industry and saving energy and reducing emission, or giving play to location advantages and promoting a coordinated development between regions, etc. This dilemma has added great difficulty to adjusting and optimizing the industrial structure and transforming the economic development pattern, and has also indicated that this is a long-term and complex, strategic task.

However, the history of economic development has revealed that you cannot make omelets without breaking eggs, i.e. it seems impossible for us to accomplish the industrial adjustment and transformation of the economic development pattern in a comfortable way; after all, who can have his cake and eat it too? When we are dealing with the relationship between short-term benefits and long-term benefits, we should seek consistent thinking, smooth away any difficulty, and make sacrifices in short-term development benefits to foster the adjustment of the industrial structure and the transformation of the economic development pattern and promote the sustainable development of the economy.

2 Prime considerations for adjusting and optimizing industrial structure and transforming economic development pattern

Since it is a long-term strategic task, we must clearly understand that it is also a long-term and complex task while stressing its urgency, and should take into consideration the following factors when we propose the task, set goals, and make plans and policies:

(1) Properly analyzing China's economic traits and economic development stage

The economic structure is changing and also closely related to economic traits and the economic development stages of each country. By comparison of economic structure in the United Kingdom, the United States, Germany, Japan, South Korea, and China's Taiwan, there are by and large two types of economic structure: the first type, represented by the United Kingdom, the United States, Japan, South Korea, and China's Taiwan, is based on the development of three industries on the scale of 3:2:1 in the whole process of industrialization where the secondary and the tertiary industries are growing rapidly; the second type, represented by Germany, is based on the development of three industries on the scale of 2:3:1, with the secondary and tertiary industries growing rapidly in the process of industrialization.

Nevertheless, they have one trait in common: after industrialization is realized, the tertiary industry kept on growing rapidly and increasing in proportion while the secondary industry decreased in proportion, transforming into the development pattern on the scale of 3:2:1. The United States completed this transformation in the 1960s with a decreasing proportion of the secondary industry but an increasing proportion of the tertiary industry. So did the United Kingdom after 1955. Thanks to these changes, Daniel Bell, an American scholar, created a concept of post-industrial society in 1959 and published two papers – *Post-Industrial Society: Forecasting the United States after 1985* and *Reading Notes on Post-Industrial Society* respectively in 1962 and 1967; then he set up a system of his ideas in these articles and published his book *The Coming of Post-Industrial Society: A Venture in Social Forecasting*[4] in 1973. Germany, as a big country of manufacturing industry, completed the transformation in 1980 with a decreasing proportion of the secondary industry but an increasing proportion of the tertiary industry; Japan, also as a big country of manufacturing industry, was later than European and American countries in industrialization, with a decreasing proportion of the secondary industry but an increasing proportion of the tertiary industry after 1990; South Korea began to witness a decreasing proportion of the secondary industry but an increasing proportion of the tertiary industry after 1990; and China's Taiwan did the same after 1985. See details in Fig. 2.23.1–2.23.6.

China now is at the middle and later stage of industrialization, with a decreasing proportion of agriculture. The industrialization process in other countries has indicated that at this stage there is large space for the development of the secondary industry and a huge potentiality for the development of the service industry, especially the manufacture-related service industry. Only by understanding this development law and properly recognizing China's economic development stage can we propose practical goals.

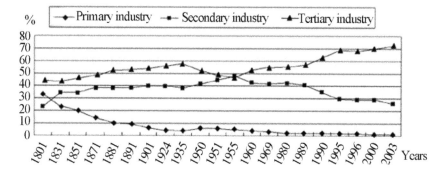

Fig. 2.23.1 Changes in Three Industries Structure of the United Kingdom

Source: Institute of World Economics and Politics of Chinese Academy of Social Sciences, *Economic Statistics Collection of Major Capitalist Countries (1848–1960)*, World Affairs Press, 1962; Wang Bin: *Introduction to Analysis of International Regional Industrial Structure*, Shanghai People's Press, 2001; the World Bank: *World Development Report (1997–2008)*

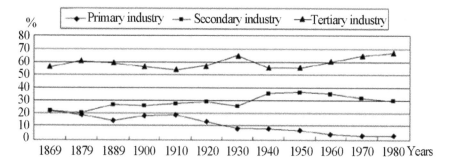

Fig. 2.23.2 Changes in Three Industries Structure of the United States

Source: Institute of World Economics and Politics of Chinese Academy of Social Sciences, *Economic Statistics Collection of Major Capitalist Countries (1848–1960)*, World Affairs Press, 1962; Wang Bin: *Introduction to Analysis of International Regional Industrial Structure*, Shanghai People's Press, 2001; the World Bank: *World Development Report (1997–2008)*

(2) Giving full consideration to unbalanced development of regional economy in China

On the whole, China now has evolved into the middle and later stage of industrialization, but economic development is unbalanced in all regions. Our studies have revealed that seven provinces and municipalities in China have realized industrialization or entered the middle and later stage of industrialization; 12 provinces, municipalities and autonomous regions are now at the middle and later stage of industrialization; 11 provinces and autonomous regions are now

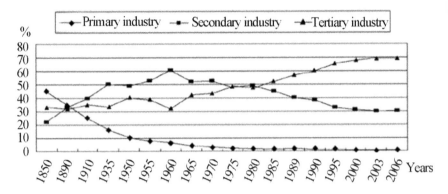

Fig. 2.23.3 Changes in Three Industries Structure of Germany

Source: Institute of World Economics and Politics of Chinese Academy of Social Sciences, *Economic Statistics Collection of Major Capitalist Countries (1848–1960)*, World Affairs Press, 1962; Wang Bin: *Introduction to Analysis of International Regional Industrial Structure*, Shanghai People's Press, 2001; the World Bank: *World Development Report (1997–2008)*

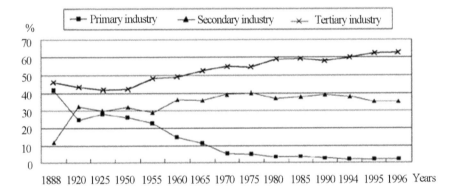

Fig. 2.23.4 Changes in Three Industries Structure of Japan

Source: Institute of World Economics and Politics of Chinese Academy of Social Sciences, *Economic Statistics Collection of Major Capitalist Countries (1848–1960)*, World Affairs Press, 1962; Wang Bin: *Introduction to Analysis of International Regional Industrial Structure*, Shanghai People's Press, 2001; the World Bank: *World Development Report (1997–2008)*

at the initial stage of industrialization; and Tibet is now at the early stage of industrialization. See details in Tables 2.23.2 and 2.23.3.

At different stages of industrialization, each region needs a different industrial structure and different tasks. For regions that have realized industrialization and entered the later stage of industrial development, their main task is finding out how to promote an upgrade of the industrial structure; but for regions that are

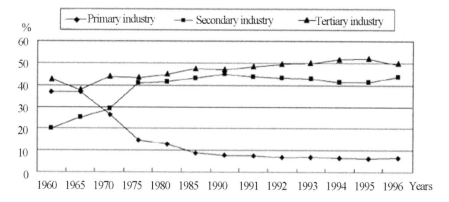

Fig. 2.23.5 Changes in Three Industries Structure of South Korea

Source: Chief Editor Fang Jia, Studies on Industrial Structure Problems, China Renmin University Press, 1997; pp. 196–223

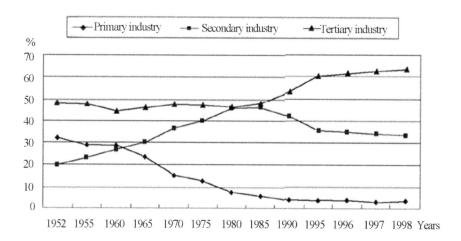

Fig. 2.23.6 Changes in Three Industries Structure of China's Taiwan

Source: Institute of World Economics and Politics of Chinese Academy of Social Sciences, *Economic Statistics Collection of Major Capitalist Countries (1848–1960)*, World Affairs Press, 1962; Wang Bin: *Introduction to Analysis of International Regional Industrial Structure*, Shanghai People's Press, 2001; the World Bank: *World Development Report (1997–2008)*

now in initial period of industrialization, their main task is to accelerate process of industrialization. In this sense, the adjustment of the industrial structure shall go through a process of gradient transfer, just like the process of economic development. A few regions do not have to go through the entire process of industrialization, including Hainan and Tibet. On this ground, a "sweeping approach" is not applicable to the adjustment and optimization of the industrial structure, i.e.

Table 2.23.2 Sentinel Value of Industrialization at Different Stages

Basic index	Pre-industrial stage (1)	Industrialization realizing stage			Post-industrial stage (5)
		Initial stage (2)	*Middle stage (3)*	*Later stage (4)*	
1. Per capita GDP (economic development level)	US$ in 1995 610–1,220	1,220–2,430	2,430–4,870	4,870–9,120	Above 9,120
	US$ in 2000 660–1,320	1,320–2,640	2,640–5,280	5,280–9,910	Above 9,910
	US$ in 2005 745–1,490	1,490–2,980	2,980–5,960	5,960–11,170	Above 11,170
2. Production value structure of three industries (industrial structure)	A>1	A>20% A<1	A<20% 1>S	A<10% 1>S	A<10% 1<S
3. Proportion of manufacturing value added in total value added of goods (structure of industry)	Below 20%	20–40%	40–50%	50–60%	Above 60%
4. Population urbanization rate (spatial structure)	Below 30%	30–50%	50–60%	60–75%	Above 75%
5. Proportion of employed persons in primary industry (employment structure)	Above 60%	45–60%	30–45%	10–30%	Below 10%

Source: Chen Jiagui, Huang Qunhui et al., *China's Industrialization Blue Book – Analysis of Industrialization Process in All Provinces and Cities,* Social Sciences Academic Press (China), 2007

accomplishing this purpose in accordance with unified requirement and uniform policy, or rather putting into practice a common but differentiated policy.

In addition, each region needs to bring its advantages into full play and highlight its industrial uniqueness based on the consideration of its resources endowment. For regions at the national level or at the levels of province, municipality, and autonomous region, emphasis shall be undoubtedly placed on the coordinated development of the primary, secondary, and tertiary industries; but for regions below provincial level, they should give full play to their advantages, focus on the development of characteristic industries, and produce an industrial chain. Only in this way can the assimilating tendency in regional industrial structure be minimized.

(3) Giving consideration to the tendency of world economic development

On the surface, the international financial crisis was caused by housing subprime mortgages in the United States; with careful study, however, we have

Table 2.23.3 Overall and Local Progress of China's Industrialization in 2007

Regional stages	Chinese Mainland	Four major economic sectors	Seven major economic areas	31 provinces, cities and regions
Post-industrial stage (5)				Shanghai (100), Beijing (100),
Later period of industrialization (4)	Second half		Yangtze River Delta (76)	Tianjin (94), Guangdong (83)
	First half	Eastern region (68)	Pearl River Delta (68), Bohai Rim (67)	Zhejiang (80), Jiangsu (80), Shandong (73),
Middle period of industrialization (3)	Second half	Chinese Mainland (52)		Liaoning (63), Fujian (59)
	First half	Northeastern region (49)	Northeastern region (49)	Shanxi (45), Inner Mongolia (43), Jilin (42), Hubei (40), Hebei (40), Chongqing (37), Heilongjiang (36), Ningxia (36), Shaanxi (33), Qinghai (33)
Initial period of industrialization (2)	Second half	Central region (24), Western region (18)	Six provinces in central region (24), Great north-western region (19), Great southwestern region (17)	Henan (32), Hunan (30), Anhui (28), Sichuan (28), Jiangxi (27), Xinjiang (26), Gansu (23), Yunnan (22), Guangxi (21), Haihe (19),
	First half			Guizhou (16)
Pre-industrial stage (1)				Tibet (0)

Source: Chief editor Chen Jiagui, *China's Economic Development: Mid-term Evaluation of the 11th Five-Year Plan and Outlook on the 12th Five-Year Plan*, China Social Sciences Press, 2010

Notes: (1) indicates pre-industrial stage (synthetic index 0); (2) indicates initial period of industrialization (synthetic index >0,<33); (3) indicates middle period of industrialization (synthetic index ≥33,<66); (4) indicates later period of industrialization (synthetic index ≥66,<99); and (5) means post-industrial stage (synthetic index ≥100). In Table 2.23.3, (2), (3), and (4) are divided into first half and second half.

noticed some underlying reasons. For instance, there are at least three reasons for international economic ailment: (i) residents' low savings and high consumption and government's high liabilities in developed countries, especially in the United States; (ii) rapid growth of exports stimulated by rapid economic growth in emerging industrial countries, which generates a large trade surplus and creditor's rights to the United States; and (iii) resources supplying countries maintaining economic prosperity after earning a large amount of foreign currency through the high price of resources. Ever since the financial crisis, all countries have rethought their economic development pattern and set about economic adjustment; for example, all developed countries, including the United States, emphasized raising residents' saving rate, reducing government deficit, and increasing exports, and some even waved the slogan of reindustrialization. As this adjustment will inevitably influence China's exports, the practice that the economic growth is stimulated by exports must be changed; if so, great pressure will be imposed on export enterprises in China. These enterprises must break the competition pattern that features mass production and low price; instead, they must build up their own brand and raise the value added of exported products.

(4) *Attaching great importance to pressure from energy saving and emission reduction and environmental protection*

As a country with enormous energy consumption and carbon emission, China is faced with the increasing pressure of energy saving, emission reduction, and environmental protection. In this respect, it will be well worth adjusting the industrial structure in addition to developing new energy resources and applying advanced technology in energy saving and emission reduction. For instance, the adjustment of light and heavy industries structure produced a significant impact on China's energy production and consumption. In the 15 years before 2003, the elastic coefficient of China's energy consumption was approximately 1:0.6; namely, if the GDP grew 1%, energy consumption would increase 0.6% only. After 2003, the elastic coefficient of energy consumption was up to about 1:1, i.e. 1% growth of energy consumption needed for 1% growth of GDP. The industrialization of heavy chemical industry and China's industrialization that have entered the middle and later period has something to do with consumption upgrading and also has much to do with the decreasing proportion of residents' consumption in the national economy, the inadequate impetus of consumption to stimulate economic growth, the excessive dependence on investment for economic growth, and selling a mass of high energy-consuming products in overseas market in recent years. We should thus adjust the distribution structure and boost the impetus of consumption for economic growth so as to facilitate the structural adjustment of light and heavy industries and the optimization of the industrial internal structure and to relieve pressure on energy saving and emission reduction.

(5) Keeping a close eye on a new tendency of world technological development and paying special attention to the progress of the new technological revolution and the development of strategic, hi-tech industries

At present, China has a low proportion of high and new technological industries and shoulders a heavy task to apply high and new technology into the transformation of traditional industries. Modern history has indicated that the rapid progress in science and breakthroughs and innovation in technology will, on the one hand, improve social productivity and change social production methods and people's life style, and will, on the other hand, inevitably give rise to a significant adjustment of the economic structure. After the outbreak of the international financial crisis, main countries in the world have placed their hopes on technological progress for the incubation of strategic emerging industries, acceleration of the economic structure adjustment and optimization, and preemption of opportunity and predominance in the new round of international competition. Emerging industries feature high technical content, high added value of products, less consumption of energy resources, less pollution of the environment, and the capability of transforming, upgrading, and updating traditional industries. Some of these industries are even capable of increasing the supply of clean energy resources and are also conducive to energy saving and emission reduction, such as solar energy, wind energy, biomass energy, and applications of many energy saving and emission reduction technologies. For this reason, we must pay close attention to the development of strategic emerging industries, including energy saving and environment-friendly industry, new generation IT industry, biological industry, high-end equipment manufacturing, new energy, new materials, and new energy automobiles, and to the significant progress and breakthroughs in basic science. We must also put more investment into these fields in order to get ahead of the curve. Meanwhile, we should deepen the reform of the scientific and technological system, accelerate the transformation of technological achievements, and quickly develop them into an industry and industrial chain.

3 Adjusting and optimizing industrial structure and transforming economic development pattern should rely on government policy and the basic role of market to allocate resources

There is no doubt that government policy plays an important role in adjusting and optimizing industrial structure and transforming economic development pattern: (1) it will make correct macroeconomic policy, keep a balanced economic aggregate, and maintain a coordinated relationship among all main economic factors so as to guarantee steady and rapid development of national economy, avoid dramatic fluctuations, and create a suitable macro environment for adjustment and optimization of industrial structure; (2) it will make a financial policy to guide development of emerging industries and disadvantaged industries, foster new economic growth points, and instruct enterprises in technical innovation to sift out backward productivity and carry out technical innovation, develop new products and enhance competitiveness on market; (3) it will adjust tax policy to encourage enterprises to carry out technological innovation and apply new technologies and techniques; and (4) it will formulate laws, regulations, and policies to facilitate enterprises' adjustment and upgrading of industrial structure, promote saving resources and energy, and protect the environment.

However, the adjustment and optimization of the industrial structure and the transformation of the economic development pattern will be eventually contingent on market forces, i.e. promoted by the basic role of the market to allocate resources and verified by the end reaction in the market. The government policy will only make the best use of the situation and increase the push power of the market. For this purpose, we must deepen the reform and improve systems that can help the market mechanism play its important roles; deepen the reform of the financial system to adjust the relationship of interests between the Central Government and local government and straighten out financial systems below provincial level; improve public finance system and standardize the transfer payment system to realize equalization of public finance; deepen the reform of the budget system and incorporate all special funds, income of state-owned enterprises, and social insurance fund, into the national budget to enhance a binding force and authority of budget; deepen the reform of the tax revenue system, implement a value-added tax transition on the large scale and accelerate the reform of both the resources tax and other tax systems; deepen the reform of the investment system, especially on the system under which no one is responsible for state investment; deepen the reform of state-owned enterprises, especially on monopolized enterprises; propel the reform of the system of administrative control to streamline administration and delegate power to the lower levels; and increase service positions and minimize government interferences in microeconomic activities.

In brief, only by deepening the reform and improving the socialist market economy system to enable the market to play its basic roles in allocating resources can we smoothly push forward the adjustment of the industrial structure and the transformation of the economic development pattern, consolidate achievements of the adjustment and transformation, and promote the sustainable development of economy.

(Published in the Journal of Graduate School of Chinese Academy of Social Sciences, Issue 2, 2011)

Notes

1 National Bureau of Statistics: *China Statistical Yearbook (2009)*, China Statistics Press, 2009 edition.
2 *China Statistical Yearbook* (2000–2009).

3 *Studies on Several Problems of National Income Distribution* by investigation group of Finance and Economic Committee of the National People's Congress, China Financial & Economic Publishing House, 2010.
4 [American] Daniel Bell, *The Coming of Post-Industrial Society: A Venture in Social Forecasting*, translated by Gao Xian and published by the Commercial Press in 1984.

Index

Note: figures and tables are denoted with italicized page numbers.

For Product Safety Concerns and Information please contact our EU
representative GPSR@taylorandfrancis.com
Taylor & Francis Verlag GmbH, Kaufingerstraße 24, 80331 München, Germany

www.ingramcontent.com/pod-product-compliance
Ingram Content Group UK Ltd.
Pitfield, Milton Keynes, MK11 3LW, UK
UKHW020952180425

457613UK00019B/650

9 780367 516628